TRAVELING BY THE STARS

CHRISTINE RAKELA

4880 Lower Valley Road, Atglen, PA 19310

Library of Congress Control Number: 2020943656

Interior design and cover design by Brenda McCallum
Type set in Bigelo Rules/Optima

ISBN: 978-0-7643-6177-7
Printed in the United States of America

Published by REDFeather Mind, Body, Spirit
An imprint of Schiffer Publishing, Ltd.
4880 Lower Valley Road
Atglen, PA 19310
Phone: (610) 593-1777; Fax: (610) 593-2002
E-mail: Info@redfeathermbs.com
Web: www.redfeathermbs.com

Although astrology is a very insightful tool, the information within is a "model" of what could occur. Due to the many variables involved, nothing can be guaranteed. This disclaimer releases the author of any and all liability including direct, indirect, incidental, punitive, and consequential damages of any kind.

I dedicate this book to my parents, Mary and Frank Rakela.
Thank you for putting a roof over my head and food on the table,
instilling solid moral values, and sending me to a parochial
grammar school. It was all I needed to survive in the world. And for
being my best friends later in life, I will travel anywhere for you.

TABLE OF Contents

ACKNOWLEDGMENTS

First and foremost, I would like to thank God for the opportunity to have my book successfully published.

Second, I am grateful to all the people who have supported me in this project. My intention while living on this planet is to write books that people will truly benefit from in their daily lives. This one surely will, and it gives me great joy to have it come to fruition.

Third, I would like to thank the people who have supported me: my parents, Mary and Frank Rakela; my daughter, Chrystal Rakela; my siblings, Nancy, Kathy, and Theresa Rakela; and my friends Jan Shulman and Renay Diamond.

For their professional contributions, I would also like to thank Fei Cochrane, president of Cosmic Patterns Software Inc., at www.AstroSoftware.com, and astrologers Penny Thornton and Jacqueline Pentek.

Last, I would like to thank the entire Schiffer Publishing team for all their support and professionalism during the process of publishing my book Traveling by the Stars.

INTRODUCTION

Travel timing has been an interest of mine for over 30 years due to my bicoastal connection with my residence in New York City and my family in California. Starting out as a glance at the transits to see if the planetary influences were relatively okay, then turning into a serious study to make absolutely sure that I not only arrived safely but also had a good flight and trip, inspired my study of *Traveling by the Stars*. Over the years, several clients requested information on safe and productive travel as well. I decided that to avoid the negative travel times would be the best way to ensure safe passage. To enhance my knowledge, I started tracking accidents and crashes throughout the world. In doing so, the consistency of basic planetary patterns could be plotted to predict adverse traveling incidents. At times, the accuracy of exact aspects used in astrology to reflect a traveling disaster was startling. September 11, 2001, certainly changed my as well as the world's perspective on traveling. However, I was not afraid when I flew out of the New York City area two weeks after 9/11. Although the airport was barren and the look of fear was rampant throughout the terminal, I was one of the fortunate ones, for I was armed with the knowledge of when to travel. Even if an accident were to have happened due to human error, I would still be grateful for the fact that my journeys were without fear, due to my confidence in the mathematical science of astrology. For I traveled for nothing less than the sheer pleasure of it. I am convinced that we live in a world where we can enhance our lives by utilizing the knowledge that exists all around us. I share this information with you in the hope that you might enjoy the wonders throughout the world, regardless of the fluctuating times.

—Christine Rakela

Chapter 1

TRAVEL PATTERNS

Travel used to be so predictable, a normal occurrence of departing from one destination to arrive at another. However, with all of the chaos and uncertainty going on in the world, we are all more concerned about what we might encounter when we travel. The "fear" of what might be the result of traveling has gripped our society in an adverse manner. Especially in the United States when we were attacked by terrorists on September 11, 2001, when four American planes were hijacked. This was nothing short of a national catastrophe. Being an astrologer, I couldn't help but wonder—*There must be a way to avoid such a disaster. Why should we have to live in "fear" when considering a trip?* Could we possibly determine a "travel strategy" that enhances our traveling experiences, whether they be local or abroad?

Since astrology is based on mathematical angles to planets, called *aspects*, if these aspects are recurring, we can establish a pattern that reflects traveling conditions. Consistent astrological patterns that occur during a trip can guide us in constructing a traveling profile that can help us plot great traveling experiences or be aware of travel disasters. When we note recurring patterns in any type of research, the pattern becomes significant because of the consistency of the evidence. In this case, the evidence is based on astrological connections that occur as we move through time and space, and reflect whether or not an accident or sabotage will occur.

After many years of research, the travel patterns that emerged were so obvious that even the common layman could be convinced. Chart after chart, the planetary angles pinpointed the accidents and traveling disasters, as well as the wonderful traveling experiences, with total accuracy. The traveling profile displayed a valid pattern that could not be disputed. Here, a recurring planetary scheme allows us to foresee a possible future outcome while traveling. What was also discovered was that not only was a pattern found, but the astrological description of the pattern was a true reflection of what happened, whether it be a tragedy or the trip of a lifetime. If the intricate interpretation of an astrology chart can be an accurate description of what happens in an accident, then timing in life is a mind-boggling experience understood only by a divine intelligence far beyond our own. The inner workings of astrology can be conceived and defined by only one source—God. Astrology is not a belief; astrology is happening all around you. It is a means of gathering information that can benefit your life. It happens every moment of every day. Its timing revolves around you as accurately as a satellite timepiece.

Precision

Numeric values, however, are more easily read, for our whole life encompasses them. All of life is based on math and various mathematical equations. Why? Because it *works*. Math is a form of perfection in and of itself. If one point is at 2 degrees on an angle and another is at 2 degrees coming in from another angle, through time and space they will meet. Such are the angles that turned up in the thousands of astrology charts that were researched to reach one conclusion. The best times for travel can be predicted.

Such precision can assist us in navigating our travel experiences and outcomes. It can also calm our fears and anxieties when we are armed with the facts. Our exploration will take us into categories involving accidents, crashes, hijackings, and bombings, especially linked with sabotage and terrorism. Having access to this information will empower you. *You will gradually discover the hidden concepts behind planning a trip for your ultimate benefi*t. Not only will you be able to avoid disastrous traveling experiences, but you will also have the opportunity to plan trips that support business opportunities, personal growth, a romantic rendezvous, or family vacations. You will be rewarded through careful, meticulous planning. Some advantageous as well as catastrophic influences are easily spotted, while others will require a more diligent approach to secure a good if not great traveling experience.

All astrological aspects will be thoroughly discussed to ensure the best results. To summarize an excellent traveling experience, we will be working with daily transits, aspects to the natal birth chart, New and Full Moon phases, Sun-sign third- and ninth house travel sectors, Sun-sign travel, Sun-sign compatibility while traveling, and relocation and astrocartography, all of which are thoroughly described in this book. When we combine the patterns of all these significant factors, timing is truly everything when it comes to planning your journey.

Accidents—Sabotage

Accidents are accidents, and therefore the patterns indicated reflect an out-of-control, unexpected, or unpredictable situation occurring. A planned course of action like sabotage or terrorism, involving crashes, hijackings, and bombings, reflects covert operations and conspiracy; therefore the patterns will be different. However, accidents, crashes, hijackings, and bombings are unpredictable only when we don't have inside information that can be easily acquired through astrology. *If you know that an accident or sabotage is likely to occur because of a certain consistent astrological pattern reflecting accidents or sabotage, then you can avoid this particular time period.* If this pattern is also showing up in other astrology charts such as your solar return (your birthday chart for the year), then I double-caution you! When you and/or your loved one's lives are on the line, risks are not to be taken.

Of course, we can't stop living when avoiding certain adverse travel times. An unfavorable Mars (cars, trucks, etc.)/Saturn (restraint, delays, authority) aspect connection could have you driving carefully in traffic to the airport behind three huge semitrucks that are obeying the truck speed limit that day. If you know this in advance, leave earlier and know that you will be delayed one way or another on your trek to the airport. Better to go through some personal frustration than a nasty accident. Saturn, in particular, always encourages us to be cautious, so whatever aspect it is making, I suggest you slow down, take your time, think things through, and plan carefully. If we work with the energy around us, we don't have to feel such great limitation.

However, statistics show that there are approximately 12 million car accidents, 5,800 train wrecks, and 178 plane crashes every year. Over 45,000 people die when perhaps it could be avoided. If the timing of traveling can be predicted, then as a society, we should use this information to improve our lives. Otherwise, statistics speak for themselves.

Our journey through life will involve travel—some more, some less. You can leave the outcome up to fate or you can apply the knowledge at hand to assist you. Even a little forethought will go a long way and may turn out to be your greatest protection.

Using Travel Patterns

Yes, there are travel patterns that one can avoid to bypass negative influences that unknowingly promote difficult and/or dangerous traveling conditions. Traveling patterns involving sabotage differ from accidents, whether they be minor or fatal. One of the worst combinations of planetary energies is an adverse Mars/Saturn/Pluto (intense destruction) transit combined with an adverse Moon (the flow of an event) aspect. Many years ago, I almost died in a terrible car accident under a nefarious Mars/Saturn/Pluto progression, and the Moon was in an adverse square aspect to a Mars/Neptune conjunction that day when a car ran a red light. I have often thought, *Could that have been avoided?* Still etched in my consciousness, I can now answer my own question and also help guide others to safer traveling experiences.

You will notice in my many examples, including the one just provided, how the Moon has a tendency to set off many adverse angles that are just waiting to ignite. One of the most volatile influences that will set off an accident or disaster is an adverse Moon/Mars (dangerous flow of energy) transit. When an unfavorable Moon/Mars transit occurs, plans go awry. And if you are driving on the road going 65 miles per hour or sitting in a plane moving at 350 miles an hour, this influence may unfold in a destructive manner, especially when set off by other adverse influences.

For your convenience, the days that adverse Moon/Mars aspects occur are listed on my website. You can look them up at: ChristineRakela.com

Chapter 2

OPTIMAL TRAVELING: ENJOYING VACATIONS AND TRAVEL PLANS

Finding the most advantageous times to travel is where we want to invest our energy. Here, we discover that consistent patterns are also found with positive traveling experiences. There are several encouraging travel patterns that not only offer protection on your trip, but will also bring more joy and excitement while on your journey. Enhancing your travel plans with these astrological patterns will ensure a terrific trip with excellent results, whether it be for business or pleasure. The idea behind traveling is to enjoy your trip by being comfortable with your traveling itinerary.

The concept behind leisurely travel is to relax and get away from it all, the stress and anxiety of daily living. When we relax while traveling, we feel rejuvenated and are thus able to put in a more productive workday upon our return. Also, a clearer vision of our goals in life may enter our consciousness, creating a brighter future. Finding more stress on your trip does not contribute to the pleasant vacation or productive business trip that you had imagined. Working with traveling patterns, we can design a trip that accommodates your needs and desires.

Optimal traveling patterns can be calculated that will result in a wonderful experience, whether it be traveling by car, train, boat, or plane. Saturn, which represents limitation, will have a tendency to restrict your travel plans, whereas Jupiter, which represents expansion, will encourage travel. Since Jupiter holds rulership over the ninth house sector of travel, especially to foreign countries, our tendency will be to lean toward favorable Jupiter influences. Leisurely travel is usually inspired by Jupiter in positive aspect to most of the planets. When you want to get away from it all, favorable Jupiter transits will help tremendously. You will also experience luck with rekindling that romantic fire, enjoying family relations, or once again becoming inspired to write a novel or paint a masterpiece. Usually, vacations allow us to recuperate from a hectic world and find some serenity. When we are in an environment that appeases our senses, we accomplish this objective. However, if our timing is wrong, more tension is added to the picture. With the valuable insights of travel timing, there isn't any excuse for not having a wonderful, refreshing journey every time you venture away from your familiar surroundings.

Business trips tend to be more productive when Jupiter's expansive and opportune qualities are in favorable aspect to the Sun, Mercury (which promotes good communication), Mars, Jupiter, and Pluto. For business travel, we want to feel confident, able to negotiate our way to land a deal. Jupiter's opportune manner allows us this possibility. We are successful in reaching a sought-after goal when plans go smoothly. Especially when it comes to business, following the favorable patterns involving Jupiter to enhance your journey and bypass the traveling pitfalls will allow you to be as industrious as you would like to be. This gives new meaning to "the sky's the limit."

Of course, there are those who see travel as pure adventure, a time of exploration and self-discovery. Jupiter's influences can certainly assist you here in designing a fascinating trip just for you. Conquering unknown territory on an excursion in a foreign land, such as Tibet, the Yucatan Peninsula, Scandinavia, Ireland, or New Zealand, could be the trip of a lifetime. Care in planning is sure to make your trip a success no matter what comes about to change your itinerary.

We don't have to deprive ourselves of the terrific journeys that we hope to make in our lifetime, whether they be at home or abroad. Taking in an exquisite sunset over the Taj Mahal, grasping the scenic splendor of Yellowstone National Park, admiring the wondrous treasure of the statue of Venus de Milo in Greece, or whatever your fascination might be can all be a part your world. Through implementing the benefits of astrological traveling patterns, taking a trip can be the great experience that it was meant to be.

Although our traveling experiences are questioned when we allow fear to enter the picture, fear has its place in cautioning us to be aware of our environment and whether it is in our best interest to be traveling at this time. If there is a government travel announcement that warns us not to go abroad to certain unstable countries, then you must listen to the warning and take heed. Regardless of the planetary influences, common sense should be exercised, especially when the risks are so great.

For Astrology Beginners

If you have limited knowledge of astrology, I suggest that you familiarize yourself with it by reading chapters 4, 5, 6, and 7 on the planets, Sun-sign travel, Sun-sign third and ninth travel sectors, and Sun-sign travel compatibility. In this way, you will be better able to appreciate more of *Traveling by the Stars.*

Chapter 3

THE TRAVEL STRATEGY

There are certain astrological influences that, when happening simultaneously, can affect your trip in a positive manner. The following influences describe the traveling strategy that, if put to good use, will enhance your traveling experiences and protect you from setbacks and disasters.

Utilizing New-Moon / Full-Moon Cycles

The Moon designates the ebb and flow of the tides, when it's time to come in and time to go out. But not only does the Moon generate the flow of the tides—it generates the flow of everything! Therefore, following Moon cycles can be very beneficial even when traveling. Traveling after the Full Moon and closer to the New Moon is recommended.

Since the New Moon promotes a new cycle, it is usually best to take off when a New Moon is occurring, for this supports the trip. I don't advise travel around the Full Moon, for there is too much tension in the air when the luminaries are in opposition to each other. For the best results, initiate a trip on or during a New Moon phase and return before the Moon is full. Keep in mind that Full Moons have a plus or minus four days of influence surrounding them.

The Full Moon should be avoided whenever possible, especially the exact day. The Full Moon will bring emotional issues to the surface, and confrontations are likely. Since the Sun and Moon are in opposition with each other on a Full Moon, the emotions and the will are not in alignment; therefore there are disagreements and situations that occur that just don't go your way. Obstacles will arise that test your patience. Hopefully the Full Moon will not get the best of you, but what it will do is cause delays and upsets to your daily routine that are frustrating, especially when on a trip somewhere. The Full Moon may even stop your trip altogether.

Traveling after the Full Moon is best because you have the opposition behind you, and the Sun and Moon will gradually come into favorable alignment by conjunction, which is the New Moon. The New Moon represents new starts or beginnings, or at least the opportunity for a new outlook. When applied, you will feel like your plans are running more smoothly, as the luminaries of the Sun and Moon are supporting each other. It's usually best to initiate a trip on the New Moon and consider returning before the Full Moon, unless the trip is one of long duration.

All Full Moon and New Moon dates are listed on my website at: ChristineRakela.com.

Avoid Moon/Mars Aspects While Traveling

I can't think of anything more important than to tell you about the malefic Moon/Mars influence while traveling. Since there is a chance of you experiencing an accident, it's not worth taking the risk. You will find that your schedule seems to go awry or a problem arises that may be difficult to resolve. If an argument occurs, you may find yourself appeasing your traveling partner throughout the length of your trip instead of enjoying it. *As documented in this book, adverse Moon/Mars influences are the major cause of accidents.* If it's not an accident, a problem will most likely be encountered. If you have to travel on a day when the Moon adversely aspects Mars, make sure you are on the ground and not in travel mode at least two hours before and two hours after the exact aspect. Due to midpoint aspects that could set off a Moon/Mars adverse influence at any time during the course of a day, it's advised to avoid that day altogether. The following is an example of a malefic Moon/Mars transit and the horrific event that occurred.

On January 31, 2000, at 4:19 pm. PST, Alaska Plane 261 crashed in Point Mugu, California, killing 88 people on board. There was an exact adverse aspect, Moon at 21 degrees Sagittarius square Mars at 21 degrees Pisces. Saturn was also in square aspect to the Sun that ill-fated afternoon.

Moon/Mars transits need to be taken into consideration when traveling or planning a trip, whether they be adverse angles and/or midpoint angles.

All Moon/Mars transits are listed on my website at: ChristineRakela.com. Just look up the day you are traveling to see if there is a Moon/Mars connection present.

The Void-of-Course (v/c) Moon

One of the most frequently asked questions is: Can I travel on a void-of-course Moon? This is when the Moon has made its last aspect of the day to another planet and is said to be wobbling in its orbit, or void of course, until it moves into the next zodiac constellation. As the void-of-course Moon emanates an influence that causes our daily flow to be interrupted, it is not advisable to plan your journey or initiate traveling under a void-of-course Moon. More often than not, plans may go awry. When the Moon is v/c, it's all right to pursue routine tasks. However, when traveling, you should start your trip when the Moon is direct in its orbit, so you are initiating things taking off in the right direction. A simple pocketbook planetary guide can assist you in tracking the void-of-course Moon, which is also listed on my website. A v/c Moon can be for only a few minutes or continue throughout the day, depending on when the Moon's last aspect to a planet takes place.

Traveling or Arranging Plans under a Mercury Retrograde

Given that Mercury is the planet that rules over the third house sector of travel in astrology, traveling under a Mercury retrograde can be very precarious, as this influence does not always support plans following through with the anticipated result. Thus, the desired trip may not manifest as expected or will involve complications along the way. If the travel strategy is followed, you are apt to have more control over the outcome of your journey. Nevertheless, there may still be setbacks. I suggest making all of your traveling plans before Mercury goes retrograde, especially if you are traveling during a Mercury retrograde. It's also not advisable to be arranging your travel itinerary during a Mercury retrograde. You will find that your plans are likely to change or not happen at all. When Mercury retrograde falls in the third or ninth house sector of travel or the fifth house sector of leisure life, you will be inclined to reevaluate your traveling agenda. Even though you might be at somewhat of a standstill, the underlying motive will persuade you to move ahead with your plans.

Traveling Windows of Opportunity

To further enhance your traveling strategy, the following sections detail the beneficial transiting influences that will favorably assist you on your journey, whether it be brief or of a long duration. The more that you have of the travel strategy, the better your trip will be. You can refer to a planetary pocket guide, where these daily influences are calculated for you as transits for each day, or you can work with a planetary ephemeris and calculate them yourself. There are also transits to your natal chart to consider. Besides the transits, progressions and solar-arc directions should also be taken into consideration in determining your traveling experience.

Sun/Jupiter

SUN CONJUNCT JUPITER

When the Sun is in aspect to Jupiter, we are meant to expand our horizons in life, and since Jupiter rules over travel, the Sun only accentuates this more. Under a Sun conjunct Jupiter influence this is a great time to travel, as now you have the enthusiasm to venture out into the world. You are looking for more freedom and adventure. A newly found confidence not only brings joy, but attracts good fortune your way. Benefits and favors are bestowed upon you, especially if you are not looking for them. Don't be surprised if you find yourself meeting up with the higher echelon while touring the world. A more distinguished appearance will also add to your elegant stride. You may wish to further your understanding of other interesting cultures. Your philosophy could be changed dramatically by the impact of distinct civilizations. Wherever you decide to journey, you will thoroughly enjoy life's treasures, big and small. A highly significant journey may occur with progressed Sun aspecting progressed Jupiter.

JUPITER TRINE/SEXTILE SUN

A Jupiter trine Sun influence offers great protection, besides a wonderful traveling experience, while the sextile aspect is more subtle. This influence is especially pronounced when Jupiter resides in the third and ninth travel sectors, or the fifth sector of romance and leisure life. A sense of freedom persuades you to journey to new vistas. You may also wish to travel in style. Feeling confident, you will seek favors to win the ideal seat assignment. Your good fortune may find you sharing the trip with an important figure in society. Feeling good along with having a high vitality, you will increase your activities and take advantage of opportunities as they appear. Gaining the trust of important individuals finds you in a strong position where others will follow your leadership abilities. As you set great aims, you soar to new horizons that broaden your perspective on life.

JUPITER SQUARE SUN

Feeling restless, you may want to break out of your normal routine and explore new vistas. However, you may be so concerned with getting away from it all that your social etiquette is lacking. You may also find yourself spending more on a trip, since you are not wanting to wait for a good deal. As you will not be sure whom to trust, honor only proven contacts. Wanting to enjoy yourself to the fullest promotes overindulgence that will end up being costly. Even so, you will attract some goodwill to make your traveling experience worth your while. You may feel restraint in conforming to formalities yet will keep your composure so you are presentable while on your journey.

JUPITER OPPOSITION SUN

You are ready for more adventure and will feel the need to broaden your horizons. Planning that big trip is on the agenda. Seeing new sights will certainly add to your personal growth. You may even seem to be overwhelmed at times with your experiences. Being too generous or self-indulgent could overtax your pocketbook. Be prepared to address high expenditures as everything will seem overpriced. Nevertheless, you will still come out winning, having the time of your life traveling as long as your expectations are not overrated.

Moon/Jupiter

JUPITER CONJUNCT MOON

Situations in life are bound to go smoothly. With the optimism you feel, this is an excellent time to travel. Those around you will sense a happy disposition and will be eager to please. The energy you put into a project you will definitely get back in return. Any journeys you embark on will create an even more positive attitude toward your future. Although your trip might be expensive, it's worth the investment. While on the road, relationships can be reconciled and family affairs are handled with ease. This is a beneficial period where there are good returns. Travel will be quite pleasant, and every opportunity should be pursued. Family ventures prosper, and excellent connections with women are noted.

JUPITER TRINE/SEXTILE MOON

When Jupiter is in trine aspect to the Moon, this tends to be a harmonious and cheerful period with the sextile aspect being more subtle. Any stress between family members and loved ones is eased, so you are able to immerse yourself into the expedition of your dreams. Jupiter's placement in the third or ninth sectors of travel, or the fifth sector of romance and leisure life, will significantly enhance your journey. Your relaxed and joyful persona wishes to absorb all of life's wonderful experiences while you tour parts of the world. As you are hopeful and optimistic about your future, your travels are truly delightful. Purchases and investments made during your trip are favorable and only add to the pleasurable highlights around you.

JUPITER SQUARE MOON

Any optimism about traveling out of town may be put to rest as family and loved ones cause emotional strain and need to rely on you for support at this time. Visiting relatives may also tax your energies. Taking care of others could lead to high expenses that deter you from arranging your travel plans. Even so, you have the ability to remain cheerful amid the commotion, recognizing that travel plans can still be pursued.

JUPITER OPPOSITION MOON

Although travel options are possible, you will also find it to be stressful at times as family and loved ones make demands on your time and energy. This will surely interrupt your idea of the ideal vacation. As you contend with friends, family, and relatives, you may also find that you are running up a high tab on costly expenditures. This may not be the way you had hoped to expand your personal growth. So, think in terms of broadening your understanding of those around you to make the best of your circumstances.

Jupiter/Mercury

JUPITER CONJUNCT MERCURY

When Jupiter conjuncts Mercury, a positive mental outlook steers you in the direction of broadening your horizons. This is a favorable time to embark on a traveling experience that will expand your philosophy of life. You will hear good news concerning your journey and meet up with inspirational individuals who encourage your ambitions. Your traveling itinerary will be a success from start to finish. Your curious mind will want to travel around the globe, yet even a brief excursion out of town could be highly stimulating. Exercising good judgment, you are likely to find exceptional deals along your trip that keep your finances in good shape. Be open to receiving gifts and rewarding opportunities that promote your traveling agenda. Under Mercury/Jupiter influences, travel, one's occupation, and personal interests will prosper, especially those involving the communications field. Good news is uplifting.

JUPITER TRINE/SEXTILE MERCURY

When Jupiter is in favorable trine aspect to Mercury, this is considered to be an excellent time for travel, especially when Jupiter resides in the third or ninth sectors of travel or the fifth sector of romance and leisure life, while the sextile aspect is more subtle. Feeling mentally bright and ready to embark on a wonderful adventure, you are sure to gain from any traveling venture. You will benefit from the choices you make at this time, whether it be now or in the future. The company of loved ones is to be enjoyed. The advantages of learning will inspire you beyond your expectations. Navigate your way through unknown territory to truly capture the essence of your world. Prestigious individuals offer support and stimulating conversation. Financial decisions are rewarding.

JUPITER SQUARE MERCURY

Overrated optimism may not be in line with reality. Watch that you don't depend too much on others, as they may promise more than they can deliver. Still, you will have great expectations until you discover your mishap. As those around you lack the intellectual exchange you prefer, you may feel frustrated with sharing your views. If your philosophies or personal beliefs clash, don't push your luck. You can still enjoy your trip. Better to exercise tolerance and perhaps a sense of humor to see you through your traveling experience. Chances are you might encounter delays, formal procedures, and uncomfortable accommodations that test your patience. Nevertheless, getting out of town may still lift your spirits.

JUPITER OPPOSITION MERCURY

Feeling mentally restless, you are desiring more freedom and adventure in your life, but if you overextend yourself during this period, you could encounter a minor disappointment. Relax and enjoy yourself. Keep your expectations in check and recognize that those around you may not be up for the intellectual exchange you prefer. Expensive purchases may consume your funds quickly, especially if traveling. Even your personal growth is limited as other matters take precedence. Although your journey may experience delays and uncomfortable accommodations, you may still be glad you had the opportunity to leave town. If you do travel under this influence, try dealing with the formal procedures and setbacks with a sense of humor.

Jupiter/Venus

JUPITER CONJUNCT VENUS

As you long for peace, beauty, and love, you are stirred by magnified emotions that amplify your journey. Luckily, you attract serene environments on your traveling expedition that persuade you to appreciate what you have. A pronounced sensitivity makes you more receptive to others as you look after their needs while on the road. Visiting friends and loved ones can be a warm and joyful experience. Your social circle may involve fashion, art, music, and entertainment that capture your imagination as you explore new vistas. You may win favor and approval from prestigious individuals that enhance your journey away from home. Watch that great expectations don't interrupt a pleasant family outing or a romantic rendezvous, for these events will end up being outstanding anyway. Under a progressed Venus/Jupiter aspect, great happiness occurs, such as a fabulous vacation or marriage. As you are feeling so good, possible indulgence and weight gain could occur. However, financial and social success is noted.

JUPITER TRINE/SEXTILE VENUS

Jupiter in auspicious trine aspect to Venus promises a wonderful traveling experience filled with happiness and romance, especially when one of these planets occupies the third or ninth sectors of travel or fifth sector of romance and leisure life, while Jupiter's sextile to Venus will be more subtle. Your evenings out may seem like a party or wedding atmosphere filled with glamour and surprises. You will find family and loved ones, as well as those around you, to be generous and cooperative making your traveling agenda a success. Although extravagant, any purchases at this time are a good investment. The viewing of artistic treasures will be pursued to inspire you along the way. As you journey to new surroundings, enjoy the hospitality around you, for it is well deserved.

JUPITER SQUARE VENUS

If you are traveling during this period, social and emotional setbacks will need to be handled graciously. You may be desiring more love, harmony, and acceptance, but the right person is not being receptive and the one who is interested doesn't satisfy your needs. Desiring more fun, romance, and sensual pleasure is met with obstacles that curtail some of your enjoyment on your trip. You may need to relax and delight in the simple pleasures to help ease any traveling tensions. As your impulsive judgment could cause you to throw caution to the wind, a risky love affair filled with hope promises more than it delivers. Being patient and having faith in those who are trustworthy will secure your itinerary. Involving yourself with art, entertainment, or parties could still be met with emotional interference that requires your utmost cooperation in going with the flow.

JUPITER OPPOSITION VENUS

Although you will feel relatively content, there is an underlying longing for more love, approval, and social acceptance while on your journey. You may be overly sensitive to the response of others, so try not to expect more than others can give. Engaging in a romantic affair along the way is not advised unless you are with a partner who understands your needs. The people you wish would pay attention to you may not, and the ones that do are not your type. Friends and family may not seem to offer the support you are looking for. Perhaps you are just trying too hard. Put on a relaxed persona and others will follow your lead. Your trip will be fine if you show compassion toward others and not focus on your own emotional needs. Artistic ventures or an entertaining venue are bound to lift your spirits.

Jupiter/Mars

JUPITER CONJUNCT MARS

You will find yourself very busy and challenged with an active traveling agenda when Jupiter conjuncts Mars. Try directing your drive and energy into constructive projects that reap positive results. You may be impulsive in spending extravagantly on your trip, but this may improve your lifestyle as well as add to your enjoyment. A passionate, romantic rendezvous could certainly be a part of exploring a newly discovered land. Seeking out adventure, especially with your traveling companions, may become excitingly competitive. Luckily, you are protected even when encountering a volatile situation. Under progressed Mars/Jupiter aspects, a high vitality enhances traveling. Take the initiative to capitalize upon great opportunities on the horizon.

JUPITER TRINE/SEXTILE MARS

Jupiter in auspicious trine aspect to Mars encourages you to pursue an exciting traveling adventure, especially when Jupiter is residing in the third or ninth sectors of travel or the fifth sector of romance and leisure life, while Jupiter's sextile to Mars will be more subtle. As your vitality and confidence are energized, this is an excellent time to be touring the wonders of the world. Adventurous travel will open up your perspective on people, religion, and life. While spending wisely on your journey, your purchases will be a good investment and may enhance your standard of living. An abundance of enthusiasm will also inspire your love life. Whether you are single or a couple, you may attract romance your way. With luck and protection around you, the advantage is on your side.

JUPITER SQUARE MARS

Sudden optimism may have you biting off more than you can chew. Your traveling plans may be met with unforeseen delays, formal proceedings, and difficult-to-resolve problems that limit your progress and cause great stress. Careless planning and scattering your forces will only end up being unproductive as fights, accidents, fevers, and financial loss are experienced. Try channeling this misguided energy into competitive sports, a wild adventure, an aggressive hike, or passionate romance. Exercise tolerance, especially in a rowdy and unpredictable environment.

JUPITER OPPOSITION MARS

You may wish to suddenly seek out more adventure in your life, yet demands may have you on the go. Overextending yourself on your journey may be unproductive and very physically taxing. Delays and extra expenditures will add to an already hectic day. Being careless during your trip may lead to financial loss through impulse buying or theft. Disagreements, frustration, and formal procedures may also be limiting. With great enthusiasm, you can tackle many activities at once. However, you may find that some projects will have unsuccessful results. Recreational activities, exercise, passionate romance, or a wild adventure are ways to channel this misdirected influence while traveling.

Jupiter/Jupiter

JUPITER CONJUNCT JUPITER

This is an excellent time to travel, especially abroad. You are wanting to enlarge your experiences of life by exploring new vistas. Your educational outlook and philosophy will expand as you absorb the meaning of breathtaking views, historical sights, or other cultures. During your journey, you attract goodwill, favors, and recognition, where differences can be reconciled and a bond of trust established. Traveling for business or pleasure, you set the pace for successful growth. Financial investments denote lucrative deals that account for your generosity while traveling. Your enthusiasm is seen by all as friendly and inviting.

JUPITER TRINE/SEXTILE JUPITER

Jupiter in favorable trine aspect to Jupiter makes this a wonderful time to travel and see the sights, especially when Jupiter is occupying the third or ninth sectors of travel or the fifth sector of romance and leisure life, while the sextile is more subtle.

Fascinating adventures expand your faith and philosophy. You will attract luck, favors, and recognition that assist you everywhere you go. As you extend your generosity, new environments are friendly. Honorable contacts make your trip even more of a delight. If you are financially secure, any purchases only enhance your style of living. Your travels can be an enriching experience that adds to your personal growth, both mentally and spiritually.

JUPITER SQUARE JUPITER

Overexpansion may be your tendency, especially in the areas of travel, philosophy, and religion. As you are open-minded to learning, there is much to be gained. Yet, people and situations are overrated. Traveling and accommodations may be costly, so plan for this in advance. Personal growth may be stymied by limitations and business affairs nonproductive. Unless you want to take on the planets, this is not the best time to pursue that magnificent journey; however, you will still be inclined to travel. Trusting familiar faces and having realistic expectations will support your expansive ideas.

JUPITER OPPOSITION JUPITER

Overrated confidence has you taking on more than you can handle. You can still make progress with your traveling itinerary, but you may have to bypass certain sights that don't fit into your agenda. Remaining optimistic, you are open to learning and new experiences that enhance your personal growth. However, you may have to contend with delays and formalities that interrupt your desire for touring the world. Your journey may be expensive, so be sure to plan ahead. It's wise to do everything in moderation. Financial loss through theft or misplaced trust may also occur. Yet, you will still be keen on embracing an adventurous trip that expands your philosophical views of life.

Jupiter/Saturn

JUPITER CONJUNCT SATURN

Having to be realistic with your traveling agenda makes this a transit that is better suited for business than pleasure. A responsible and tolerant attitude will have you planning carefully for solid results. This is a great time to conclude your duties by organizing your life. Here, a restricted condition of the past is alleviated to allow you to advance with ease as you emanate a cheerful disposition while proceeding with your work. Travel will have an orderly tone, yet much can be accomplished.

Although your freedom is limited, working hard and applying yourself toward any goal is a good investment.

JUPITER TRINE/SEXTILE SATURN

When Jupiter is in positive trine aspect to Saturn, a solid sense of confidence increases your ambition to travel, especially when Jupiter is residing in the third or ninth sectors of travel or the fifth sector of leisure life, while the sextile is more subtle. Gradual expansion of your goals gives you the reassurance you need to excel in a new direction. A cheerful attitude shows in the satisfaction of your work. As wise economic planning promotes security, only practical expenditures will be considered. While on your trip, handle yourself in a dignified manner to catch the eye of your superiors.

JUPITER SQUARE SATURN

You may be required to take on more responsibilities to see a job through to completion. Luckily, you are confident you can handle the workload and be productive. This may severely hinder your opportunities to travel. Nevertheless, you make the best of it. Your freedom may be limited by extra obligations or someone in need. Better to serve your time, as indulgence can be more than costly.

JUPITER OPPOSITION SATURN

Since you are subject to additional responsibilities that limit your freedom, you may need to postpone your trip for a later date. Any travel purchases will be deemed a poor investment. You may be overwhelmed with work that requires long hours. As you are shouldering extra responsibilities, progress is slow. You may be required to take care of someone in need. As you are being tested, hold tight to your dignity and work hard to secure your position.

Jupiter/Uranus

JUPITER CONJUNCT URANUS

Given that this is a fabulous time for self-discovery and growth, take the initiative to travel to a new, attractive place that inspires your passion for living. Change will work to your advantage and instill a confidence that bolsters your individuality. Feeling a great sense of freedom and expansion, seize the chance to pursue your independent goals. Business dealings are also apt to go smoothly. Purchases, especially of innovative products, work to your advantage. While on your trip, exciting insights will be acquired through philosophy, religion, science, esoteric practices, or other cultures. Surprise favors or invitations may arrive unexpectedly to add to an otherwise uplifting vacation. New ventures or people will open doors of opportunity that benefit you in the future.

JUPITER TRINE/SEXTILE URANUS

When Jupiter is in an auspicious trine aspect to Uranus, discovering new lands becomes a fabulous experience, especially when Jupiter occupies the third or ninth sectors of travel or the fifth sector of romance and leisure life, while the sextile is more subtle. Windfalls of luck could make this an excellent time to see the world under the Jupiter trine Uranus influence. You will be thrilled with the genuine treasures you find while on your journey. Extraordinary individuals may further your growth and dramatically change your life. Progress may be made in the areas of philosophy, science, religion, esoteric practices, or other cultures. Support, gifts, and invitations are a welcomed surprise as you tour your chosen destination. A freer and buoyant outlook enhances your travels and potential for success.

JUPITER SQUARE URANUS

The changes you hope to make are out of sync with your expectations. Unexpected situations push you to come up with an original strategy concerning your travels. An overwhelming independent streak encourages you to expand your perception of the world. Although you can trust yourself with newly implemented plans, you may question other people's reliability. Trips, domestic or abroad, are exciting yet meet up with scheduling changes and erratic circumstances that challenge you every step of the way. The timing is not supportive of your need for freedom and exploration. You might want to indulge yourself in unusual subjects such as enlightening philosophy, esoteric practices, religion, or the occult. Even these topics may seem too far-fetched for your interests. Economic and business transactions tend to be overrated. Someone you meet may have a flamboyant style that is appealing yet unstable. Gather your insights together, as this is a time of preparation.

JUPITER OPPOSITION URANUS

You may feel the need to start a new cycle in your life, which may involve travel, but the freedom you desire is hindered by unstable situations that require more time to be resolved. Expectations of your future are overrated. The timing is premature for you to move too quickly into a new direction or plan that great trip. Advances made now could be disruptive to your normal routine. You may need to curb your demand for more freedom and growth until things settle down. Erratic situations can cause much tension. Purchases are also unwise at this time and are apt to be expensive. Any gifts or favors may come with stressful obligations. A new individual, although interesting, may be too eccentric for your style. Keep your original ideas intact, as they will serve you in the near future. Further yourself through philosophy, religion, esoteric practices, other cultures, or independent realizations.

Jupiter/Neptune

JUPITER CONJUNCT NEPTUNE

The ideal trip or vacation can be experienced under this influence. As you attract goodwill, you are protected in any new environment. A gentle persona is more interested in enjoying the colorful, eventful journey that captures one's imagination in every respect. You will be moved by exotic lands with scenic landscapes. Drawn to the creative arts, mystical religions, and spiritual philosophies, your open-minded manner is well received. Conceptual growth far outweighs any business or financial considerations. You will be prone to dreaming of the ideal traveling experience as you desire more adventure and freedom. Realistic plans will help you achieve this idyllic goal. If your trip's itinerary is not up to par, make the best of it. You can still have a great vacation. Beware of financial schemes that guarantee a splendid vacation. If you are careful with those who might squander your money, you can relax with ease enjoying your adventure.

JUPITER TRINE/SEXTILE NEPTUNE

Jupiter in favorable trine aspect to Neptune highlights a magnificent journey, especially when Jupiter is in the third or ninth sector of travel or the fifth sector of romance and leisure life, while the sextile is more subtle. The trip of a lifetime is frequently experienced under the trine aspect. Here, newly discovered cultures will fascinate you. Enjoy the scenic splendor that captures your imagination, and you will surely be moved. Whether you are spending on traveling necessities or luxury items, the advantage is on your side. Be creative and open to the inspiration around you.

JUPITER SQUARE NEPTUNE

A vague restlessness will promote visiting a tranquil environment. Taking a pleasure trip or recuperating at a peaceful retreat is a possibility. Plan carefully, as everything is subject to uncertainty. Overrated expectations may come to pass as your agenda doesn't materialize as planned. Right now, you cannot count on anyone but yourself. Even financial dealings are suspect to fraud, so keep your wits about you. In showing compassion for those in need, you will receive an unexpected benefit.

JUPITER OPPOSITION NEPTUNE

You may need to guard against overoptimism and misplaced trust, as you are not being very realistic. That great journey that you have had planned may be delayed or encounter disappointments. Still, you are confident that things will work out. Since you are vulnerable to scandal, watch your expenditures. If you are not traveling, you certainly will be daydreaming on the job of the ocean voyage or scenic expedition that you could be enjoying.

Jupiter/Pluto

JUPITER CONJUNCT PLUTO

Travel opportunities offer wonderful personal and business success. Confidence in your plans attracts goodwill and cooperation from others. An all-consuming journey will bring great depth and meaning into your life experience. A new perspective on your past, present, and future will ensure the progress of your ambitions. Your negotiating power will book that special expedition or land that great deal. Insight into philosophy, spirituality, or religion intensifies your beliefs. You are self-assured in all of your actions. You are encouraged to cooperate with others to gain their trust and pursue your freedom, as you know with compromise you can advance your position. Being agreeable and optimistic in group situations will work in your favor. As you desire adventure and personal growth, travel is on the agenda. You must have faith in your philosophy and goals, as you might be tested. Any subtle manipulation by others can be resolved. Travel will be enjoyed under this influence as long as you are willing to make adjustments.

JUPITER TRINE/SEXTILE PLUTO

Jupiter in positive trine aspect to Pluto brings a superb traveling adventure, especially when Jupiter is in the third or ninth sector of travel or the fifth sector of romance and leisure life, while the sextile is more subtle. Confident in your chosen itinerary, you are sure to experience a meaningful journey. As the advantage is on your side, you easily persuade others to bring out their best, so everyone benefits. An optimistic outlook encourages goodwill and inner strength. Spiritual, religious, and philosophical growth inspires greater future achievements. Business and economic transactions attract lucrative results while traveling.

JUPITER SQUARE PLUTO

An intense period of expansion lies ahead of you. Traveling, although opportune, is hindered by setbacks. Business affairs too are riddled with complications. You must hang on to your personal faith to guide you through this challenging time. Everyone needs to benefit from negotiations; otherwise, a one-sided deal will escalate existing difficulties, especially while traveling. Compromising where possible will elicit more cooperation from those around you and allow your greater potential to be seen. If you are subject to others' philosophical or religious ideas, keep your perspective on maintaining moral values. Your own truth lies in your actions.

JUPITER OPPOSITION PLUTO

Although you wish to expand upon your personal growth, you may need to understand your past experiences to acquire a full perspective. Insightful realizations in philosophy, spirituality, or religion offer you guidance, even while on the road. Still, travel plans may encounter some resistance. Business and economic dealings may be difficult to negotiate. Have faith in yourself and compromise where it is needed. Cooperating with others and winning their confidence will ensure the best results.

Positive Influences in the Third and Ninth Travel Sectors

The astrology chart is divided into twelve sectors, and when it comes to traveling, the third house sector in astrology rules over brief trips and the ninth house sector rules over distant travel. If there is a positive influence in either of these sectors, then your traveling experiences are bound to go smoother. Having Venus and/or Jupiter, the benefic planets in astrology, in one of these house sectors of the astrology chart will attract benefits and goodwill while traveling, whereas having Saturn here might attract delays or obstacles. It is recommended that a favorable influence is in or affecting your travel sectors to ensure a good and safe trip. You may also want to consider having planets make positive aspects to your third and/or ninth house sector cusps of travel, such as Jupiter in favorable trine to the third house cusp and thus in favorable sextile to the ninth house cusp.

Even though you may be experiencing and leaving for your trip under good transits to the third and ninth house travel sectors, the Moon in adverse angle to Mars, the Moon in adverse aspect to Uranus, and Mars in adverse aspect to Saturn, Uranus,

Neptune, or Pluto are to be avoided when starting your trip. You can track the adverse transiting Moon/Mars influences on my website: www.ChristineRakela.com. For more information on adverse transits, please refer to chapter 12: Adverse Travel Times.

Positive Aspect to the Ascendant of Your Natal Birth Chart

Since the Ascendant indicates how you are going about approaching a certain goal, it's important to check the Ascendant to see if there are any adverse aspects from other planets occurring when starting out your journey. Never leave when it's approaching or under a Uranus adverse aspect such as a square or opposition angle. This is just way too volatile, like a Mars (Ascendant) / Uranus aspect that can cause the unexpected to occur. Your travel excursion may not turn out as planned, and an accident may be in the offing.

(Please refer to your natal astrology chart to ascertain whether there are any adverse influences to your Ascendant before traveling.)

Although your traveling profile will be informative, no matter who is traveling, adverse influences will still cause difficult and sometimes disastrous traveling occurrences. The adverse daily influences need to play out. However, when using the "travel strategy," you can skirt around them to avoid the potential problem. And remember, just because your astrological transits are relatively good, if the daily transits indicate a major accident, this may happen. Everything must be taken into consideration.

The travel strategy is a planetary outline that is sure to encourage a favorable traveling experience if properly followed.

Chapter 4

HOROSCOPE SIGNS AND TRAVEL

Besides using the travel strategy, getting along on a day-to-day basis while traveling can also be influenced by your horoscope Sun sign. The tropical zodiac is used here in this chapter. Dates may vary depending on the date, time, and place you were born. Refer to your astrology chart for greater accuracy.

Aries (March 21–April 19)

Aries will undoubtedly want to be the first one to arrive at any destination. You may at times feel like you are competing with others in a race to the finish line, but others have to admire your pioneer spirit of adventure. With suitcases packed, you are ready in a flash to travel the world. Your fearless demeanor is always open to new discoveries, especially in unexplored territory. Charting new terrain and visiting fascinating regions of the planet will pique your curiosity. Journeying about from place to place agrees with your style as well. Your quick-witted persona will find you venturing off into many new directions. Embarking on a journey to pursue unseen landscapes will arouse great excitement. Although you prefer being the leader, you will follow as long as you feel like an equal with your tour guide. Even then, you are inclined to persuade your guide to move in your desired direction. Known for your independent nature, you are keen on doing your own thing. Your travel companion had better be as fast-paced as yourself to promote a successful trip. Although you are highly motivated to see all the sights you can in one day, this hectic pace may also arouse your temper, as patience is not one of your virtues. While on the road, a splitting headache might be the only thing that deters you from reaching your destination, so be sure to bring along some water and aspirin. The nice thought about traveling for Aries is that you can always travel down a different road, and every one holds great excitement!

Taurus (April 20–May 20)

Although you can make the best of it while on the road, you prefer more comfortable and luxurious accommodations when it comes to traveling. You like the idea of making your trip secure and will slowly but surely acquire the travel plans that work best for you. As long as your journey is well thought out, you can relax and have fun with every aspect of your traveling expedition. Others may not always appreciate your slow pace, until they recognize that this is a great way to enjoy a terrific trip. You know that partaking in a fine dining experience, strolling through newly discovered sights, or basking in the sun on a sandy beach is the ultimate in travel. In arranging your trip, you will be looking for every deal you can, not spending a penny more than necessary. In shopping around, you will eventually find an inexpensive trip that still provides comfy accommodations. The more you are pampered, the more you dream of your next vacation spot. Since you may not always be prompt, especially starting your journey or at checkout time, leave early and plan ahead for delays. Traveling under stress will bring out the worst in you and possibly cause throat or neck problems. A stubborn attitude could also put a damper on your trip. Cooperating with others broadens your social life and enhances your overall journey. Aiming toward a peaceful and pleasant trip will attract the comfort you seek.

Gemini (May 21–June 20)

Being true to the duality of your Sun sign, you will prefer to visit at least two places on your trip to satisfy your versatile nature. Involving yourself in a multifaceted journey will not only inspire you, but keep you from experiencing boredom along the way. Since you have a thirst for knowledge, you want to exercise your freedom to absorb all of what life has to offer. As long as you are mentally intrigued, you will enjoy any out-of-town excursion. Your versatility and adaptability are quick to accommodate any unexpected changes to your travel itinerary. You greet each and every travel opportunity with great anticipation, as the sky's the limit in exploring new discoveries. Thriving on nervous energy may cause you to burn out, catch a cold, or be prone to arm, shoulder, or chest injuries. Broken collarbones are not uncommon. Regardless, you experience a quick recovery, for life can't wait when it comes to traveling the world. Since you are a wonderful conversationalist, you will want to be well informed on every subject matter, possibly studying up before you embark on your journey. Learning new and fascinating pieces of information will excite your travels and settle a restless mind. Only on occasion will your fickleness deter you from clarifying your position about a travel itinerary. Nevertheless, your swift thinking is soon to recover from any lagging plans and stimulate a new interest in your journey. Quick wit can be appreciated in any traveling experience, yet developing a broader understanding of different cultures is more rewarding than superficial knowledge.

Cancer (June 21–July 21)

In planning your trip, you are keen about trusting your intuition for the best advice. You will surely be guided to an inviting place that you can call home as you nestle in for the night. Accommodations that allow you to feel safe and sound are important, so you can relax and enjoy your surroundings. Appetizing meals must also be provided or in close proximity to keep you nourished and happy. Afterward, a moonlit walk on a sandy beach will draw your attention. The best way for you to feel comfortable while traveling is to be able to create a homelike ambiance wherever you go. Occasionally, your moods may sometimes interfere with your traveling experiences, but your instincts are always on target and will steer you into some very exciting places that include a safe place to nest. Wanting to feel like you belong, you may be more comfortable visiting the same old familiar places. You are especially at home when in an accommodating environment serving delicious food. You also prefer to cuddle after you explore the town, which encourages both romantic and family outings. You may find that only stomach problems interfere with your enjoyment of new traveling experiences, so be careful of what you eat. You are naturally assertive, but will become aggressive if your surroundings are threatened in any way. The wonderful memories you accumulate will continue to inspire more and more traveling escapades in the future.

Leo (July 22–August 21)

You are keen on enjoying yourself to the fullest. Reveling in holiday travel and pleasure trips, you use your creativity to plan for a fabulous trip. Your travel itinerary will expose you to the delights of royalty in Monte Carlo or braving it through the jungles of the Amazon. You take pride in planning the best trip of them all. Since you wish to win the approval of others joining you on your journey, you will go to great lengths to seek the ideal accommodations for everyone. Inspiring others, you are confident that things will go smoothly. During your excursion, you can be quite the entertainer. Usually you exercise a warm disposition, but if you channel your occasional demands, your traveling experience may be close to perfect. Being stubborn may also alienate you from communing with those around you. Since you expect a lot of yourself, you could overdo it on your journey, causing aches and pain with your back. The idea is to enjoy your trip; otherwise, further stress could lead to heart problems. Your courageous survival instincts will encourage you to venture into any environment. Most will admire your leadership ability and look to you to be their travel guide. Appreciating the attention you receive, you will gladly take center stage to lead your group into a memorable adventure.

Virgo (August 22–September 22)

When it comes to traveling, your detailed agenda does not overlook anything. You are organized to a "T," which includes every compartment in your luggage as well. Although you are adaptable, you prefer that everything go smoothly, and in most cases it will since you've planned well. A cerebral approach will have you analyzing each day of your trip and allowing you to accomplish everything on your agenda. The excitement you feel in getting things done will fuel your vitality to achieve more. Your traveling companions can relax knowing that you've planned your trip better than a travel guide. With such high expectations of yourself, you may expect the same from others. Watch that critical observations don't spoil the journey. Approaching problems from a practical point of view will be helpful in resolving them. Being too picky will only lead to digestive trouble, so attempt to be carefree and enjoy the sights around you. Whether it be roughing it in the wilderness or dining like royalty, you are impeccably dressed for all occasions. Your logical inclinations will come in handy when calculating the overall expenses. Wanting to thoroughly understand every aspect of your traveling excursion, your curiosity is aroused with each place that you visit. Such information not only will be mentally stimulating, but will inspire you to explore other traveling vistas. You may be especially attracted to places of refinement. Your keen eye for detail will appreciate the splendor of ancient castles or a modern-day, stratosphere skyscraper. You are convinced that sticking to your agenda will allow you to see more in less time. Now you must convince others of that fact! In aiming for the perfect trip, you will find great satisfaction in any journey.

Libra (September 23–October 22)

You truly enjoy visiting new places as it allows you to expand your social circle, even connecting with those of a higher echelon. Since you prefer sharing your experiences with others, you may always have a traveling companion with you. Of course, it's much more fun this way too! You tend to gravitate toward beautiful surroundings. While on the road, you desire first-class service everywhere you go. Your diplomatic approach is sure to improve accommodations not up to your expectations. No other sign knows how to turn on the charm and persuade others to your point of view, which will come in handy while traveling the world. Being attracted to places of refinement, you aim toward the best in travel so you can have fun and relax with the ambiance. You know that keeping the peace will create a harmonious environment, appreciated by all. However, your physical health may suffer under too much stress or arguing, thus causing problems with your kidneys. Normally you are quite cooperative, but you can become very defensive if plans don't go your way. Your willingness to converse and generate feedback from others may solve any dilemma. Whether it be a walk on a sunny beach or a ballroom gala, you are well dressed for any occasion. Sometimes you may feel that the riches of life are for you, yet you are willing to compromise if it calms everyone's nerves. You are aware that for a trip to be fulfilling, everyone must play fair. Your social etiquette will be appreciated by all. Only the frustration of indecision will delay you in embracing a great travel adventure.

Scorpio (October 23–November 21)

You are intensely driven to put together the best travel itinerary to get the most out of your trip. In-depth research may require extra time, but will pay off in a beautifully planned excursion. Once you are involved with your journey, you are keen about seeing as much as you can. You are attracted to places that pique your curiosity, and may find yourself obsessed with certain sights that will be frequently visited at a later date. Although you are sure to enjoy your solitude, your dynamic personality draws well-wishers your way. Wanting to increase your understanding of a particular place, you will go to great lengths in probing into everything to satisfy your need for knowledge. Your traveling peers will view you as a charismatic leader and will authorize you to be their guide. Fortunately, you can rely on your resourcefulness to acquire safe passage to any destination. While traveling, you can appreciate time alone in having a meaningful experience with what's around you. As a couple, however, you can have a passionate romance that takes your breath away. You will have better results when your intense energy finds outlets that channel any pent-up feelings. Even so, your need to be in control of your environment may put others on the defensive. Relax—it's a vacation! You can be either charming or scary. Being charming will get you to more places, especially with the elite.

Sagittarius (November 22–December 21)

Given that you are the sign that rules over travel, you will either feel a natural affinity to exploring the world or be able to quickly gather yourself together when called for to partake in an adventuresome journey. Always wanting to experience new environments and people, you are excited at the prospects before you. Your strong desire for freedom will have you spontaneously packing your bags and venturing out. Traveling is also mentally stimulating for you, from the beginning stages of planning your journey to actually taking it. Bold Sagittarius will travel anywhere for mental, social, and physical stimulation. Experiencing the journey is what you find intriguing. With such a strong sense of independence, you can easily travel alone. You prefer seeing everything you can, enjoying each sight to the fullest. Every trip you embark on may be an educational experience as well, which certainly suits your style. Your aim is not just to gather new insights, but to acquire a deeper understanding of every place visited. Although you thrive on taking risks, you also have a tendency to bite off more than you can chew and become consumed with your traveling itinerary. This could easily wear and tear on you and your traveling partner. Your hips and thighs may be strained from overexertion. Luckily, your lively sense of humor will keep your spirits high and crown you a wonderful traveling companion. In describing your journey, you are a terrific storyteller, attracting the ears and eyes of all those around you. Whether you travel overseas or domestically, you are sure to explore the treasures of one town after another, all the while discovering more and more about what exists in your world.

Capricorn (December 22–January 19)

Your no-nonsense manner will be appreciated by all in your surroundings. Exercising a strong persona, you are sure to acquire what you want in travel accommodations. You've earned it, so why not have the best. Taking a practical approach to your traveling agenda will also secure a great trip. Others will prefer your reliable manner, knowing that you are someone they can depend on if need be. The patience you display will be admired by others. You know you will be rewarded for time spent organizing your trip's itinerary. Calculating the ideal route will add to the pleasantries of your traveling experience. Securing your journey with a clear outline will put yourself and others at ease. Why leave anything to chance? With everything so well thought out, you are bound to capture the true essence of every place on your agenda. You will go to great lengths to make sure your trip is a success, due to the many sights and meaningful experiences you will attain. Traveling high and low, however, may take a toll on your knees, joints, bones, or teeth. You may need to exercise some caution, so as not to interrupt your journey. You are willing to address any challenge that you encounter along your trip, including overcoming a lack of confidence to expand your social circle. This may be easily pursued if you work alongside others, as opposed to taking command. However, your leadership ability will be applauded when you prove yourself through hard work and consideration for others while on your journey.

Aquarius (January 20–February 18)

Your freedom-loving sign is always intrigued with traveling to new, exciting places. You insist on being unique in planning your trips and creating your own rules along the way. You favor meeting new faces and developing interesting friendships that enhance your exhilarating journey. Many will appreciate you for your uplifting approach and refreshing insights. While traveling, your intuition will act as a terrific guide. You welcome spontaneity and the fun that it brings. Always a humanitarian, you will direct people toward fair play. Although you don't mind traveling independently, embarking on a journey with a companion or group suits your fancy just fine. You are keen on trekking through unexplored territory and sharing your insights with others. When it comes to traveling the world, mental stimulation is all around you. In order to keep you inspired, you jump at the chance for fascinating discoveries. Your innate restlessness encourages you to quickly reach your destination. However, it may be at the expense of hurting your ankles and knees. Erratic gestures could also cause accidents, so be especially careful when rushing. Trying to catch the tour bus isn't worth it if you sprain your ankle in the process. Pacing yourself will allow you to make progress while traveling and avoid the unpredictable. If you decide to be a rebel at heart and avoid the rules and regulations set by your traveling companions, you may end up traveling alone. Although you will still find some enjoyment on your own terms, having another partake in your journey will be especially fulfilling.

Pisces (February 19–March 20)

As a dreamer, you may have a desire to travel the world. You have a tendency to bond emotionally to whatever you are exposed to while visiting new places. Being able to adapt easily to any surrounding will be an asset when traveling from place to place. You may prefer environments that are adjacent to rivers, lakes, or oceans. Occasionally, your ambiguous mannerism will throw others off track, even though you still have an idea of where you're headed. You will especially feel right at home when traveling as a group. Escaping from reality might be what drives you to explore uncharted terrain or appreciate a frequently visited site. Your romantic style is appealing while traveling with a lover. Because of your compassionate ways, you may need to guard against others taking advantage of you. Utilizing your perceptiveness will steer you in a positive direction, bypassing misleading elements. Although your view is not always realistic, you can see the best in a person or situation. Those you feel a connection with, you may feel obligated to help along with their journey. You like to plan a trip that offers some great moments and flexibility with your itinerary. Exploring the mysteries of the world or seeing the splendor of nature captures your attention. While trekking through the mountainside or wading through the ocean waters on a sandy beach, your sensitive feet may experience some aches and pains if you overdo it on prolonged excursions. Nevertheless, you will still be intrigued with the captivating world of traveling.

Chapter 5

THE TRAVEL SECTORS

The astrology chart is divided into 12 sectors, and there are two house sectors in the chart that promote travel, the third sector and the ninth sector. The third and ninth house cusps of these sectors describe traveling conditions for each horoscope sign. Below, you can look up your horoscope sign to find out more about your travel sectors. In this section, we are discussing your Sun's horoscope signs on your third- and ninth house travel sectors.

Travel and the Third House Sector

The third house sector of one's astrology chart represents short trips, such as brief excursions, weekend getaways, and daily treks, including quick road trips. The horoscope sign ruling the third house sector describes how you will plan your trip, what you will most likely enjoy while traveling, and what kind of a journey you will experience. Since this is also known as an area of basic education, you will learn a lot while on your trip. Planets in this sector in your natal astrology chart will also determine the outcome.

Travel and the Ninth House Sector

The ninth house sector represents long, distant trips, such as traveling to another state, voyages to another continent, extensive expeditions, and explorations of foreign countries. Travel in the ninth house sector is for journeying abroad or covering a greater distance and length of time. The horoscope sign here describes how you will approach planning for your journey, what you may appreciate doing, and what kind of experience you will have while traveling to faraway places. Since the ninth house is known as the area of the higher mind, education, legalities, spirituality, religion, philosophy, and other cultures, your traveling experiences are bound to have quite an impact on you, especially when visiting other countries.

For Aries

THIRD TRAVEL SECTOR: GEMINI

Traveling to multifaceted places will not only inspire you, but keep you from becoming bored along the way. Since you like the idea of going from one experience to the next, having at least two places to visit will agree with this sign's duality in the area of travel. As long as you are mentally intrigued, you will enjoy your traveling excursions out of town. There is a need to feel free to take in all of what life has to offer. However, thriving on nervous energy, you could easily burn out or be prone to arm, shoulder, or chest injuries. Catching a cold or experiencing a broken collarbone is not uncommon. Regardless, you are sure to plan fascinating trips that lift your spirits. Your versatility and adaptability have you ready to change your itinerary at a moment's notice like it was part of the old, original schedule. You know that every traveling opportunity has so much to offer as you soar to new heights of intellectual discovery. Only your fickleness may get in the way. Being well informed on your visits will make you quite a conversationalist. Your restless mind has a chance to learn new and interesting pieces of information that continue to excite your travels. Remember that it's one thing to be quick and witty and another to cultivate a deeper understanding of other stimulating cultures.

NINTH TRAVEL SECTOR: SAGITTARIUS

You were born to travel and have an innate desire to see the world. As you thrive on risk-taking, you enjoy the challenges met with each new traveling expedition. Your eternal optimism keeps you mentally stimulated, encouraging you to seek out new and fascinating horizons. As your expanded outlook gradually brings more meaning into your life, a new philosophy is developed. You like the idea of always having a trip to look forward to on your itinerary. You are drawn to diversity, so exploring foreign countries will be intriguing. Your open-mindedness will take you to many places that will have a tremendous impact on you. In seeing the larger picture, you are able to express a broader viewpoint. While traveling, your enthusiasm is contagious, easily inspiring those around you. Throwing caution to the wind, your freedom-loving style spurs you on to bigger and better vistas. Excessive or overrated journeys could be overwhelming, causing you undue stress to your liver, hips, or thighs. Also, stay clear of confrontations, as an overly blunt opinion could lead to an embarrassment. Since you are concerned with going beyond the experience and bringing more meaning into your life, your journeys are assessed for their philosophical value. Cultivating more wisdom will unlock social doors, establish ethical principles, and take you on a magical mystery tour of discovery.

For Taurus

THIRD TRAVEL SECTOR: CANCER

You are guided by your intuition and feelings to plan for the best travel experience. As long as you know you are safe and sound with warm, inviting accommodations and healthy provisions, you can relax and appreciate the sights. A moonlit walk on a tropical island may attract your attention. You may feel the need to set up a homelike ambiance wherever you go. Feeling comfortable, you can nestle right into any new surroundings. You may especially be at home when you are prancing about on the beach, accompanied by a few of your zodiac "crab" comrades. As long as you can cuddle, you can be geared up for both romantic or family trips. Although your instincts may steer you into some new, exciting places, you may always be looking for a safe nest. Wanting to belong, you may find yourself visiting the same familiar places. Only stomach problems will keep you from thoroughly enjoying new traveling vistas. You are naturally assertive, but will become aggressive if your environment is threatened. Your moods may sometimes get in the way of your traveling experiences, but you can always rely on wonderful memories to inspire you toward more pleasurable journeys in the future.

NINTH TRAVEL SECTOR: CAPRICORN

You are good at combining pleasure trips with business to get the most out of your traveling experience. Of course, the plus side to this arrangement is that traveling expenses could easily turn into business expenses. While on your journey, you like to be seen as a person held in high regard and will be very calculative with your opinions. In putting your organized plans into action, you work within certain boundaries that make you feel safe, especially when traveling overseas. You may be inclined to visit places of historical interest. Traditional values may persuade you to explore your ancestry in another country. You will develop a better understanding of the importance of your greater role in society. Social accomplishments are earned and should be prized. It is not in your best interests to take advantage of someone's accommodating nature along your journey. Respecting yourself means respecting others. Your ambitious attitude is to be admired and you may find yourself attracted to the idea of conquering Pikes Peak, but if knee or joint trouble flairs up, stick to lesser heights. Even though pessimistic at times, no matter how hard the journey, you are determined to go the extra mile required to reach your destination. Although you will implement rules, law, and order as a routine on your trip, your journey abroad is sure to be a well planned success.

For Gemini

THIRD TRAVEL SECTOR: LEO

You are definitely one for holiday travel and pleasure trips. Your aim is to enjoy yourself to the fullest. Being creative with your traveling itinerary may have you exploring the wild jungle or visiting a sultry desert island. Wherever you are, it's important you are able to move about and experience your own exciting discoveries. A desire for fulfillment will find you planning the best vacations of all. If traveling with others, you will want to know that your important contribution of traveling ideas is applauded. Being sure on your feet, you approach new journeys with confidence in your objectives, which makes you a great traveling companion. Wherever you are taking in the sights, you are delightfully entertaining and exercise a warm disposition. You can't help but express your opinion on all that is learned along the way. If you can channel your occasional demands, your trip may be close to picture perfect. You expect a lot of your physical self, which could lead to back pain. Keeping stress to a minimum will allow you to enjoy your journeys and avoid a heart attack! Being stubborn may also alienate you from communing with others. Revealing your spirit for survival encourages those around you to do the same. It takes courage to venture beyond our known environment. As others look to you as a leader, you could be a terrific travel guide that unveils the mystique of new adventures.

NINTH TRAVEL SECTOR: AQUARIUS

You truly enjoy traveling the world and are at ease with strangers and foreigners. An element of wanderlust surrounds you, inspiring the discovery of fascinating places. Much can be learned from listening to your intuition and planning your trip accordingly. You move beyond a predetermined path, breaking out of rigid conditioning. You may even reinvent yourself along the way, changing your philosophy completely. A traveling partner will appreciate your humanitarian spirit and admire your ingenuity. You can easily fit in with either the higher or the lower echelons of society. Your instinctive insights lead you to exciting and enchanting civilizations that fuel the intellect. Your independent nature allows you to explore the marvels of life while traveling. Touring with a group is also fulfilling when the mood strikes. Since you need space, being on your own promotes deep thought and study. However, watch that a too-detached attitude doesn't create loneliness on the road. Jaunting from one area to another at a hurried pace could cause an unexpected accident. Protect your knees and ankles by relaxing at rest stops, and try taking everything in stride, even rushing to see the largest stargazing observatory. An enthusiastic nature is always motivating you to follow your individuality. Fortunately, your rebellious tendencies are in line with knowing that you are part of an ever-changing society.

For Cancer

THIRD TRAVEL SECTOR: VIRGO

When it comes to traveling, you are well organized, right down to luggage that has a compartment for everything you will need. You are impeccably dressed for all occasions, whether you are visiting historical sites or appreciating a fine dining experience. Analyzing each day of your trip will encourage you toward planning to perfection. If needed, your statistical manner will be useful in keeping a financial account of expenses. You may expect others to be as neat and together as you are. Don't let a too-critical attitude spoil the venture. It's much better to enjoy the perfection of the Eiffel Tower than allow worry and nitpicking to upset your digestive system. Constructive solutions will have you arriving at your destination sooner. Wanting to thoroughly understand every aspect of your journey, your curiosity is aroused with each place visited. Such great mental stimulation will have you off exploring the world in no time. Places of refinement will be especially enjoyed. Your keen eye for detail will allow you to appreciate the splendor of snow-capped mountains or a tantalizing waterfall in spring. Aiming toward a specific agenda will have you exploring more sights in less time. You know that sticking to the schedule will promote a smooth journey. Yes, your ideas on achieving the perfect trip can be realized.

NINTH TRAVEL SECTOR: PISCES

You are destined to traveling overseas to uncharted areas. Fascinating civilizations come alive to open your cultural perspective like never before. By visiting such magical surroundings, your philosophy and spiritual beliefs are reinforced. You envision mystical waters, enchanting castles, and moonlit mountains. On your quest to navigate unknown territories, you are sure to find peace within yourself. Because you are more connected to the cosmos than others, you have a broader understanding of the elements in our universe that persuade our soul. Your innate compassion causes you to extend yourself to others to draw upon a larger realization of the world that can be experienced through contact with other cultures. Once it's learned, you are a magnet for higher knowledge that encourages travel in the future. As your journey unfolds, don't let flighty plans or people ruin a good time away. Be clear with your traveling schedule and avoid devious types. Long hours of seeing the sights on your voyage may take a toll on your feet. Comfortable shoes will allow your mind and body to continue to wander. Wisdom coupled with creative visualization equals a fabulous trip. Vast horizons lie before you, waiting to be awakened by your presence. Your ideals can be reached when you are realistic in pursuing the goal.

For Leo

THIRD TRAVEL SECTOR: LIBRA

While traveling, you enjoy being socially connected, especially to the higher echelon of society. You like the idea of sharing your experiences with another. Receiving feedback from your traveling ideas develops a healthy balance. You gravitate toward beautiful, luxurious surroundings, preferring first-class service if possible. Even when your accommodations are not up to par, your diplomatic approach will win favor with the hotel clerk. Wanting peace at all costs makes you a wonderful traveling companion. Disagreements and stress are sure to cause havoc with your physical health, especially the kidneys. A romantic rendezvous on a moonlit trail in wine country calms your senses. You are attracted to places of refinement where you can relax and appreciate the ambiance. You are well dressed for all occasions, whether it be a sunrise walk on the beach or attending a ballroom gala in the evening. At times, you might feel you were born to enjoy the good life. You are happy to compromise where it is needed. You know that in interacting with others, there must be fair play for your trip to be rewarding. As you naturally want to get along with everyone, you display renowned etiquette. Only the frustration of indecision will delay you in embracing a great adventure.

NINTH TRAVEL SECTOR: ARIES

Reaching for new, exciting horizons, you will not hesitate when it comes to traveling, especially abroad. You are quick to plan your traveling itinerary, pursuing a direct course of action. Your desire for adventure and interacting with fascinating new cultures will have you spontaneously boarding a plane to a faraway land. Countries that maintain a hot climate or sport a rebellious demeanor will appeal to you. Considering yourself a pioneer in the truest sense, you will conquer new territory as if it was to become your own. On your journey, this exciting influence can lead to sudden one-night or weekend stays that lift your spirits. For traveling instills in you a feeling of freedom to explore all parts of the world whenever the need arises. Filled with enthusiasm, your mind is ever ready to change its philosophy at a moment's notice from the influence of other stimulating cultures. You are thrilled with the idea that there is so much to explore on your traveling adventures. A courageous persona will confront any challenges along the way, such as a too-hectic schedule that could lead to headaches. Nevertheless, your energetic spirit will not only keep you motivated, but also will inspire any traveling companions. If you can remember to keep your impetuous nature in check, your journeys are bound to be exhilarating.

For Virgo

THIRD TRAVEL SECTOR: SCORPIO

Your intense effort in planning trips will pay off, as every place will have a chance to be visited. You are drawn to adventure and intrigue and may find yourself obsessed with certain sights, with a need to revisit these places in the future. Your interesting and dynamic persona attracts well-wishers your way. A strong, charismatic image will elect you to be the leader of the traveling pack. Luckily, you can rely on your never-ending resourcefulness to guide you safely. Not only are you capable, but your keen perceptiveness is an asset in reaching each destination. Carefully probing everything in sight, you hope to acquire a great deal of knowledge that can be used to enhance your understanding. Traveling alone gives you the chance to have a deeper and more meaningful experience. You also have the opportunity to experience intense romance as a couple. Keeping busy with a full itinerary will only add to your trip as you release any repressed feelings. Still, you may want to manipulate others in your surroundings, putting them on the defensive. Coercing those around you to your point of view will not win the favor of others. However, being your charming self will attract more opportunity, even with the higher echelon.

NINTH TRAVEL SECTOR: TAURUS

Your journey abroad will be a well-planned success aimed to please even the toughest customer. Whether it be a long-awaited cruise or visiting a foreign country, your travel plans will be secure to ensure you of the best trip possible. Although you are always looking for a great deal, first-class accommodations are what you desire. You prefer being pampered, but your stamina will see you through a long journey. Truly wanting to appreciate the beauty of "Mother Nature," you are eager for adventure as long as it is on your own terms. A slow, steady, and pleasant trip will knowingly bring fulfillment. Satisfying personal self-indulgence, you are keen to pursue luscious meals, tantalizing sunsets, and spa treatments. Liking permanence, staying at the same hotel with familiar faces will add to your comfort. You are certainly open to new situations or exploring the unknown, as long as these excursions are planned in advance; no surprises, please! Usually you are considered to be a docile creature; that is, until someone provokes the raging bull. You may also encounter neck pain or throat ailments that cause delays. Aim toward having leisurely time and you will sail with ease. Although you are not known to change your philosophy, you may find yourself taking on a more profound mindset by thoroughly understanding the background of other interesting cultures.

For Libra

THIRD TRAVEL SECTOR: SAGITTARIUS

A strong desire for freedom has you busy drawing up new travel plans when the mood strikes. Traveling by road, sea, or air will be sure to purge any mental cobwebs. Just the thought of taking a trip is bound to put you in a good frame of mind. However, you are eager to embark on your journey, possibly to distant lands, not just think about it. You are meant not only to expand your outlook, but also to cultivate a greater understanding of your world. With such a curious mind, each pleasure trip turns into a brilliant, educational venture full of fun and excitement. You may thrive on taking risks that others would shy away from, as your spontaneous nature looks for adventure. Your only fault might be biting off more than you can chew and becoming overwhelmed by your travel agenda. The strain may be felt in your hips and thighs, which might need a good massage following your trip. When it comes to describing your journey, you are a great storyteller and are sure to spice up your jaunt out of town to appeal to your enthralled audience. Your sparkling sense of humor makes you an excellent traveling partner. You may feel inclined to visit relatives or siblings, with happy results. If you travel abroad, you will find yourself sightseeing the treasures of one town after another, not spending a lot of time in one place. Your discoveries may lead you to many rainbows and inspire your presence in the world.

NINTH TRAVEL SECTOR: GEMINI

Mental expansion agrees with you, thus spurring on many traveling opportunities. Here your mind is stimulated by learning about the background of other cultures. A Gemini influence loves to accumulate information from foreign lands. While on your journey, you are quick to move about from place to place and gain from your traveling experiences. Don't be surprised if you find yourself acquiring new languages, as your active mind is prone to accepting new avenues of communication. Since you have the ability to see things from more than one point of view, absorbing a foreign perspective will fascinate you. You prefer arriving on time and are swift to check in and out, as required. Sleeping little, your restless mind is more interested in seeing the sights than staying in your hotel. The more variety that is in your day, the more energy you seem to have. However, a scattered disposition could throw you off schedule, stress out your nervous system, and, in a worst-case scenario, cause harm to your arms, shoulders, or chest. Exercising a more cerebral approach will help integrate ideas and contribute to your overall health. Your philosophy of life will be greatly affected by your captivation with various cultures. You will only be further encouraged to travel the world.

For Scorpio

THIRD TRAVEL SECTOR: CAPRICORN

A pragmatic approach to traveling gets your trip off to a good start. Others may find your sensible and reliable style a relief, as they know you are someone they can depend on. You are also able to exercise a great deal of patience while on your journey. Leaving nothing to chance, every inch of your trip has been mentally calculated. For the diligent effort you make with your traveling itinerary, you will be well rewarded. Your "think first and act later" attitude has you well ahead of others, especially where being on time is concerned. Although you might prefer an earthbound experience like hiking in the Grand Canyon, your knees are a weak spot, so slow down and move with care. Defining the territory with which you wish to explore makes you and your traveling companions more secure on your journey. Nevertheless, you are ready to tackle any challenge, big or small, that appears along the way. Your aim is to have a successful trip that involves seeing meaningful, selected sights that confirm your traveling experiences. You will be keen on overcoming a lack of confidence at times in interacting with others by establishing a social circle at the beginning of your trip. However, working with people as opposed to trying to take advantage of someone's kindness will win friends more easily, and allow you to feel like you've achieved a windfall of success socially and personally.

NINTH TRAVEL SECTOR: CANCER

The serenity of oceans, lakes, and streams will be very appealing in your traveling experiences. Moved by emotion, you will trust your "gut feeling" when venturing out into the world. You know your philosophy will be greatly affected by the people of newly visited lands. Yet, wanting to be in protective surroundings while traveling will be paramount. As long as a culture appears to be nonthreatening, you are receptive. You will be sure to set up a cozy home environment, whether it be on a sandy desert island in the Caribbean or atop the Himalayas. Once you feel relaxed, you are off to enjoy an enriching adventure. You may prefer traveling with a group or will develop your own clan as you journey from place to place. Being in touch with everything around you, you are aware of people's motivations and can persuade them to follow your agenda. Your moods may cause you to change your traveling itinerary on a daily basis. Try being flexible and watch that stomach trouble doesn't delay you. Here, your sharp intuition will turn out to be one of your greatest assets and will have you absorbing and utilizing information rapidly. In storing all those wonderful memories, you will have many stories to tell about your inspiring trips.

For Sagittarius

THIRD TRAVEL SECTOR: AQUARIUS

A strong desire for personal freedom has you thriving on each traveling adventure. Your freedom-loving sign is always intrigued with traveling to new, exciting places, and your unique style will clearly want to plan a traveling agenda that's just right for you. Insisting on being unique in planning your trips, you create your own rules along the way. You love meeting new faces and developing exciting friendships on your excursions in or out of town. Most people admire your refreshing spirit and fun way of thinking. Along your journey, your intuition will act as a wonderful guide. You will be articulate in persuading others how the daily schedule should go. Although you like to travel independently, you may also enjoy your excursions with a group, where sharing your original thoughts with others is inviting. Visiting unexplored sights is also mentally stimulating. Acquiring insightful knowledge will only inspire you to hurry up and plan your next trip. Deep down inside, you know that without interesting discoveries, life is boring. As you want to quickly reach each destination, the strain on your knees and ankles could frustrate your upbeat persona. Undirected energy could also lead to accidents. It's fine to express the excitement of embarking on a fascinating trip, but you will make more progress during your journey by pacing yourself. If you decide to rebel against rigid rules and ideas conveyed by those around you, be prepared to travel alone. Even in the midst of isolation, you will still be thrilled with surprising encounters along the way.

NINTH TRAVEL SECTOR: LEO

You prefer to travel in style. Comfort and elegance appeal to your royal tastes. Traveling first class allows you to project your regal image and attract prestigious contacts. Although luxurious settings are appealing, you will also enjoy being entertained by dramatic trips, especially abroad. You wish to explore all risk-taking adventures, as you are confident with your own expertise. Born to be a natural leader, you may find yourself guiding your traveling companions. You will gain much respect if you lead with your heart as opposed to your ego. As you have no trouble holding the interest of your audience, others may seek you out just to hear you describe your thrilling journeys. The overabundance of energy you put into your travel ventures may take a toll on your heart, spine, and back, especially if you are lifting heavy suitcases. You may want to roam the jungle of many places, but take your time and watch overexerting yourself. Your vacation plans are important to you and will cultivate a broader understanding of life. Spectacular, extraordinary, and breathtaking trips will continue to fascinate you, where traveling becomes a pursued hobby. You will especially find romance fulfilling while visiting another country. In creating a purpose-filled trip, watch that your demands don't interfere with what might be the opportunity of a lifetime.

For Capricorn

THIRD TRAVEL SECTOR: PISCES

You may find great satisfaction visiting oceans, lakes, and rivers. They agree with your meditative outlook. Fishing in a quiet stream, you can escape into moments of pleasant solitude. Wanting to experience the unknown, you are open-minded to adjusting your trip's itinerary. As you are a dreamer, you desire to travel overseas and dive into the culture of unexplored worlds. Along your journey, you are sure to find good in the people you encounter. You may also feel obligated to help guide them. Your compassionate and understanding nature is appreciated. Your perceptiveness will steer you around those who seem to be misleading. Regardless of this, your trips will bring wonderful experiences that delight your imagination. The more creative, the better. Once in a while, wishy-washy plans may cause an unproductive trip. Luckily, you are balanced by the polarity of Virgo on the ninth cusp, which can assist you in devising a meticulous approach to redefine your goals. Your voyage to new places offers you the chance to be an innovative visionary. Areas of mystique or nature's charm capture your attention. While wading in the ocean or hiking through the wilderness, your feet could encounter some aches and pains. Could it be that you are carrying too many unresolved issues? Have faith that your life experience will once again be enchanting, like a captivating waterfall in spring.

NINTH TRAVEL SECTOR: VIRGO

Your organized manner is a blessing every time you pack and travel, especially overseas. Everything is in order as you manage your trip with ease. You like clothes that are functional yet reflect your well-groomed image. Your mental skills are great at drawing up plans for a rewarding traveling experience. Each adventure is well thought out, which will satisfy your cerebral capacity for more information. You may discover that you are acquiring healthier habits with each trip you embark on from your itinerary. You exercise high standards, and your accommodations must be well kept, offering superior service. If your expectations are not met, watch that a puritan or complaining attitude doesn't undermine your journey. Think about appreciating the intricacies of a Tibetan sand mandala instead of stressing out your nervous system with anxiety. Rowdy environments are also to be avoided, and tasteful, charming places should be visited. Areas of historical value may appeal to you. Foreign countries, in particular, will inspire a new outlook on life. Your matter-of-fact viewpoint will purposely analyze others' philosophies and religious beliefs. Although they may not agree with your own views, you will still be influenced by gaining significant knowledge of other cultures. Exploring many of the vast regions of our world to enhance your intellectual potential will always intrigue you.

Aquarius

THIRD TRAVEL SECTOR: ARIES

When it comes to traveling, you embrace a pioneer spirit of adventure. Always wanting to be where the action is, you will spontaneously pack your bags and journey into exciting, unexplored territory. You have no fear in what may lie ahead, for it will be experienced only as a new discovery. Visiting unseen regions and charting new terrain will pique your curiosity. As staying in one place for a long period could become boring, jaunting from one area to the next is more your style. Your quick-witted nature will find you venturing off into many new directions. Even your drive to the grocery store will have you coming up with an original route to arouse enthusiasm. Not only will you find new roads to travel, but your drive to the store will never be the same drive on your return home. While getting started, you do not care to be delayed for a moment too long. As your independence streak runs high, you are keen on doing your own thing. If someone wishes to join you, they had better be as fast-paced as you, so your trips go smoothly. Occasionally, a raging headache will deter you from reaching your destination. Once relieved, you are back in action in no time. Although you are highly motivated to accomplish many errands throughout the course of a day, you need only to be careful that your impatience doesn't get the best of you while on the road. Your daring persona is sure to revive your vitality.

NINTH TRAVEL SECTOR: LIBRA

Attracted to refinement, you will seek out fascinating places, beauty, and harmony. Luxurious hotels that offer the opportunity to meet up with high-caliber people call your attention. Your classy persona easily attracts social invitations. Never at a loss for good manners and appealing attire, you shine. While traveling, you are good at seeing both sides of the coin and then making an objective decision. When anything goes awry, you are quick to restore order. Chaotic situations could put extra stress on your kidneys, which may find relief taking in a radiant sunset, preferably in some exotic land. You are not your average tourist and are willing to compromise where it is needed to support daily excursions. You may be more assertive in establishing a traveling companion so you don't have to be alone. Since you make friends easily, this should not be a problem. Sharing your trip with another satisfies just about every need. A worldly philosophy keeps you open-minded to foreign ideas, food, and living. Although intrigued, you are not so willing to give up your upscale traveling lifestyle that offers every comfort. Generally speaking, you love people and visiting places of elegance. Only an overly sophisticated attitude will limit the possibility of meeting some terrific people on your journeys.

For Pisces

THIRD TRAVEL SECTOR: TAURUS

Since you desire comfort with every traveling experience, you may prefer a down comforter and pillows in a hotel as opposed to camping out. Making sure travel plans are secure will also put your mind at ease. You know that taking your time on a well-planned journey will allow for a more enjoyable and relaxing time. Basking in the sun while sipping an island drink, partaking in a fine dining experience in your luxurious hotel, or leisurely taking in the sights with a travel guide is traveling at its best. The more you are pampered, the more you dream of your next vacation spot. In booking your trip, you will be money conscious, looking for a good deal. Shopping around, you will find the traveling itinerary that's right for you, but excellent accommodations must be provided. Since you are not one to be prompt, leave ahead to arrive at your destination on time. You don't particularly care to travel under stress, as it may cause throat and neck problems. Your stubbornness may also create difficulty. Cooperating with those around you will generate a smoother traveling experience. Developing a lively social circle to add to your leisurely activities will create a nice ambiance that attracts pleasant memories.

NINTH TRAVEL SECTOR: SCORPIO

Your profound philosophy will encourage you to travel the world. Given that each trip may need to have a special purpose, you will feel compelled to prearrange your trip to suit your needs. Your extremist likes and dislikes of areas to travel to will have you visiting specific places that satisfy your desire for intrigue. Don't be surprised if you become totally immersed in your expedition, for you are on a mission to uncover the secrets of every traveling venture. This is why mystical lands will appeal to you. Although you love romance and unforeseen adventure, dramatic experiences may cause undue stress for you, felt throughout your entire being, especially if your physical drive is suppressed. You are driven to experience everything, so do, even if your trip may become an odyssey of stories that others may find difficult to believe.

It is also wise to keep personal and financial obligations in check so your journey is not delayed. While visiting various cultures, others may find you fascinating or militant about expressing your point of view. They may also discover that your resourcefulness is a godsend, especially when a tour guide is needed. Personally, you will gather great insight by furthering your understanding of the world we live in. Upon returning from each traveling experience, you awaken to a deeper purpose as you reflect on your journey.

Chapter 6

TRAVEL COMPATIBILITY

Are you and your traveling companion compatible? Sun-sign compatibility indicates what kind of relationship one sign will have with another. This chapter gives you an understanding of how your trip will fare with your traveling partner to bring out the best of your traveling experience together.

Aries/Aries

These two lively signs are meant to conquer new lands when traveling together. Their dynamo energies will take them on risky adventures, such as journeying to the Greek isles or the monasteries of mountainous Tibet. They enjoy the physical challenge that's involved with a bold adventure. Relaxing as they move about, they rarely need to take time out. Aries are quick to pack and quick to go. Their trip may be the result of spontaneous planning earlier that same day! Aries can be seen in the land of luxury or on hiking and camping expeditions. Wherever they are, there must be lots of activity to channel their overabundance of energy. On occasion, their itineraries may clash and a compromise is not foreseen. Cooperation is a must while traveling, and two Aries may learn the hard way that this applies to them as well. It's also important that each of them takes their share of the responsibilities in planning their journey. Once everything is decided, they are a winning team ready and willing to embark on their daring tour of the world.

Aries/Taurus

Aries and Taurus are an interesting couple who are inspired by each other's approach to life and their traveling expeditions. Taurus will prefer to formulate an organized and well-accommodated agenda that Aries will be sure to indulge in while vacationing. Aries will want to roam about, conquering every corner of the Earth that Taurus will love to see. They will seek out breathtaking views that validate the magnificence of the world around them. A romantic rendezvous in Monte Carlo may suit their tastes. Of course, Aries will have a tendency to overschedule each day, while Taurus will want to enjoy each scene in stride. It is hoped that Taurus will be willing to share in Aries's adventure; otherwise, stubbornness could stymie the day. Aries too will need to be persuaded by Taurus to slow down and embrace the beautiful sights that will only enhance their union.

Aries/Gemini

When Aries and Gemini travel together, their innate qualities genuinely complement each other, making for a wonderful traveling experience. Aries's assertive pioneer spirit mixes well with Gemini's communicative skills and quick wit in exploring new lands. Gemini will surely appreciate Aries's spontaneous nature, as this satisfies Gemini's need for environmental stimulation. A mutually desired social scene may be found in Miami Beach. Aries is thrilled with Gemini's natural ability to converse with the locals and fellow travelers along the way. Gemini may even pick up the basics of another language. Both prefer to arrange trips that accommodate their need to move from place to place at a moment's notice. Their vitality will be consumed with such places as the mighty Colosseum in Rome or the Acropolis in Athens, which are sure to fascinate this ambitious couple. They are motivated by how much they can do and see in one day. No matter what is encountered, they will thoroughly enjoy any interesting journey with such great compatibility.

Aries/Cancer

Aries and Cancer may be viewed as an unlikely duo when traveling together. Yet, these two enterprising cardinal signs are actually a well-matched pair, as long as they give each other space. Cancer may need their downtime, and Aries may prefer running off and being more independent. Diving in the Barrier Reefs off the coast of Australia or touring the fortress city of Dubrovnik and its splendor on the southern coast of Croatia may satisfy both of their needs. When they come together after a busy traveling day, it's all hugs and kisses, as the sensitivity of Cancer and passion of Aries can create quite a romantic rendezvous. Cancer will swiftly set up a comfortable home base, and Aries will scout around, figuring out the traveling itinerary for the day. Aries may need to be careful of rushing Cancer into daring situations or not allowing enough flexibility for Cancer's moods. If Aries paces themselves and makes fewer demands, they will enjoy the pleasurable company of Cancer and still make it to their destination. Cancer may need to come out of their shell and be willing to venture out, knowing that Aries will explore the terrain, making it clear for safe passage. Listening to each other's needs is required for a smooth traveling experience.

Aries/Leo

These two exhilarating fire signs are destined to experience many thrilling moments while on their journey. Aries is motivated to travel to unexplored territory, and Leo is excited to live life to the fullest with their Aries partner. They will dress and dine on a grand scale that creates wonderful memories together. Both are able to encourage one another to cover a lot of ground, putting in extra hours that are well worth it. They may prefer to enjoy the good life, where they are entertained by their surroundings. Whether it be the glamorous evening spectacle in Las Vegas or the majestic Canadian mountains comprising Chateau Lake Louise, they share in the mutual wanderlust. They will love to show off speaking a few words in a foreign language in the country they're visiting, or displaying new traveling gear that inspires their trip. Although they complement each other just fine with their ambitious energy, both Aries and Leo have strong wills and may clash when deciding who will take the lead. Conflicts may also arise in choosing a starting point as well as a destination. A compromising attitude is essential to experience a smooth sailing vacation. The reciprocal admiration that is displayed will keep this couple buoyantly compelled to appreciate each other's company.

Aries/Virgo

Although this couple seems to be at odds with each other, when Aries and Virgo are traveling together, they know what they're best at and can arrange a fabulous trip. Enjoying it might be another story. Virgo is confident about planning a vacation with every detail in place, and Aries will encourage Virgo to hurry up and pack and go. If they can aim toward establishing a great bond of friendship, they can tackle even the most difficult problems while on the road. Journeying through Cape Town, South Africa, and seeing Table Mountain and Victoria Falls will be very rewarding. If a more social/intellectual scene is needed, they may prefer the magnificent Metropolitan Museum in New York City. Virgo may need to speed up to join Aries's quick pace, and Aries may need to slow down and appreciate taking in the facts and history to really experience the moment with Virgo. Aries is fast and mentally stimulating to Virgo. The incredible knowledge Virgo has with just about every landmark in sight intrigues Aries, besides the fact that Virgo is sticking to their agenda and keeping a record of expenses. Not known to venture too far from home, this pair may find convenience and comfort in riding in their own vehicle. Aries will love being in the driver's seat as Virgo, with map or GPS in hand, charts the way to their desired destination.

Aries/Libra

Opposites attract to make this couple a great match for traveling. Aries is willing to spontaneously explore the world, as Libra will easily compromise to make everything go smoothly. Libra is excited and motivated by Aries's ambitious nature, and Aries appreciates Libra's ability to arrange travel plans with diplomatic skill and a harmonious attitude. Libra prefers the best in accommodations and will choose some very luxurious places to stay. The impressive cities of Salzburg (birthplace of Mozart), Vienna, Munich, Lucerne, and Strasbourg, with breathtaking architecture and historical value, are bound to satisfy them both. When on the road, Libra will persuade Aries to relax and enjoy the sights around them, as opposed to rushing through town. Aries's aggressive style may even be an equal conversationalist to Libra in their social surroundings. They both will truly benefit from each other's strong qualities. Of course, once in a while Aries's impulsiveness will aggravate Libra's need for calm, as Libra's indecision will frustrate Aries's tendency to move quickly toward a new destination. Through it all, their individual energies will complement their vacationing wherever they wish to go.

Aries/Scorpio

The strength of these two signs individually makes this a great pair for traveling throughout the world. Aries likes to be spontaneous and be the first in line to take that thrilling cruise or see Michelangelo's statue of David. Scorpio is determined to get the best seats in the house or tour every corner of the Louvre in France. With such fortitude, these two signs are able to conquer vast lands that hold unique vacation sites. Aries's impulsive manner will motivate them both to put their traveling ideas into action, while Scorpio will immerse themselves in arranging the ideal trip. Although these two could be terrific travel guides, they would rather just guide themselves and not waste any precious time in seeing the sights. Aries and Scorpio will be especially taken by any trip that invites intrigue and adventure. This terrific match will be found venturing into the Arctic zone or researching the volcanoes in Hawaii. Whatever seems to be off-limits is worth exploring. Aries is bound to provide tremendous encouragement while touring the planet, and Scorpio will inspire great depth of experience for every place visited.

Aries/Sagittarius

This terrific pair will be seen gallivanting throughout the world and having the time of their lives. As traveling is part of their chemistry, they are interested in venturing out into unexplored territory for the thrill of it all. Sagittarius will enjoy arranging a fast-paced trip with Aries's spur-of-the-moment advice. These two certainly prefer being waited on in the throes of a luxurious hotel; however, they are well prepared to tackle Mount Everest if it suits their fancy. Similar interests will make travel easy. Seeing many places in a day is common practice for two energetic fire signs. You can bet they will not stay in one place for too long, as they will be inspired to check out the next adventure on their itinerary as quickly as possible. Jet-skiing in Glacier National Park, Montana, or a wild Kenyan safari may call their attention. Leaving some of their plans up in the air, they both can exercise being spontaneous as they go along. Although their active schedule could be a bit accident prone, this lively duo is ready to roll to capture the exhilarating moments encountered through traveling the world.

Aries/Capricorn

Although these are both very enterprising signs, Aries and Capricorn need to express their traveling intentions to avoid a trip that is moving in two different directions. Capricorn likes to plan and be prepared for all occasions, and Aries prefers to be spontaneous, winging it for the thrill of the moment. If they can put their two heads together, they will be able to arrange a successful trip that satisfies both parties. This can be accomplished only by opening up the dialogue between them. First-class accommodations are preferred while away from home; after all, they work hard for it. However, slower-paced Capricorn may have trouble keeping up with fast-paced Aries. Though they may seem like an odd couple, they can complement each other by introducing new experiences to their partner that make traveling fun and enjoyable. Their mutually driven strength will allow them to endure long, grueling trips, such as flying from San Francisco to Paris, taking the bullet train to Switzerland, and skiing the Alps for two weeks! A vacation that we all might envy.

Aries/Aquarius

This terrific team is sure to enjoy the auspices of traveling together. The spontaneity of Aries mixed with the inspiration of Aquarius creates great excitement on any journey. This "live wire" couple will pursue the most innovative trips. Whatever hasn't been explored will be. Taking in some delicious cuisine in Split, Croatia, and then touring the islands of Brac, Hvar, and Korcula will be of interest. Each sign has an effective way of motivating the other so that the fun just continues. If they had their way, they would never stop traveling. The vision of Aquarius will be eagerly pursued by the exhilaration of Aries. Although their opinions may differ on which vacation spot to visit or which site to see next, there is never a dull moment with this globetrotting duo. Their fascination with one another's outlook on their trip keeps them inspired along the way, especially while waiting through travel delays. Their enthusiasm while touring the world is contagious and motivates other worthy travelers. You may find this couple partaking in extreme skiing, whitewater rafting, or parachuting, since the better the thrill, the more the intrigue. Their slightly accident-prone nature will not deter them from experiencing every adventure known to humankind.

Aries/Pisces

The idyllic scenario of where to travel envisioned by Pisces is sure to arouse Aries's enthusiastic side. Pisces will want to be intrigued with their surroundings, and Aries will want to conquer the world. These two signs are able to assist one another throughout their trip to get the most out of it. Aries will persuade Pisces to tour one site after another, not allowing Pisces to become too immersed in one site for too long. Pisces will encourage Aries to slow down and appreciate the intricate wonders of our world, such as the majestic snowcaps of Alaska's Glacier Bay or the Eilean Donan Castle in the Scottish Highlands. Pisces's sometimes ambiguous approach will force Aries to take control and make sure all of the reservations are set and the right travel gear and attire are packed. As long as both are able to pursue their vacation preferences, they'll be happy on the road, in the air, or on the seas.

Taurus/Aries

Aries and Taurus are an interesting couple who are inspired by each other's approach to life and their traveling expeditions. Taurus will prefer to formulate an organized and well-accommodated agenda that Aries will be sure to indulge in while vacationing. Aries will want to roam about, conquering every corner of the Earth that Taurus will love to see. They will seek out breathtaking views that validate the magnificence of the world around them. A romantic rendezvous in Monte Carlo may suit their tastes. Of course, Aries will have a tendency to overschedule each day, while Taurus will want to enjoy each scene in stride. It is hoped that Taurus will be willing to share in Aries's adventure; otherwise, stubbornness could stymie the day. Aries too will need to be persuaded by Taurus to slow down and embrace the beautiful sights that will only enhance their union.

Taurus/Taurus

As two Tauruses can totally rely on each other, traveling together will be a warm and relaxing experience. Both know that for a great trip to happen, it has to be well planned, with follow-up reservations secured. Plush five-star hotels are preferred with down pillows and comforters and the ability to indulge in earthly delights. Since Taurus loves the idea of vacationing, taking time off to travel is always on their agenda. Strolling through the ancient ruins of Rome or sailing on the Adriatic Sea will be an appealing holiday retreat. They will also want to savor sumptuous dining and fine wine. A moonlit walk on the beach enhances an already romantic atmosphere that both Tauruses find quite pleasurable. Quiet time is respected, perhaps with an enticing book, and socializing is enjoyed, especially when seeing the sights. As long as they keep any stubbornness in check, sharing each other's company is a joy as they embrace the wonders of the world.

Taurus/Gemini

We might call this twosome an odd couple that is somehow able to come together when traveling. Taurus will be concerned with creating a solid trip with confirmed reservations at every location. Upgraded accommodations and superb dining are preferred. Gemini will figure out ways to enhance this traveling agenda to make the journey exciting, spontaneous, and carefree. An aerial view of the Hoover Dam and the Grand Canyon are sites not to be missed. Gemini will appreciate Taurus's reliable planning, just as Taurus will appreciate Gemini's interesting and uplifting approach to a traveling experience. Where they differ, however, could cause discord along their journey, as the stubbornness of Taurus may not agree with Gemini's willingness for change and taking risks. Although Taurus may be a little more particular, both can adapt to new environments in their own way. If they can overlook each other's worst quality, they can partake in the many cultures around them, finding a renewed sense of self while traveling the world.

Taurus/Cancer

Traveling together can be calm and relaxing with this zodiac team. As a couple, they have an innate understanding of what the other is thinking about, which makes for a nice rapport. Taurus can be relied upon to plan a solid trip that makes Cancer feel secure while being away from home. Both will prefer comfortable accommodations and take pleasure in fine dining. Leisurely walking through the streets of Venice as if they were back in time would certainly be enjoyed. Relaxation may also be found at a resort spa in Telluride, Colorado. For a day trip, Taurus and Cancer will enjoy visiting Lake Havasu City, where the original London Bridge that existed over the Thames River is now located. They both like an itinerary that gives them some direction, but allows for new places to be observed as well. At times, Cancer's moodiness may be provoked by the stubbornness of Taurus. Both need to be aware of their weaknesses and not give into them, allowing for a splendid trip.

Taurus/Leo

The tenacious spirit of these signs will allow them to survive any trip and build stronger bonds together. Both signs will want to partake in experiencing the luxurious surroundings of a vacation resort with all the trimmings. Once Taurus is convinced to take the time to dress up, this couple will be an elegant display in any dining quarters. They may need to spend more hours organizing a pampered, relaxing, and satisfying trip. The end result is a vacation worth talking about for years to come. Their mutual, uncanny perceptiveness will tune into each other's needs and desires for the ultimate in fulfillment. Taurus and Leo are inclined to take a cruise in the South Pacific or embrace the illustrious Niagara Falls. Similar interests will bring harmony as they visit every special sight. Setting stubbornness aside, they are bound to accomplish their planned agenda. Leo likes being the center of attention and directing the traveling itinerary of the day, as Taurus gravitates toward the charming, social persona of Leo. In journeying together, they realize the significance of having a well-suited partner with whom they can explore the planet.

Taurus/Virgo

The practical, organized skills of Taurus and Virgo may be the envy of everyone, especially when traveling. Their shared discipline keeps them on track with their well-thought-out agenda. They know that to have a great trip, taking their time in securing the hotel accommodations, a rental car, dinner reservations, and the daily tour schedule, is well worth it. Whether it be relaxing in the sun or enjoying an appetizing meal, Taurus and Virgo will ease into their vacation as it should be. If plagued by weather or transportation problems, they will stand steadfast until the situation is resolved. This efficient duo has no issue with sticking to a detailed agenda, budgeting as they go, and following a map or GPS to make their trip seem like a success on a daily basis. They may be inclined to visit Mount Rushmore National Memorial in South Dakota, where they will see the granite presidential monuments of Washington, Jefferson, Lincoln, and Teddy Roosevelt. Traveling light with casual attire streamlines extras that are not necessary. Their love of charting a new journey will find them researching books, magazines, and the internet to make sure they've thoroughly explored all of the options. With such intensive and careful planning, you will find this daring team thrilled with discovering the lands of Russia, India, or Australia.

Taurus/Libra

These two social signs trotting around the globe will find much enjoyment in traveling. They will visit the most beautiful, scenic, and relaxing places, such as Tuscany or Monte Carlo. Old World charm is very appealing to this duo. Wining and dining in style, they will seek out the finest in food and ambiance. Taurus will be wise and practical with drawing up a wonderful itinerary for their trip. Libra will depend on their social prowess to put those travel plans into action. They will be easily persuaded into touring towns that hold classical art and architecture that resides in ancient Rome and other parts of the world. Although this pair is selective about what they see, their primary concern is having a terrific time while traveling. Conversing about one special sight after another will keep them thoroughly inspired along their journey. This delightful team makes great traveling companions, and they know how to indulge in the most restful vacations.

Taurus/Scorpio

One of the most compatible opposites is Taurus and Scorpio, and because of it, they travel well together. Taurus provides what Scorpio needs, and Scorpio has a knack for knowing what Taurus desires. When designing their trip, Taurus will want to have everything in place for a secure and comfortable journey, and Scorpio will give the trip depth and meaning to bring back special memories. They might thoroughly enjoy traveling to Saint Petersburg, Florida, and viewing the fabulous Salvador Dalí Museum, which holds seven magnificent murals among his other major works of art. Occasionally, their naturally stubborn natures will have difficulty agreeing on a particular destination, but eventually their practical side will kick in to draw up a compromised itinerary. They are both drawn to hot climates, such as the Caribbean. Basking in the sun can be very rejuvenating. Understanding other cultures is also appealing to their knowledge. They acquire the most from their travels when becoming totally immersed in the journey.

Taurus/Sagittarius

Although Taurus and Sagittarius have different characters, somehow they manage to get along quite nicely while traveling. Charting a course of action will be preferred by Sagittarius and tempered down by Taurus, so they can appreciate the scenes around them without being too rushed. Taurus will be glad to draw up a traveling itinerary that's safe and sound, allowing them to gently ease into their trip. Sagittarius will encourage Taurus to take risks that they otherwise would not entertain while traveling. Sagittarius likes Taurus's reliability, and Taurus likes Sagittarius's positive attitude. When on their trip, they are both good with maps, GPS, and transportation, which enables them to visit more scenic locations than most. As one seeks out adventure and the other beauty, you may find this couple journeying to France to see the Louvre, the Musee d'Orsay, and Monet's Gardens in Giverny. Historical sites, where there's something to be learned, will also be very appealing. If they can be patient with each other's desires to visit certain places, they will both gain from each other's perspective while discovering what exists on Earth.

Taurus/Capricorn

The result of two earth signs coming together equals a very successful trip, especially when it's Taurus and Capricorn. Efficient planning and packing is a must. Both have an agenda that needs to be met for the effort they're putting into their journey. This team is practical on all they say and do. They prefer traveling when the reservations and accommodations are secure, for only then can they relax. Since they both desire to be greatly moved by their journey, their itinerary will be scheduled to a "T." They also hope to take advantage of the best travel package. Bargain hunting will drive them. They will be most comfortable on a Mediterranean cruise or European tour, as they are able to thoroughly enjoy the highlights of various sites without being rushed. With such wonderful compatibility, this pair could eventually tour all the corners of the world.

Taurus/Aquarius

When Taurus and Aquarius travel together, the "bull" and the "water bearer" join forces to create a great team while venturing out into the world. A well-orchestrated trip allows them both to have a fabulous time. Aquarius's intuitive know-how is used as a terrific travel guide as Taurus's pursuit of logic gives the trip a solid foundation that's hard to beat. Although Taurus looks for a bargain, they desire first class if it is available, whereas Aquarius is comfortable anywhere. As a couple, they prefer doing the unusual, like trekking through the magnificent pyramids in Mexico's Yucatan or venturing on a train through the Himalayas in Tibet. They prefer to see rare events in places few visit. Only their stubbornness will stall the great moments yet to be experienced on a trip. When they are ready to see each other's point of view, they can blend their ideas for a monumental journey.

Taurus/Pisces

This calm duet is very compatible while traveling. The insightful compassion of Pisces is well received by the receptive and, in turn, nurturing Taurus. Pisces will dream up a wonderful vacation, while Taurus is busy weaving it all together. Pisces is convinced that a trip that includes a humanitarian effort will give their journey more meaning. Taurus, preferring a relaxing trip with no concerns, at the request of Pisces will learn to explore their philanthropic side while away from home. Together, they can bring goodwill into the world. Basic accommodations and necessities may not fare as well for Taurus as it does for Pisces, so there may have to be a compromise here. Their travels may take them to the Peace Corps efforts in Kenya or the Hawaiian Islands, paradise on Earth. Their romantic expectations can be easily satisfied by a glorious sunset overlooking the ocean. Both can enhance each other's view of the world by appreciating what each other has to offer when exploring new lands.

Gemini/Aries

When Gemini and Aries travel together, their innate qualities genuinely complement each other, making for a wonderful traveling experience. Aries's assertive pioneer spirit mixes well with Gemini's communicative skills and quick wit in exploring new lands. Gemini will surely appreciate Aries's spontaneous nature, as this satisfies Gemini's need for environmental stimulation. A mutually desired social scene may be found in Miami Beach. Aries is thrilled with Gemini's natural ability to converse with the locals and fellow travelers along the way. Gemini may even pick up the basics of another language. Both prefer to arrange trips that accommodate their need to move from place to place at a moment's notice. Their vitality will be consumed with such places as the mighty Colosseum in Rome or the Acropolis in Athens, which are sure to fascinate this ambitious couple. They are motivated by how much they can do and see in one day. No matter what is encountered, they will thoroughly enjoy any interesting journey with such great compatibility.

Gemini/Taurus

We might call this twosome an odd couple that is somehow able to come together when traveling. Taurus will be concerned with creating a solid trip, with confirmed reservations at every location. Upgraded accommodations and superb dining are preferred. Gemini will figure out ways to enhance this traveling agenda to make the journey exciting, spontaneous, and carefree. An aerial view of the Hoover Dam and the Grand Canyon are sites not to be missed. Gemini will appreciate Taurus's reliable planning, as Taurus will appreciate Gemini's interesting and uplifting approach to a traveling experience. Where they differ, however, could cause discord along their journey, as the stubbornness of Taurus may not agree with Gemini's willingness for change and taking risks. Although Taurus may be a little more particular, both can adapt to new environments in their own way. If they can overlook each other's worst quality, they can partake in the many cultures around them, finding a renewed sense of self while traveling the world.

Gemini/Gemini

Two mentally stimulated Geminis will definitely enjoy traveling the Earth, with so many sights to see and people to meet. Enthusiasm runs high, from making reservations to involving themselves in an exciting traveling excursion. This duo is quick to pack and discover new horizons. All brochures or travel guides on their destination will be read and new cultures welcomed. Of course, lots of variety is what's needed to totally satisfy these mentally hungry travelers. They will have fun entertaining themselves and conversing with locals and fellow travelers while on their journey. In this case, the slogan, "the more, the merrier" is appropriate. Traveling by train or plane through America or Europe allows them to cover a lot of ground. They are happiest when making new friends, pursuing spontaneous ventures, and learning about their environment. When a trip is really impressive, superficial knowledge turns to wisdom.

Gemini/Cancer

When Gemini and Cancer travel together, they are bound to share their thoughts and feelings with each other, allowing each of them to appreciate what the other has to offer. Quick-paced Gemini will be the one who motivates Cancer to see the sights, as Cancer offers food and comfort along the way. Checking out the Napa Valley wineries and touring the countryside on a luxurious dining train will be a winner on their traveling itinerary. At times, Gemini may insist on staying out all hours of the night to discover what a town has to offer, whereas Cancer would rather be nesting in a cozy five-star hotel. Cancer may be keen on persuading Gemini to relax and enjoy the peaceful side of an environment or community, taking in the true culture that lies around them. Mentally inclined Gemini will welcome the exchange of information, as both signs benefit from exploring the wonders of planet Earth. You may find them roaming through the Yanks Air Museum in Chino, California, which holds over one hundred vintage airplanes completely restored to their original design. Although both Gemini and Cancer may need to compromise, doing so sets the pace for an amicable trip.

Gemini/Leo

The stimulating energy of Gemini and Leo inspires jaunts to every corner of the globe. Their delightful, playful manner encourages romps near an ocean resort, such as Monterey Bay. Their restless motivation will have them touring every site on the vacation guide map, especially to capture a glimpse of the spectacular ancient Roman gardens at the J. Paul Getty Museum in Malibu, to enthusiastically converse about it later that night. Since they can't seem to sit still, they may rush having dinner and sleeping, just to hurry up, get out, and see the sights scheduled for the day. Luckily, Gemini is happy to quickly draw up an agenda that allows Leo to experience what the world has to offer. Their curiosity will drive them to learn as much as they can, if only to motivate them toward more travel. Gemini and Leo will want to capture their rare moments on film, which is why you will see them sporting a camera that may even bear a tripod. Much can be gained from scheduled tours, but the idea of wandering into a town that offers a genuine experience will be quite enticing.

Gemini/Virgo

Gemini and Virgo are an intellectual duo who will be practical with every traveling detail. Both signs like to partake in drawing up an itinerary for the fascinating excursions they plan to take. They share the responsibilities while traveling, as well, but exercise a different approach when on a trip. Virgo will design an itinerary that is efficient so they are able to see all of the sights before moving on to the next stop. Fast-paced Gemini will not appreciate long visits, preferring to sprint from site to site and city to city. One way to balance their desires is to spend a little time apart, while both get to observe what they want to see. As Gemini and Virgo like to think things through, these two signs will enjoy their journey more if they have some quiet time to digest all of the new information. Visiting Ford's Theatre (where President Lincoln was assassinated), viewing the many educational sights at the Smithsonian, and touring the nation's capital in Washington, DC, will give you much to talk about. At night, relaxing with a good book or jotting down notes in a daily journal may be preferred over going out. Both signs are thirsty for mental stimuli, and if they can compromise on their approach, they will be considered terrific traveling buddies for life.

Gemini/Libra

These two easygoing air signs are well matched when it comes to traveling. They both like to be educated on the many places they will be visiting before embarking on a journey. Reading all of the historical facts or descriptions along the way will also be enticing. Their relaxed style brings harmony into any situation. This team will truly appreciate great conversation with other travelers on the road as well. Participating in festivities in a foreign country will be a must on their itinerary. Exploring the traditions and ancient ruins of Italy in Verona, Tuscany, Florence, and Rome will be a delight, both mentally and romantically. They both will display good taste and elegance and be appropriately dressed for the occasion. Once in a while, both of them will have trouble making up their minds, although Gemini might be quicker to arrive at an answer. With such great overall interaction, this duo will gladly enjoy every wonderful vacation experienced.

Gemini/Scorpio

The intensity of Scorpio will complement the quickness of Gemini in touring the world with great tenacity. Long journeys, where they can become involved with their intriguing surroundings, are preferred. Touring the world-famous Casablanca, the El Badi Palace in Marrakesh, and the ancient city of Volubilis will surely capture both signs' attention. Since Gemini is very adaptable to any new environment and Scorpio is driven to explore every site, you may find this couple traveling for weeks or months at a time. Nothing is too dull or too glamorous for Gemini and Scorpio, as they will appreciate a variety of vacation spots. This pair will have fun seeing great historical sites, glitzy city life, moonlit beaches, and camping out in new terrain. Their depth for intrigue keeps them motivated to conquer new destinations. Both are good conversationalists, especially when they are traveling the globe, for there's so much to talk about! Even when there is stress, Gemini will lighten the heaviness sometimes experienced by Scorpio, and Scorpio will have Gemini inspired by coaxing them to the next fun-filled or romantic rendezvous.

Gemini/Sagittarius

Gemini's wit and Sagittarius's fiery ambition are a powerful combination for traveling the globe in style. Besides enjoying life to the fullest, they will challenge one another to bring out the best in each other. Although this pair will appreciate luxurious hotels, they are just as comfortable camping under the stars, for they are more concerned about the meaningfulness of their traveling experience. Gemini and Sagittarius are keen on expanding their mental and physical prowess by exploring life in different parts of the world. They will pack their bags at a moment's notice and be off to the next exciting adventure that may be found in speedboating off the breathtaking shores of Split, Croatia, or hot-air ballooning in Albuquerque, New Mexico, where the world's largest ballooning event is held. Sagittarius may prefer outdoor activities and taking risks, while Gemini, needing cerebral stimulation, will enjoy learning about foreign languages and other cultures. These fire and air signs are well matched as they inspire each other to new heights while on their fascinating journeys.

Gemini/Capricorn

Carefree Gemini and structured Capricorn may have some challenges while traveling together. This unlikely duo must be willing to compromise to make any journey a success. Capricorn will prefer following an outlined itinerary for the best results, whereas Gemini is more comfortable with being spontaneous and winging it. Here, Capricorn will need to be more flexible and recognize that while on vacation, you can break the rules and have fun. Although Gemini can appreciate Capricorn's structured and reliable manner, the easygoing spirit of Gemini thrives on new experiencess so Capricorn needs to loosen up. Since they both want to accomplish getting to their destination, there is some mutual agreement, yet they may have varying ideas on which path to take. They will both like seeing the historical past, such as visiting the sites of Hungarian coronations, touring the Schonbrunn Palace in Vienna, and cruising on the Danube, which is bound to conjure up some great conversation. Capricorn will want to be in charge, but Gemini will add the final touches. As long as they are open to what each other has to offer, they will surely benefit while exploring the world.

Gemini/Aquarius

These two cerebral signs are a great match for traveling together. They are keen on motivating each other to enhance their insightful wit, especially while gallivanting throughout the world. There will never be a dull conversation between them, only a delightful rapport that lasts throughout the day. With Gemini's keen perceptiveness and Aquarius's grand intuition, they can plan an incredible vacation complete with all the perks. Since they both love their freedom, traveling by car or RV gives them the independence they need to carry out their own agenda. Jet-setting around the globe to distant lands such as Ecuador and the Galapagos Islands or the beautiful, Old World city of Prague, Czech Republic, will satisfy their thirst for intrigue. Since this pair needs excitement, you will not find them glued to one place for too long. They can easily wander in any direction, as they are adaptable to new surroundings. They are the best of friends, with Gemini arranging their travel itinerary and Aquarius steering them in the right direction. With such a great partnership, before a trip has ended, they are already planning the awesome details of their next one.

Gemini/Pisces

These two will enhance each other's best qualities while traveling together. Gemini's wittiness is sure to realize Pisces's dream vacation. The result is that both are happily satisfied while on their fabulously planned journey. Gemini, needing mental stimulation, will want to move quickly from place to place, while Pisces may be happy with just enjoying the impact of their immediate surroundings. Both may find satisfaction touring the legendary ruins of Pompeii or trekking through the Scandinavian countries. They may prefer their own transportation with travel gear it tow. Food can always be found along the way, with an interesting variety for anyone's palate. Their ability to be flexible and adapt to any new environment is a plus. However, there will be times when they are both wondering which way to go and end up delayed or not going at all. It's best if they decide their itinerary early on, before embarking on their anticipated journey. Once a trip is finalized, they can delight in the wonders of the world.

Cancer/Aries

Cancer and Aries may be viewed as an unlikely duo when traveling together. Yet, these two enterprising cardinal signs are actually a well-matched pair, as long as they give each other space. Cancer may need their downtime, and Aries may prefer running off and being more independent. Diving in the Barrier Reefs off the coast of Australia or touring the fortress city of Dubrovnik and its splendor on the southern coast of Croatia may satisfy both of their needs. When they come together after a busy traveling day, it's all hugs and kisses, as the sensitivity of Cancer and passion of Aries can create quite a romantic rendezvous. Cancer will swiftly set up a comfortable home base, and Aries will scout around, figuring out the traveling itinerary for the day. Aries may need to be careful of rushing Cancer into daring situations or not allowing enough flexibility for Cancer's moods. If Aries paces themselves and makes fewer demands, they will enjoy the pleasurable company of Cancer and still make it to their destination. Cancer may need to come out of their shell and be willing to venture out, knowing that Aries will explore the terrain, making it clear for safe passage. Listening to each other's needs is required for a smooth traveling experience.

Cancer/Taurus

Traveling together can be calm and relaxing with this zodiac team. As a couple, they have an innate understanding of what the other is thinking about, which makes for a nice rapport. Taurus can be relied upon to plan a solid trip that makes Cancer feel secure while being away from home. Both will prefer comfortable accommodations and take pleasure in fine dining. Leisurely walking through the streets of Venice as if they were back in time would certainly be enjoyed. Relaxation may also be found at a resort spa in Telluride, Colorado. For a day trip, Taurus and Cancer will enjoy visiting Lake Havasu City, where the original London Bridge that existed over the Thames River is now located. They both like an itinerary that gives them some direction, but allows for new places to be observed as well. At times, Cancer's moodiness may be provoked by the stubbornness of Taurus. Both need to be aware of their weaknesses and not give into them, allowing for a splendid trip.

Cancer/Gemini

When Cancer and Gemini travel together, they are bound to share their feelings and thoughts with each other, allowing each of them to appreciate what the other has to offer. Quick-paced Gemini will be the one who motivates Cancer to see the sights, as Cancer offers food and comfort along the way. Checking out the Napa Valley wineries and touring the countryside on a luxurious dining train will be a winner on their traveling itinerary. At times, Gemini may insist on staying out all hours of the night to discover what a town has to offer, whereas Cancer would rather be nesting in a cozy five-star hotel. Cancer may be keen on persuading Gemini to relax and enjoy the peaceful side of an environment or community, taking in the true culture that lies around them. Mentally inclined Gemini will welcome the exchange of information, as both signs benefit from exploring the wonders of planet Earth. You may find them roaming through the Yanks Air Museum in Chino, California, which holds over one hundred vintage airplanes completely restored to their original design. Although both Gemini and Cancer may need to compromise, doing so sets the pace for an amicable trip.

Cancer/Cancer

Of course, two Cancers together can set up a pleasant home wherever they go. Both of them will be adamant about having accommodations that are comfortable and cozy, and so should the transportation for getting there. Although they will enjoy sumptuous dinners out, they may find that cuddling up together after a long day of sightseeing is very appealing. Since the Moon, which affects one's daily moods, rules their sign, they may need to respect each other's requests so that moodiness doesn't disrupt their entire trip. They will also need to watch what they eat, as a long day of traveling could cause an upset stomach. A moonlit walk on the Cayman Islands will help ease any tension. Trusting that natural Cancerian intuition as their guide is advised, especially when the unexpected enters the picture. Going with the flow will surely be appreciated when embarking on their journey.

Cancer/Leo

It's surprising how a water sign and fire sign can make a great match, but it's true. Since Leo enjoys the limelight, they are bound to tour the hot spots in Hollywood, Graceland, or Broadway, New York, in search of celebrities. Both signs agree that first-class reservations and luxurious accommodations will provide the status and comfort they desire while on their exciting journey. They will also find themselves prone to overpacking, as Cancer likes all the creature comforts of home and Leo likes to be prepared for every occasion. Dining in style is a must, as this pair will display elegance at every turn. In most cases, they both will compromise on which places to visit. Leo may not care to tolerate any moodiness from Cancer, and if Leo is stealing all the spotlight, Cancer will quickly feel ignored. Being grateful for each other's company will keep them both quite happy. Although they like to spend when they are having a good time, they both still have a knack for being economical.

Cancer/Virgo

Cancer and Virgo are a very organized team when traveling the planet. Cancer will appreciate Virgo's meticulous approach so that everything is secure. The trip will work like clockwork, and both signs will feel at ease. It's possible with such great planning skills that they will be helpful with each other's traveling itinerary, since they've already done the research. Touring enchanting Ireland and visiting Saint Patrick's Cathedral, Blarney Castle, and the three Lakes of Killarney is a memorable experience. Their own calculated trip may involve keeping track of a budget, setting a daily traveling agenda, and logging in the miles from one place to another. Cancer will be grateful for Virgo's intellectual way of figuring things out. However, Cancer will prefer to rely on their intuitive skills to lead the way. With Cancer's silent strength to persevere and Virgo's ability to easily adapt to any environment, these two are a fabulous duo promoting a long-term union. Their mutual respect for each other is a refreshing sight.

Cancer/Libra

The fine rapport that develops between Cancer and Libra is sure to make this match a winner. The need of Cancer to link emotionally with his or her partner is complemented by Libra's desire to interact one on one in a relationship. They are both keen on comfort and beauty and will book accommodations in the finest places with the most exceptional view. The stunning landscapes and social scene of Sydney, Australia, or the panoramic wonders on a Mediterranean voyage are sure to impress this couple. Yet occasionally, Libra's indecision or Cancer's moodiness will have them not seeing eye to eye. Nevertheless, they will enjoy discussing the trip from the beginning stages to the end. Still, they both are respectful of each other's space and quiet time. Either one could take the lead while the other gleams over the beautifully scenic landscape, thoroughly enjoying their journey away. Tours and package deals or preplanned trips work well with this pair, as neither of them wants to miss out on any special sight.

Cancer/Scorpio

When Cancer and Scorpio travel together, there is a deep, understood emotional bond that guides their trip on an intuitive level. If anything, there needs to be a more meaningful reason as to why they are venturing out to new horizons locally or around the globe. Involving themselves with humanitarian enterprises, such as rescuing animals from an oil spill overseas or journeying to Southern California to save the beached whales, will be fulfilling. Relishing their privacy, they would also find pleasure in exploring Lake Tahoe or Yosemite National Park, for starters. Since Cancer and Scorpio are both water signs, they will blend together like two merging streams. This strongly connected duo will bypass superficial touristy sights in lieu of more moving experiences while traveling. They both will truly enjoy their quiet time, whether it be relaxing in their hotel suite or basking in the sun on a tranquil beach. Overseas, they would be intrigued with the coast of Portugal, which holds the Jeronimos Monastery and the 14th-century Alcazar. This pair does not care to be fettered by "extras." They will pack what is necessary, knowing that the idea is to have a great time traveling and enjoying themselves while en route to their desired destination.

Cancer/Sagittarius

This passionate duo is actually very compatible, although they are bound to learn a lot from each other. Sagittarius will need to be more sensitive to Cancer, and Cancer will need to be more outgoing with freedom-loving Sagittarius. Neither will react well when plans go awry. Sagittarius will be angered when the unexpected appears, and Cancer will feel overwhelmed by the tension felt. Still, they will both appreciate each other in different ways, which will continually build the bond between them. Their pensive intuition will act as a great travel guide along their trip. They will be mindful of using their sixth sense to tap into one another for the best results. Being flexible with their itinerary, both will find pleasure in the scenic drive on California's coastal highway or dining and being entertained in Caesars Palace in exciting Las Vegas. Friendly Sagittarius will always be there, providing the emotional support that Cancer requires, drawing Cancer out of their shell. Cancer will provide a cuddly, nurturing environment while on the road. Sagittarius likes the exhilaration felt in traveling to new places. Although supportive of Sagittarius, Cancer may prefer to play it safe, not wanting to venture too far from home base, even when tempted to explore new vistas. Cancer, once comfortable, will be inspired by Sagittarius to venture out, and Sagittarius will appreciate Cancer's warmth and homespun atmosphere wherever they both go.

Cancer/Capricorn

When Cancer and Capricorn travel together, opposites do attract. In this case, the strength of both signs creates a relationship foundation that succeeds at conquering any obstacle. This pair will agree on staying in a safe haven, like the charming Grand Hotel on the pristine, secluded Mackinac Island off the coast of Michigan. This summer hotel, built in 1887, offers Old World hospitality. Even in planning their trip, it will be a step-by-step process that leads to the accomplished goal, a sound and reliable trip. They will go out of their way to seize even the smallest reward. Spending days following up on a vintage stamp collection is not uncommon. Capricorn is driven to calculate their spending limit, prepare all of the accommodations and modes of travel, and double-check all tours on their journey's itinerary. Cancer never overlooks the necessities of home while traveling, bringing slippers, pajamas, whatever it takes to create a warm ambiance. Occasionally, Cancer's moodiness may interfere with Capricorn's structured manner or vice versa. Here, both need to respect the feelings and needs of the other to smooth over any rough spots. Regardless, these are two strong-minded signs that will endure any hardship to complete their exciting and well-planned journey.

Cancer/Aquarius

There is one element that draws these two signs together for a traveling experience; they are both incredibly intuitive and can rely on their intuition to steer them in the best direction with travel plans. Even though they seem to be miles apart, their sixth sense drives them right back to each other. They are humanitarians by nature, Cancer being more sensitive to conditions that affect humanity and Aquarius being more intellectual about how to approach a widespread problem concerning the masses. Aquarius will certainly pursue an unconventional venue when it comes to traveling, while Cancer will feel emotionally motivated to stay at home. Through Aquarius's exciting manner, Cancer is inspired to pack their bags and travel with abandonment as long as their Aquarius partner is right beside them. Venturing out to Cape Cod and Martha's Vineyard will satisfy both signs. Cancer, more interested in setting up comfortable lodging quarters, will rely on impressive and sociable Aquarius to book the proper accommodations and travel arrangements for an exciting time. Whether it's on the road or in the air, these two unlikely signs find a way to complement each other and travel the world like no other two zodiac signs.

Cancer/Pisces

When Cancer and Pisces tour the world together, these two water signs are an excellent match that will hold up through the years. The compassionate gestures of Pisces will be highly supportive of Cancer's emotional need for stability. Catering to Cancer's needs, Pisces will bring all sorts of goodies to make any journey, short or long, a truly comfortable one. Pisces can be easily diverted to embark on any traveling excursion, whereas reclusive Cancer will engage in traveling only when they are both financially and emotionally ready to explore new sights. Cancer may need to be gently persuaded and also have sound reassurance from their sometimes evasive Pisces traveling companion. Journeying through the Napa Valley vineyards on an elegant dining train and wine tasting in their grandiose wineries may easily satisfy both zodiac signs. Their intuitive qualities will allow them to succeed at planning a wonderful trip with little effort. As long as they have each other, they are ready to travel cross-country in a sporty convertible or discover new terrain in a foreign country just for fun.

Leo/Aries

These two exhilarating fire signs are destined to experience many thrilling moments while on their journey. Aries is motivated to travel to unexplored territory, and Leo is excited to live life to the fullest with their Aries partner. They will dress and dine on a grand scale that creates wonderful memories together. Both are able to encourage one another to cover a lot of ground, putting in extra hours that are well worth it. They may prefer to enjoy the good life, where they are entertained by their surroundings. Whether it be the glamorous evening spectacle in Las Vegas or the majestic Canadian mountains comprising Chateau Lake Louise, they share in the mutual wanderlust. They will love to show off speaking a few words in a foreign language in the country they're visiting, or displaying new traveling gear that inspires their trip. Although they complement each other just fine with their ambitious energy, both Aries and Leo have strong wills and may clash when deciding who will take the lead. Conflicts may also arise in choosing a starting point as well as a destination. A compromising attitude is essential to experience a smooth-sailing vacation. The reciprocal admiration that is displayed will keep this couple buoyantly compelled to appreciate each other's company.

Leo/Taurus

The tenacious spirit of these signs will allow them to survive any trip and build stronger bonds together. Both signs will want to partake in experiencing the luxurious surroundings of a vacation resort with all the trimmings. Once Taurus is convinced to take the time to dress up, this couple will be an elegant display in any dining quarters. They may need to spend more hours organizing a pampered, relaxing, and satisfying trip. The end result is a vacation worth talking about for years to come. Their mutual, uncanny perceptiveness will tune into each other's needs and desires for the ultimate in fulfillment. Taurus and Leo are inclined to take a cruise in the South Pacific or embrace the illustrious Niagara Falls. Similar interests will bring harmony as they visit every special site. Setting stubbornness aside, they are bound to accomplish their planned agenda. Leo likes being the center of attention and directing the traveling itinerary of the day, as Taurus gravitates toward the charming, social persona of Leo. In journeying together, they realize the significance of having a well-suited partner with whom they can explore the planet.

Leo/Gemini

The stimulating energy of Leo and Gemini inspires jaunts to every corner of the globe. Their delightful, playful manner encourages romps near an ocean resort, like Monterey Bay. Their restless motivation will have them touring every site on the vacation guide map, especially to capture a glimpse of the spectacular ancient Roman gardens at the J. Paul Getty Museum in Malibu, to enthusiastically converse about it later that night. Since they can't seem to sit still, they may rush having dinner and sleeping, just to hurry up, get out, and see the sites scheduled for the day. Luckily, Gemini is happy to quickly draw up an agenda that allows Leo to experience what the world has to offer. Their curiosity will drive them to learn as much as they can, if only to motivate them toward more travel. Leo and Gemini will want to capture their rare moments on film, which is why you will see them sporting a camera that may even bear a tripod. Much can be gained from scheduled tours, but the idea of wandering into a town that offers a genuine experience will be quite enticing.

Leo/Cancer

It's surprising how a water sign and fire sign can make a great match, but it's true. Since Leo enjoys the limelight, they are bound to tour the hot spots in Hollywood, Graceland, or Broadway, New York, in search of celebrities. Both signs agree that first-class reservations and luxurious accommodations will provide the status and comfort they desire while on their exciting journey. They will also find themselves prone to overpacking, as Cancer likes all the creature comforts of home and Leo likes to be prepared for every occasion. Dining in style is a must, as this pair will display elegance at every turn. In most cases, they both will compromise on which places to visit. Leo may not care to tolerate any moodiness from Cancer, and if Leo is stealing all the spotlight, Cancer will quickly feel ignored. Being grateful for each other's company will keep them both quite happy. Although they like to spend when they are having a good time, they both still have a knack for being economical.

Leo/Leo

Two vivacious Leos trotting the globe are out to have a fabulous time. Only first-class accommodations will do, as both of them relish in the lap of luxury. Exotic excursions, elegant hotels, and fine dining agree with their decadent tastes. Socializing with the higher echelon, they feel right at home. Sleeping in and spending precious time in the morning to look their best at all times may be a strong part of their routine. Prancing through glamorous Las Vegas or South Lake Tahoe, they are sure to show up at the fanciest casinos and still be there until closing at the famous dance clubs at night. Pursuing a wild shopping spree complete with photo ops adds to the already impressive journey. Since they love each other's company so much, they will be talking about their next vacation on this trip. As long as they pay attention to each other, every getaway is the joyous adventure they seek.

Leo/Virgo

Virgo will love to do all of the planning for a perfect trip, and Leo is there to enjoy and be proud of the meticulous organization of their Virgo partner—what an asset! However, they both will need to learn to be patient with each other, as they work on different time clocks. Leo likes to take their time, and Virgo prefers to get things done. Virgo might feel cheated from having some quiet time and a down-to-earth traveling experience that Leo may not be so inclined to provide. Still, Leo will appreciate the detail that goes into everything that Virgo does, especially in drawing up the ideal traveling itinerary, as Leo likes to look good while on the road, in the air, or out on the seas. They may both find pleasure with star-studded performances on the world's stage at Lincoln Center in New York City. Exciting and mentally stimulating, they are captivated by the best talent around. Their attire also makes a nice impression. Virgo's neat packing will include an outfit for every travel occasion, and Leo dressing to impress will complement their partner quite nicely. Although this duo seems like an odd couple, Virgo can use their wit to enlighten Leo to the world around them, and Leo can encourage reserved Virgo to take on a wild expedition and have the time of their life. If Leo curbs their dominating persona and Virgo steps up to the plate, both can achieve a satisfying vacation together.

Leo/Libra

Leo and Libra are an excellent match while traveling together. Their complementary dispositions generate much cooperation, as an innate understanding looks after each other's needs and desires. Vacationing with class and style is always preferred and will attract prestigious individuals and elegant social festivities. This lively pair will be a couple on display with their elegant attire. Even in the midst of unexpected disruptions while traveling, Leo and Libra radiate their togetherness through lavish socializing events and extravaganza, as seen at Rockefeller Center in New York City, or world-renowned Rodeo Drive in Beverly Hills. Harmony permeates the atmosphere with this couple's presence, and they in turn have a splendid day and evening while vacationing. Libra prefers refinement and beauty, and their Leo companion likes the glitz and glamour of an exciting city. Both learn from each other and appreciate each other's interests. Compromising as they journey from place to place, they will arrive at their destination with excitement and promise of the world around them.

Leo/Scorpio

When Leo and Scorpio are traveling together, they are a powerful, driven, and active pair that can move mountains to get to where they need to go. Once the two of them make up their mind on which places to visit, they intensely pursue securing accommodations and arranging tours and places to explore. They may be interested in venturing into the picturesque Yellowstone National Park or traveling the back roads of Tuscany. This duo could win an award for perseverance in maintaining their traveling itinerary, equal to scaling Mount Everest or sailing around the globe, where they may even achieve substantial notoriety. They may be viewed as the ideal traveling couple, yet these two signs also clash, but never in public. After all, Scorpio is an introvert and Leo an extrovert. Both must respect the feelings and wishes of the other for true compatibility. Leo likes to see their diligent work appreciated, and Scorpio likes the respect and excellent rapport they have established with each other. Both take pride in their well-rehearsed social skills, which land them what they want every time. Their strong loyalty makes these two a good match and promotes the longevity of their relationship, as they vacation through the years. Only their mutually stubborn manner will deter them from enjoying their surroundings while away from home.

Leo/Sagittarius

The vision of Leo and Sagittarius gallivanting from one vacation site to another is not surprising. These two fire signs are extremely compatible, especially while embarking on a fabulous journey. Both are natural risk takers, desiring to party hard and experience life on a grand scale. They can dine in style in a luxurious restaurant in New York City or be spontaneous with a candlelit dinner on the beach in Puerto Vallarta. Either way, they are happy to be with one another, having a blast with each new location visited. This pair competes for fun, which only adds to the excitement of their traveling rendezvous. Seeking out adventure, you may find them in the most unusual places. As both will challenge the other to bring out their best, Leo and Sagittarius together will exhibit a classy performance. Sagittarius may prefer more philosophical pursuits that challenge the mind, body, and spirit, which may help channel Leo's prideful manner or lust for entertainment. If you happen to encounter this lively couple while on your journey, you will love their company and be inspired to join along and revel in their marvelous moments.

Leo/Capricorn

When Leo and Capricorn tour the world, they put themselves and others at ease in securing comfortable accommodations, dining, and entertainment that feels like they've accomplished quite an endeavor. Capricorn will be keen on arranging the trip that Leo is sure to enjoy. Leo will acknowledge and respect Capricorn's wisdom for a job well done. Yes, with a little effort Leo and Capricorn can unite in a strategy that proves rewarding while vacationing. This couple is a strong pair that can endure the wilds of nature, such as touring the Tigris River or any daring adventure that calls them. Even though they can rough it, they do have a flair for style and will appreciate dining out in a chic restaurant, satisfying Capricorn's etiquette and Leo's flamboyance. Taking in a gala performance at the San Francisco Opera House would also be quite fulfilling. Capricorn's practical sense keeps them adhering to a budget, being on time, and aware of one's surroundings, keeping Leo in check. Leo encourages Capricorn to move beyond his or her conservative boundaries and enjoy what life has to offer when seeing the sights. This hardworking and appealing couple will be moved to find enchantment, whether they have to take the most challenging road to get there or not.

Leo/Aquarius

The foresight and creativity that this union emanates will generate a sparkling aura for all to see. In this case opposites attract, displaying such a flair for socializing and excitement. This amazing duo can be seen running a bed-and-breakfast, being tour operators, or overseeing a travel agency. Their love for journeying the globe will keep them involved with some aspect of travel. Aquarius's insights and Leo's smarts are able to formulate the best vacation itinerary for their needs. As a team, their productive, humanitarian, and outgoing manner finds them volunteering for the Peace Corps or assisting abandoned children overseas. They are willing to tread through any country, purging their fears and learning from every incredible experience that beholds them. Easily adjusting to other cultures and languages, they are welcomed by the inhabitants of a new land and enjoy the challenges that face them. Leo and Aquarius can be spotted counting the stars and appreciating the destiny behind each one of them. When all is said and done, this couple will wine and dine in style as Leo shows off their flashy attire and Aquarius invites publicity with their unique fashions. A weekend out in the Hamptons on Long Island is the pleasant, upscale environment they may seek. An occasional misstep may impede their trip, but this couple will still delight in all that can be attained.

Leo/Pisces

Tremendous creative energy will make this couple very appealing, even though their styles are different. The compassionate and introspective Pisces is happy to go along with their partner, as Leo's strong persona will dominate by organizing the trip and packing their bags. They both may plan many more vacations than what they actually take, for it is thinking up the possibilities that excites them. Looking through travel magazines or browsing the internet for vacation deals is a great way for this couple to pass the time. Since Leo and Pisces are both dreamers, when traveling they will shoot for the perfect trip and then dream away. Leo will direct them both through amazing jungles or the wild streets of civilized societies. They may enjoy the magnificent, romantic Eiffel Tower just as much as the panoramic view of Vancouver Island. Pisces will be supportive of their partner and definitely fascinated by it all, looking up to Leo with gratitude. Being a great host and hostess, Leo and Pisces may look for friends or traveling companions to display their social skills and artistic prowess. As long as Leo allows Pisces's perceptiveness to assist with the plans and doesn't dominate or show a lack of appreciation for what Pisces has to offer, and Pisces doesn't become too evasive with their itinerary, these two signs can happily travel the Earth together.

Virgo/Aries

Although this couple seems to be at odds with each other, when Virgo and Aries are traveling together, they know what they're best at and can arrange a fabulous trip. Enjoying it might be another story. Virgo is confident about planning a vacation with every detail in place, and Aries will encourage Virgo to hurry up and pack and go. If they can aim toward establishing a great bond of friendship, they can tackle even the most difficult problems while on the road. Journeying through Cape Town, South Africa, and seeing Table Mountain and Victoria Falls will be very rewarding.

If a more social/intellectual scene is needed, they may prefer the magnificent Metropolitan Museum in New York City. Virgo may need to speed up to join Aries's quick pace, and Aries may need to slow down and appreciate taking in the facts and history to really experience the moment with Virgo. Aries is fast and mentally stimulating to Virgo. The incredible knowledge Virgo has with just about every landmark in sight intrigues Aries, besides the fact that Virgo is sticking to their agenda and keeping a record of expenses. Not known to venture too far from home, this pair may find convenience and comfort in riding in their own vehicle. Aries will love being in the driver's seat as Virgo, with map or GPS in hand, charts the way to their desired destination

Virgo/Taurus

The practical, organized skills of Virgo and Taurus may be the envy of everyone, especially when traveling. Their shared discipline keeps them on track with their well-thought-out agenda. They know that to have a great trip, taking their time in securing the hotel accommodations, a rental car, dinner reservations, and daily tour schedule, is well worth it. Whether it be relaxing in the sun or enjoying an appetizing meal, Virgo and Taurus will ease into their vacation, as it should be. If plagued by weather or transportation problems, they will stand steadfast until the situation is resolved. This efficient duo has no issue with sticking to a detailed agenda, budgeting as they go, and following a map or GPS to make their trip seem like a success on a daily basis. They may be inclined to visit Mount Rushmore National Memorial in South Dakota, where they will see the granite presidential monuments of Washington, Jefferson, Lincoln, and Teddy Roosevelt. Traveling light with casual attire streamlines extras that are not necessary. Their love of charting a new journey will find them researching books, magazines, and the internet to make sure they've thoroughly explored all of the options. With such intensive and careful planning, you will find this daring team thrilled with discovering the lands of Russia, India, or Australia.

Virgo/Gemini

Virgo and Gemini are an intellectual duo who will be practical with every traveling detail. Both signs like to partake in drawing up an itinerary for the fascinating excursions they plan to take. They share the responsibilities while traveling, as well, but exercise a different approach when on a trip. Virgo will design an itinerary that's efficient so they are able to see all of the sights before moving on to the next stop. Fast-paced Gemini will not appreciate long visits, preferring to sprint from site to site and city to city. One way to balance their desires is to spend a little time apart while both get to observe what they want to see. As Virgo and Gemini like to think things through, these two signs will enjoy their journey more if they have some quiet time to digest all of the new information. Visiting Ford's Theatre (where President Lincoln was assassinated), viewing the many educational sights at the Smithsonian, and touring the nation's capital in Washington, DC, will give you much to talk about. At night, relaxing with a good book or jotting down notes in a daily journal may be preferred over going out. Both signs are thirsty for mental stimuli, and if they can compromise on their approach, they will be considered terrific traveling buddies for life.

Virgo/Cancer

Virgo and Cancer are a very organized team when traveling the planet. Cancer will appreciate Virgo's meticulous approach so that everything is secure. The trip will work like clockwork, and both signs will feel at ease. It's possible with such great planning skills that they will be helpful with each other's traveling itinerary, since they've already done the research. Touring enchanting Ireland and visiting Saint Patrick's Cathedral, Blarney Castle, and the three Lakes of Killarney is a memorable experience. Their own calculated trip may involve keeping track of a budget, setting a daily traveling agenda, and logging in the miles from one place to another. Cancer will be grateful for Virgo's intellectual way of figuring things out. However, Cancer will prefer to rely on their intuitive skills to lead the way. With Cancer's silent strength to persevere and Virgo's ability to easily adapt to any environment, these two are a fabulous duo promoting a long-term union. Their mutual respect for each other is a refreshing sight.

Virgo/Leo

Virgo will love to do all of the planning for a perfect trip, and Leo is there to enjoy and be proud of the meticulous organization of their Virgo partner—what an asset! However, they both will need to learn to be patient with each other, as they work on different time clocks. Leo likes to take their time, and Virgo prefers to get things done. Virgo might feel cheated from having some quiet time and a down-to-earth traveling experience that Leo may not be so inclined to provide. Still, Leo will appreciate the detail that goes into everything that Virgo does, especially in drawing up the ideal traveling itinerary, as Leo likes to look good while on the road, in the air, or out on the seas. They may both find pleasure with star-studded performances on the world's stage at Lincoln Center in New York City. Exciting and mentally stimulating, they are captivated by the best talent around. Their attire also makes a nice impression. Virgo's neat packing will include an outfit for every travel occasion, and Leo dressing to impress will complement their partner quite nicely. Although this duo seems like an odd couple, Virgo can use their wit to enlighten Leo to the world around them, and Leo can encourage reserved Virgo to take on a wild expedition and have the time of their life. If Leo curbs their dominating persona and Virgo steps up to the plate, both can achieve a satisfying vacation together.

Virgo/Virgo

When two Virgos are traveling together, harmony prevails, for you can bet their trip has been planned with great attention to detail. Their mental skills love the idea of being put to good use by researching every travel guide to finally devise the perfect vacation. These two signs may consider an excursion to Windsor Castle, the oldest inhabited castle, or seeing the perfection of mystical Stonehenge. With such meticulous planning, Virgo is always looking out for a great deal on a hotel, rental car, or flight, and usually finds one. Accommodations don't have to be first class, but they do have to be neat, clean, and private. When embarking on a journey, two Virgos know how to give each other space to relax or perhaps do some reading. Although Virgos travel with an outfit for every occasion, they are well equipped with maps, books, a camera, and a cell phone that sports an easy-to-access calculator, compass, currency converter, and language translator to make extra sure their journey is a success. First-aid kits may also be close at hand. Such great preparation and keen insight that Virgos possess will lead them to an idyllic travel experience that they will always treasure.

Virgo/Libra

When Virgo and Libra travel together, the interesting blend of harmony and intelligence fares well in arranging and venturing out on any journey. Since they both appreciate beauty, design, and culture, they will travel to places that offer an authentic experience that satisfies their taste for artistic and cultural adventure. They may be found taking a flight to see the splendor of Buckingham Palace or discover the pyramids of Egypt. Since they both are ambitious about their travel agenda, they will capitalize on their efficient style to get the most out of their trip. Virgo and Libra will be happy under an adobe roof of a small country home in Portugal instead of a touristy hotel in Tinsel Town. Preferring to travel light, they are able to adjust to any situation without a lot of extras. Interestingly enough, these two signs are an excellent pair, synthesizing their diplomatic and mental skills to attain a rewarding trip.

Virgo/Scorpio

When Virgo and Scorpio travel together, they are bound to plan the most terrific trip. The detail-mindedness of Virgo coupled with Scorpio's intense involvement produces a complete travel itinerary that others would envy. Leaving no stone unturned, they both will explore all of the options before embarking on a journey that covers all the bases. Feeling that they can represent their own travel agency in arranging their trip, they thoroughly investigate the possibilities. Forget about the tourists, as Virgo and Scorpio will prefer a trip that offers lots of privacy, like being by themselves on an island beach. One place worth visiting might be the Coral Coast of Fiji, where you can relish in the sun and participate in a traditional feast. A road trip may also be inviting for this pair as they drive through uncharted territory. One appealing stop could be Utah's Canyonlands National Park, full of sculptured treasures, geological marvels, and ancient fossils worth exploring. Although they can be particular about their vacation, as long as they have each other, they will travel anywhere. From packing their bags to eagerly making their own discoveries while on their expedition, Virgo and Scorpio have a secret pact that enables them to share in a fulfilling journey every time.

Virgo/Sagittarius

These two mentally stimulated signs travel well together. They are both interested in visiting the sights and historical places that pique one's curiosity. Virgo will want to read up on all of the brochures and check out the tourist maps. Sagittarius will encourage Virgo to reach new horizons and find depth and meaning with every traveling experience. They both will find other cultures intriguing, which may easily take them on a voyage overseas. Enjoying the treasures of Notre Dame Cathedral in Paris or the Sistine Chapel in Vatican City; both are inspiring sights. The knowledge gained while on their adventures is invaluable. Throughout their ventures, great conversation is easily inspired by the world around them. They are great roommates wherever they go, never short of words between them. They can travel in style or rough it, as getting something out of the trip is what is most important. Virgo may need to learn to adapt to a less rigid schedule and spend extra time away, while Sagittarius may need to curb overly risky ventures. All in all, this pair is likely to tour countries that offer a captivating experience, one they'll always remember.

Virgo/Capricorn

This no-nonsense couple makes a great team when traveling together. They both approve of being functional and efficient, from making reservations to embarking on a spectacular expedition that includes the magically ornate structures of Saint Petersburg, Russia, and the ancient architecture that you will find in Saint Basil's Cathedral in Moscow. Practical to a "T," they like being organized with the proper traveling gear and attire. Virgo will like taking care of the details, while Capricorn wants to control how the journey will actually unfold. Their particular tastes may be demanding of others to make their trip as wonderful as can be. With the use of their intellectual brilliance, they will work hard to accomplish whatever goal they set out to acquire. Both will plan and coordinate their trip, looking for the best deal around. They will be intrigued with prearranged tours. Being economical is a strong priority, even in purchasing souvenirs. Little can come between this resourceful couple, who make excellent traveling companions.

Virgo/Aquarius

These two exceptionally bright signs are fine partners when it comes to traveling together. The natural intuitive wit of Aquarius combined with the practical intelligence of Virgo makes this a duo that is able to delve into the illuminating recesses of the mind to guide them both toward the most rewarding places to see while on their journey. They will be fascinated with exploring the many universes in our galaxy. Here on planet Earth, Virgo and Aquarius may want to visit the ornate Saint Stephen's Basilica in Budapest or delight in the unique architectural treasures of Istanbul. Virgo needs to appreciate Aquarius's intuitive insights, and Aquarius needs to appreciate Virgo's logic. Both can learn and gain from each other while experiencing the wonders of the world. If they allow their differing views to clash, their illustrious vacation will fall short of their expectations. Also, Virgo likes to be precise and on time, whereas Aquarius may be open-minded to exploring various options as they appear. Compromising is the key to keep this journey moving in a mentally intriguing direction.

Virgo/Pisces

These two opposites combine their unique qualities to enhance their journey together. The practicality of Virgo blends with the creativity and vision of Pisces to create wonderful traveling excursions. Virgo is keen on making sure everything is in order with their itinerary, right down to the smallest detail. Pisces visualizes the entire journey and relays this to Virgo. Pisces will appreciate the specific information that Virgo has researched on every place they visit. Virgo will enjoy Pisces's relaxed and dreamy approach so they both can experience a great vacation. What Virgo lacks, Pisces makes up for, and what Pisces lacks, Virgo makes up for, which creates an excellent balance while traveling. Here, they are able to strike a nice balance that meets each other's needs while touring the globe. Their compassion and willingness to be of service to others draw them to remote and underprivileged areas, where they are rewarded with the satisfaction of helping others. You may find them trekking through the provinces of Africa, Asia, or South America. Collecting artifacts from other countries, they decorate their home as a memorandum of their travels. In discovering more about people and other cultures, they are continually fascinated with the world around them.

Libra/Aries

Opposites attract to make this couple a great match for traveling. Aries is willing to spontaneously explore the world, as Libra will easily compromise to make everything go smoothly. Libra is excited and motivated by Aries's ambitious nature, and Aries appreciates Libra's ability to arrange travel plans with diplomatic skill and a harmonious attitude. Libra prefers the best in accommodations and will choose some very luxurious places to stay. The impressive cities of Salzburg (birthplace of Mozart), Vienna, Munich, Lucerne, and Strasbourg, with breathtaking architecture and historical value, are bound to satisfy them both. When on the road, Libra will persuade Aries to relax and enjoy the sights around them, as opposed to rushing through town. Aries's aggressive style may even be an equal conversationalist to Libra in their social surroundings. They both will truly benefit from each other's strong qualities. Of course, once in a while Aries's impulsiveness will aggravate Libra's need for calm, as Libra's indecision will frustrate Aries's tendency to move quickly toward a new destination. Through it all, their individual energies will complement their vacationing wherever they wish to go.

Libra/Taurus

These two social signs trotting around the globe will find much enjoyment in traveling. They will visit the most beautiful, scenic, and relaxing places, like Tuscany or Monte Carlo. Old World charm is very appealing to this duo. Wining and dining in style, they will seek out the finest in food and ambiance. Taurus will be wise and practical with drawing up a wonderful itinerary for their trip. Libra will depend on their social prowess to put those travel plans into action. They will be easily persuaded into touring towns that hold classical art and architecture, in ancient Rome and other parts of the world. Although this pair is selective about what they see, their primary concern is having a terrific time while traveling. Conversing about one special site after another will keep them thoroughly inspired on their journey. This delightful team makes great traveling companions, and they know how to indulge in the most restful vacations.

Libra/Gemini

These two easygoing air signs are well matched when it comes to traveling. They both like to be educated on the many places they will be visiting before embarking on a journey. Reading all of the historical facts or descriptions along the way will also be enticing. Their relaxed style brings harmony into any situation. This team will truly appreciate great conversation with other travelers on the road as well.

Participating in festivities in a foreign country will be a must on their itinerary. Exploring the traditions and ancient ruins of Italy in Verona, Tuscany, Florence, and Rome will be a delight, both mentally and romantically. They both will display good taste and elegance and be appropriately dressed for the occasion. Once in a while, both of them will have trouble making up their minds, although Gemini might be quicker to arrive at an answer. With such great overall interaction, this duo will gladly enjoy every wonderful vacation experienced.

Libra/Cancer

The fine rapport that develops between Libra and Cancer is sure to make this match a winner. The need of Cancer to link emotionally with his or her partner is complemented by Libra's desire to interact one on one in a relationship. They are both keen on comfort and beauty and will book accommodations in the finest places with the most exceptional view. The stunning landscapes and social scene of Sydney, Australia, or the panoramic wonders on a Mediterranean voyage are sure to impress this couple. Yet occasionally, Libra's indecision or Cancer's moodiness will have them not seeing eye to eye. Nevertheless, they will enjoy discussing the trip from the beginning stages to the end. Still, they both are respectful of each other's space and quiet time. Either one could take the lead while the other gleams over the beautifully scenic landscape, thoroughly enjoying their journey away. Tours and package deals or preplanned trips work well with this pair, as neither of them wants to miss out on any special site.

Libra/Leo

Libra and Leo are an excellent match while traveling together. Their complementary dispositions generate much cooperation, as an innate understanding looks after each other's needs and desires. Vacationing with class and style is always preferred and will attract prestigious individuals and elegant social festivities. This lively pair will be a couple on display with their elegant attire. Even in the midst of unexpected disruptions while traveling, Leo and Libra radiate their togetherness through lavish socializing events and extravaganza, as seen at Rockefeller Center in New York City, or world-renowned Rodeo Drive in Beverly Hills. Harmony permeates the atmosphere with this couple's presence, and they in turn have a splendid day and evening while vacationing. Libra prefers refinement and beauty, and their Leo companion likes the glitz and glamour of an exciting city. Both learn from each other and appreciate each other's interests. Compromising as they journey from place to place, they will arrive at their destination with excitement and promise of the world around them.

Libra/Virgo

When Libra and Virgo travel together, the interesting blend of harmony and intelligence fares well in arranging and venturing out on any journey. Since they both appreciate beauty, design, and culture, they will travel to places that offer an authentic experience that satisfies their taste for artistic and cultural adventure. They may be found taking a flight to see the splendor of Buckingham Palace or discover the pyramids of Egypt. Since they both are ambitious about their travel agenda, they will capitalize on their efficient style to get the most out of their trip. Libra and Virgo will be happy under an adobe roof of a small country home in Portugal instead of a touristy hotel in Tinsel Town. Preferring to travel light, they are able to adjust to any situation without a lot of extras. Interestingly enough, these two signs are an excellent pair, synthesizing their diplomatic and mental skills to attain a rewarding trip.

Libra/Libra

The cooperative spirit of two Libras traveling together makes this an excellent match for touring the world. Both will seek out a diplomatic approach in arranging and handling the itinerary for their journey. First-class accommodations are preferred; however, if plans go awry, Libra will always make the best of it to keep the peace. When in opulent surroundings, they enjoy meeting up with the higher echelon. They will be keen on appreciating all of the wonderful treasures they can see while on their trip. Places that behold beauty and romance will be appealing. The island of Bora Bora could certainly be one of them. Their calm, easygoing nature will make any traveling excursion a joy. The socializing skills of Libra will be put to use as they easily make friends along the way. Sharing all of the sights together will make both feel quite satisfied while on the road. What's nice is that they both will go to great lengths to make sure their partner is happy, which ensures a fabulous traveling experience.

Libra/Scorpio

These two signs are an odd couple that somehow find a way to get along while traveling. Intense Scorpio and harmonious Libra actually help balance each other out. Emotionally deep Scorpio will be very involved in the planning stages of their journey, as well as want to thoroughly enjoy every aspect of their trip. Libra will aim toward making sure their travels are pleasant and congenial as they visit the most exquisite sights around. For lovers, the romanticism of Libra and the passions of Scorpio ignite for an irresistible rendezvous. Libra's occasional indecision is overcome by Scorpio's persuasiveness to be direct, make a decision, and venture out into the world. Whereas Scorpio's ardent moodiness is calmed by Libra's peaceful and smoothing manner and has them both focusing on their travel itinerary once again. Scorpio will be determined to carry out Libra's idea of the perfect trip, whether it be visiting the Taj Mahal, taking an Alaskan cruise, or touring the treasures of Old Europe.

Libra/Sagittarius

This is definitely one of the most complementary pairs in the zodiac, especially when touring the globe. These fire and air signs are the best of friends as well as lovers, for they are both willing to cooperate and live life to the fullest. Libra will encourage Sagittarius to expand their social circle as they tour the planet, which Sagittarius is eager to embrace. Sagittarius will inspire Libra to appreciate other cultures and enhance their philosophy of the world. You may find them in the most luxurious hotels and dining in style with their expensive tastes. They prefer to travel with class or not at all. Having an outfit for every occasion keeps them in the eye of the public, which is bound to notice their electric flair. Since Sagittarius is known to be one of the traveling signs, Libra is more than happy to join in on this adventuresome experience. Attending every party or social festivity makes this an active couple in pursuit of fun and adventure that you might find in Rio de Janeiro. They are able to cover a lot of ground in little time, and a world tour is not uncommon. Locally, they may jaunt from the Palace of Fine Arts in San Francisco to the Golden Gate Bridge to trendy Sausalito all in one day. Their upbeat and harmonious energy allows this appealing couple to attract good luck everywhere they go.

Libra/Capricorn

This team will make the most secure trip as perfect as can be. Traveling plans aim for first class or at least close to it. Capricorn will want to address all of the traveling arrangements so everything is under control. Libra will put on the final touches, adding a more luxurious approach to accommodations and scheduling beautiful, scenic tours that you can behold on the Italian Riviera or the French Côte d'Azur. Capricorn will appreciate Libra's leisurely, romantic style while on their journey, making both feel at ease as they get the most out of their vacation. At times, however, Capricorn's rigid ways may be intentional to keep up with the itinerary, as Libra wants to relax, socialize, and spend more time enjoying a particular site. As long as they both respect the wishes of the other, they can reach a compromise, which of course Libra would prefer. If friction exists, they may need some space to pursue separate itineraries during the trip, so that both of them are happy as they discover new traveling vistas.

Libra/Aquarius

These two lively air signs create a very stimulating energy for traveling. The harmonious ways of Libra combine with the exciting, intuitive manner of Aquarius for a motivating trip. They may be considered frequent travelers, ready to go at a moment's notice. Yet, Aquarius's restlessness and Libra's occasional indecision may clash at times. Even if there is a difference of opinion, they still complement each other nicely. Since they love their freedom, they both will enjoy gallivanting around the planet. Mentally inspiring places activate great conversation along the way. Their enjoyment of stargazing may take them to the Lowell Observatory in Flagstaff, Arizona—a popular destination for tourists who enjoy astronomy, and famous for its discovery of Pluto. Their accommodations and traveling plans are handled in a quick, easy manner so as not to waste precious time. They both are interested in learning a new language, especially if it will benefit their journey. Exploring new cultures, which prevail in the traditional customs of Japan or the long-standing pride of Greece, opens them both up to a fascinating world that continues to promote travel in the future.

Libra/Pisces

The romanticism of Libra and the idealism of Pisces creates an imaginary world of traveling that is very appealing. You may find these two signs in the awe-inspiring canals of Venice or the Taj Mahal. They may also experience great pleasure in taking a voyage across the ocean, which instills fun and romance. Libra may be particular about their travel arrangements, and Pisces is likely to go along with the plan. Their mutual compassion and sensitivity draw them closer together as they jaunt from place to place, taking in the wonders of the world. Since Libra likes one-on-one communication and Pisces prefers another "fish" to swim with, they both gravitate toward each other, expressing their views and forming tighter bonds along their journey. As long as the vagueness of Pisces and the indecision of Libra are held in check, this unlikely duo can embrace every traveling experience for the fabulous expedition that it is.

Scorpio/Aries

The strength of these two signs individually makes this a great pair for traveling throughout the world. Aries likes to be spontaneous and be the first in line to take that thrilling cruise or see Michelangelo's statue of David. Scorpio is determined to get the best seats in the house or tour every corner of the Louvre in France. With such fortitude, these two signs are able to conquer vast lands that hold unique vacation sites. Aries's impulsive manner will motivate them both to put their traveling ideas into action, while Scorpios will immerse themselves in arranging the ideal trip. Although these two could be terrific travel guides, they would rather just guide themselves and not waste any precious time in seeing the sights. Aries and Scorpio will be especially taken by any trip that invites intrigue and adventure. This terrific match will be found venturing into the Arctic zone or researching the volcanoes in Hawaii. Whatever seems to be off-limits is worth exploring. Aries is bound to provide tremendous encouragement while touring the planet, and Scorpio will inspire great depth of experience for every place visited.

Scorpio/Taurus

One of the most compatible opposites is Scorpio and Taurus, and because of it, they travel well together. Taurus provides what Scorpio needs, and Scorpio has a knack for knowing what Taurus desires. When designing their trip, Taurus will want to have everything in place for a secure and comfortable journey, and Scorpio will give the trip depth and meaning to bring back special memories. They might thoroughly enjoy traveling to Saint Petersburg, Florida, and viewing the fabulous Salvador Dalí Museum, which holds seven magnificent murals among his other major works of art. Occasionally, their naturally stubborn natures will have difficulty agreeing on a particular destination, but eventually their practical side will kick in to draw up a compromised itinerary. They are both drawn to hot climates, such as the Caribbean. Basking in the sun can be very rejuvenating. Understanding other cultures is also appealing to their knowledge. They acquire the most from their travels when becoming totally immersed in the journey.

Scorpio/Gemini

The intensity of Scorpio will complement the quickness of Gemini in touring the world with great tenacity. Long journeys, where they can become involved with their intriguing surroundings, are preferred. Touring the world-famous Casablanca, the El Badi Palace in Marrakesh, and the ancient city of Volubilis will surely capture both signs' attention. Since Gemini is very adaptable to any new environment and Scorpio is driven to explore every site, you may find this couple traveling for weeks or months at a time. Nothing is too dull or too glamorous for Gemini and Scorpio, as they will appreciate a variety of vacation spots. This pair will have fun seeing great historical sights, glitzy city life, moonlit beaches, and camping out in new terrain. Their depth for intrigue keeps them motivated to conquer new destinations. Both are good conversationalists, especially when they are traveling the globe—for there's so much to talk about! Even when there is stress, Gemini will lighten the heaviness sometimes experienced by Scorpio, and Scorpio will have Gemini inspired by coaxing them to the next fun-filled or romantic rendezvous.

Scorpio/Cancer

When Scorpio and Cancer travel together, there is a deep, understood emotional bond that guides their trip on an intuitive level. If anything, there needs to be a more meaningful reason as to why they are venturing out to new horizons locally or around the globe. Involving themselves with humanitarian enterprises, such as rescuing animals from an oil spill overseas or journeying to Southern California to save the beached whales, will be fulfilling. Relishing their privacy, they would also find pleasure in exploring Lake Tahoe or Yosemite National Park for starters. Since Cancer and Scorpio are both water signs, they will blend together like two merging streams. This strongly connected duo will bypass superficial touristy sights in lieu of more moving experiences while traveling. They both will truly enjoy their quiet time, whether it be relaxing in their hotel suite or basking in the sun on a tranquil beach. Overseas, they would be intrigued with the coast of Portugal, which holds the Jeronimos Monastery and the 14th-century Alcazar. This pair does not care to be fettered by "extras." They will pack what is necessary, knowing that the idea is to have a great time traveling and enjoying themselves while en route to their desired destination.

Scorpio/Leo

When Scorpio and Leo are traveling together, they are a powerful, driven, and active pair that can move mountains to get to where they need to go. Once the two of them make up their minds on which places to visit, they intensely pursue securing accommodations and arranging tours and places to explore. They may be interested in venturing into the picturesque Yellowstone National Park or traveling the back roads of Tuscany. This duo could win an award for perseverance in maintaining their traveling itinerary, equal to scaling Mount Everest or sailing around the globe, where they may even achieve substantial notoriety. They may be viewed as the ideal traveling couple, yet these two signs also clash, but never in public. After all, Scorpio is an introvert and Leo is an extrovert. Both must respect the feelings and wishes of the other for true compatibility. Leo likes to see their diligent work appreciated, and Scorpio likes the respect and excellent rapport they have established with each other. Both take pride in their well-rehearsed social skills that land them what they want every time. Their strong loyalty makes these two a good match and promotes the longevity of their relationship as they vacation through the years. Only their mutually stubborn manner will deter them from enjoying their surroundings while away from home.

Scorpio/Virgo

When Scorpio and Virgo travel together, they are bound to plan the most terrific trip. The detail-mindedness of Virgo coupled with Scorpio's intense involvement produces a complete travel itinerary that others would envy. Leaving no stone unturned, they both will explore all of the options before embarking on a journey that covers all the bases. Feeling that they can represent their own travel agency in arranging their trip, they thoroughly investigate the possibilities. Forget about the tourists, as Scorpio and Virgo will prefer a trip that offers lots of privacy, like being by themselves on an island beach. One place worth visiting might be the Coral Coast of Fiji, where you can relish in the sun and participate in a traditional feast. A road trip may also be inviting for this pair as they drive through uncharted territory. One appealing stop could be Utah's Canyonlands National Park, full of sculptured treasures, geological marvels, and ancient fossils worth exploring. Although they can be particular about their vacation, as long as they have each other, they will travel anywhere. From packing their bags to eagerly making their own discoveries while on their expedition, Scorpio and Virgo have a secret pact that enables them to share in a fulfilling journey every time.

Scorpio/Libra

These two signs are an odd couple that somehow find a way to get along while traveling. Intense Scorpio and harmonious Libra actually help balance each other out. Emotionally deep Scorpio will be very involved in the planning stages of their journey, as well as want to thoroughly enjoy every aspect of their trip. Libra will aim toward making sure their travels are pleasant and congenial as they visit the most exquisite sights around. For lovers, the romanticism of Libra and the passions of Scorpio ignite for an irresistible rendezvous. Libra's occasional indecision is overcome by Scorpio's persuasiveness to be direct, make a decision, and venture out into the world. Whereas Scorpio's ardent moodiness is calmed by Libra's peaceful and smoothing manner and has them both focusing on their travel itinerary once again. Scorpio will be determined to carry out Libra's idea of the perfect trip, whether it be visiting the Taj Mahal, taking an Alaskan cruise, or touring the treasures of Old Europe.

Scorpio/Scorpio

Two Scorpios traveling the world wish to immerse themselves in their journey so that it is a life-changing experience. It's a serious matter when they plan their specific itinerary that allows for tremendous depth and meaning while touring their destination. The intense passion that this pair exudes will have them determined to see their journey through, no matter what the obstacles. Their sensual, romantic side can be further explored in many historical countries that have the depth Scorpio looks for when traveling. Once they grasp the world in the palm of their hands, they know they are on their way toward a fulfilling expedition, such as exploring Dromoland Castle in Ireland or discovering the Mayan ruins in Mexico. You can count on these two getting along great most of the time. However, when differences arise, their stubbornness will turn a wonderful trip sour if this disposition isn't put into check soon. Since Scorpios like to be alone at times, traveling together can ruffle some feathers unless they are both willing to make an effort. In respecting each other's space, they can plan and share what can be a fabulous journey together.

Scorpio/Sagittarius

When Scorpio and Sagittarius travel together, their resourcefulness will take them anywhere, yet their views on what to see will vary. Both are determined to reach the end of their journey as planned. Sagittarius will exercise a carefree way of venturing out to experience new vistas, whereas Scorpio will want to explore every nook and cranny. They possess a great spirit for traveling, and both want to find meaning along their journey to new lands. Other cultures will be intriguing, and much will be learned to satisfy their curiosity. The impressive Grand Kabuki Theatre in Japan or the mystical land of Bali could be sights worth seeing. Since Scorpio has high expectations, they will do the serious planning to make sure all of the arrangements are secure, and Sagittarius will add the lighter touches with some fun-filled excursions. At times, Scorpio will be unimpressed with Sagittarius's risky traveling plans, while Sagittarius may not be too thrilled with Scorpio's strong preoccupation to probe into every interesting place on the itinerary, leaving nothing unexplored. If they can find some common ground and appreciate what each other has to offer, their trips could be quite fulfilling with lasting memories.

Scorpio/Capricorn

Scorpio and Capricorn are a winning team not only in business, but travel as well. The efficient, structured side of Capricorn will want to build a solid trip that ensures a great journey. Scorpio will probe even deeper to make sure everything is in place. The individual strengths of these two signs are a remarkable testimony to a magnificent trip. They will both naturally encourage each other's growth toward a meaningful experience with ancient artifacts, historical architecture, and being among other cultures. Even though they appear sturdy and reliable, this duo may be careful, shy, and secretive at times with their plans. As long as they can have their privacy, their trip will be time well spent. Brief trips are just as significant as long ones. A fun-filled or weekend romantic rendezvous to Saint Thomas Island can be just as fulfilling as seeing the "Jewels of Alpine Europe," including Lake Geneva in Switzerland. As a couple, they are not known to be ardent travelers. However, when they get a chance to enjoy a change of scenery, their vacation will be nonetheless rewarding.

Scorpio/Aquarius

This loyal pair is an interesting couple that can benefit from each other's acquired wisdom when traveling. Scorpio will be shrewd in carrying out the whimsical ideas of Aquarius in devising an itinerary for their journey. Both can connect on a higher intuitive level to work out the details. Aquarius will be intrigued with Scorpio's depth, as Scorpio will be enlightened by Aquarius's flash insights. However, Aquarius's flightiness may be mistaken for a lack of depth by Scorpio, and Scorpio's secretive manner and stubbornness may not win approval from Aquarius's openness. Hopefully, their intellectual status will lead them back to what's important while on their journey. Since they like their privacy and freedom, kayaking down the Nile River or venturing into the lost cities of ancient Peru and Machu Picchu would be quite fulfilling. They derive great pleasure in immersing themselves in nature. Trusting their mate, they may feel comfortable enough to briefly separate and rejoin their loved one at a specified location. In this way, both are satisfied with seeing certain highlights of their trip and sharing the jubilant results with their traveling companion.

Scorpio/Pisces

Two water signs linking up for a traveling experience is an excellent match. Since they are both emotionally intuitive, they will sometimes communicate on a telepathic level and have an in-depth understanding of one another. Pisces's dream trip can be researched by intense Scorpio so that it's not only scenic, but holds great meaning. Scorpio is grateful for Pisces's vision, and Pisces is happy that Scorpio can be attentive to the details that are involved in creating a fabulous expedition. Scorpio will be tolerant of Pisces's vagueness from time to time, as Pisces will accept Scorpio's desire to be secretive. Whether they are traveling first class or camping out under the stars, they do prefer their privacy. While on their journey, Scorpio will want to investigate every fascinating site. Both will be captivated by the unforgettable impression of the luscious Costa Rican rainforests, with the most beautiful waterfalls in the world. Capturing a rare moment in silence is what is most rewarding when traveling together. Overall, this pair is an excellent partnership, walking hand in hand in exploring the planet they live on and appreciating its grandeur.

Sagittarius/Aries

This terrific pair will be seen gallivanting throughout the world and having the time of their lives. As traveling is part of their chemistry, they are interested in venturing out into unexplored territory for the thrill of it all. Sagittarius will enjoy arranging a fast-paced trip with Aries's spur-of-the-moment advice. These two certainly prefer being waited on in the throes of a luxurious hotel; however, they are well prepared to tackle Mount Everest if it suits their fancy. Similar interests will make travel easy. Seeing many places in a day is common practice for two energetic fire signs. You can bet they will not stay in one place for too long, as they will be inspired to check out the next adventure on their itinerary as quickly as possible. Jet-skiing in Glacier National Park, Montana, or a wild Kenyan safari may call their attention. Leaving some of their plans up in the air, they both can exercise being spontaneous as they go along. Although their active schedule could be a bit accident prone, this lively duo is ready to roll to capture the exhilarating moments encountered while traveling the world.

Sagittarius/Taurus

Although Sagittarius and Taurus have different characters, somehow they manage to get along quite nicely while traveling. Charting a course of action will be preferred by Sagittarius and tempered down by Taurus, so they can appreciate the scenes around them without being too rushed. Taurus will be glad to draw up a traveling itinerary that's safe and sound, allowing them to gently ease into their trip. Sagittarius will encourage Taurus to take risks that they otherwise would not entertain while traveling. Sagittarius likes Taurus's reliability, and Taurus likes Sagittarius's positive attitude. When on their trip they are both good with maps, GPS, and transportation, which enables them to visit more scenic locations than most. As one seeks out adventure and the other beauty, you may find this couple journeying to France to see the Louvre, the Musee d'Orsay, and Monet's Gardens in Giverny. Historical sites, where there's something to be learned, will also be very appealing. If they can be patient with each other's desires to visit certain places, they will both gain from each other's perspectives on discovering what exists on earth.

Sagittarius/Gemini

Gemini's wit and Sagittarius's fiery ambition are a powerful combination for traveling the globe in style. Besides enjoying life to the fullest, they will challenge one another to bring out the best in each other. Although this pair will appreciate luxurious hotels, they are just as comfortable camping under the stars, for they are more concerned about the meaningfulness of their traveling experience. Gemini and Sagittarius are keen on expanding their mental and physical prowess by exploring life in different parts of the world. They will pack their bags at a moment's notice and be off to the next exciting adventure that may be found in speedboating off the breathtaking shores of Split, Croatia, or hot-air ballooning in Albuquerque, New Mexico, where the world's largest ballooning event is held. Sagittarius may prefer outdoor activities and taking risks, while Geminis, with their need for cerebral stimulation, will enjoy learning about foreign languages and other cultures. These fire and air signs are well matched as they inspire each other to new heights while on their fascinating journeys.

Sagittarius/Cancer

This passionate duo is actually very compatible, although they are bound to learn a lot from each other. Sagittarius will need to be more sensitive to Cancer, and Cancer will need to be more outgoing with freedom-loving Sagittarius. Neither will react well when plans go awry. Sagittarius will be angered when the unexpected appears, and Cancer will feel overwhelmed by the tension felt. Still, they will both appreciate each other in different ways, which will continually build the bond between them. Their pensive intuition will act as a great travel guide along their trip. They will be mindful of using their sixth sense to tap into one another for the best results. Being flexible with their itinerary, both will find pleasure in the scenic drive on California's coastal highway or dining and being entertained in Caesars Palace in exciting Las Vegas. Friendly Sagittarius will always be there, providing the emotional support that Cancer requires, drawing Cancer out of their shell. Cancer will provide a cuddly, nurturing environment while on the road. Sagittarius likes the exhilaration of traveling to new places. Although supportive of Sagittarius, Cancer may prefer to play it safe, not wanting to venture too far from the home base, even when tempted to explore new vistas. Cancer, once comfortable, will be inspired by Sagittarius to venture out, and Sagittarius will appreciate Cancer's warmth and homespun atmosphere wherever they both go.

Sagittarius/Leo

The vision of Sagittarius and Leo gallivanting from one vacation site to another is not surprising. These two fire signs are extremely compatible, especially while embarking on a fabulous journey. Both are natural risk takers, desiring to party hard and experience life on a grand scale. They can dine in style in a luxurious restaurant in New York City or be spontaneous with a candlelit dinner on the beach in Puerto Vallarta. Either way, they are happy to be with one another, having a blast with each new location visited. This pair competes for fun, which only adds to the excitement of their traveling rendezvous. Seeking out adventure, you may find them in the most unusual places. As both will challenge the other to bring out their best, Leo and Sagittarius together will exhibit a classy performance. Sagittarius may prefer more philosophical pursuits that challenge the mind, body, and spirit, which may help channel Leo's prideful manner or lust for entertainment. If you happen to encounter this lively couple while on your journey, you will love their company and be inspired to join along and revel in their marvelous moments.

Sagittarius/Virgo

These two mentally stimulated signs travel well together. They are both interested in visiting the sights and historical places that pique one's curiosity. Virgo will want to read up on all of the brochures and check out the tourist maps. Sagittarius will encourage Virgo to reach new horizons and find depth and meaning with every traveling experience. They both will find other cultures intriguing, which may easily take them on a voyage overseas. Enjoying the treasures of Notre Dame Cathedral in Paris or the Sistine Chapel in Vatican City; both are inspiring sights. The knowledge gained while on their adventures is invaluable. Throughout their ventures, great conversation is easily inspired by the world around them. They are great roommates wherever they go, never short of words between them. They can travel in style or rough it, as getting something out of the trip is what is most important. Virgo may need to learn to adapt to a less rigid schedule and spend extra time away, while Sagittarius may need to curb overly risky ventures. All in all, this pair is likely to tour the countries that offer a captivating experience, one they'll always remember.

Sagittarius/Libra

This is definitely one of the most complementary pairs in the zodiac, especially when touring the globe. These fire and air signs are the best of friends as well as lovers, for they are both willing to cooperate and live life to the fullest. Libra will encourage Sagittarius to expand their social circle as they tour the planet, which Sagittarius is eager to embrace. Sagittarius will inspire Libra to appreciate other cultures and enhance their philosophy of the world. You may find them in the most luxurious hotels and dining in style with their expensive tastes. They prefer to travel with class or not at all. Having an outfit for every occasion keeps them in the eye of the public, which is bound to notice their electric flair. Since Sagittarius is known to be one of the traveling signs, Libra is more than happy to join in on this adventuresome experience. Attending every party or social festivity makes this an active couple in pursuit of fun and adventure that you might find in Rio de Janeiro. They are able to cover a lot of ground in little time, and a world tour is not uncommon. Locally, they may jaunt from the Palace of Fine Arts in San Francisco to the Golden Gate Bridge to trendy Sausalito all in one day. Their upbeat and harmonious energy allows this appealing couple to attract good luck everywhere they go.

Sagittarius/Scorpio

When Sagittarius and Scorpio travel together, their resourcefulness will take them anywhere, yet their views on what to see will vary. Both are determined to reach the end of their journey as planned. Sagittarius will exercise a carefree way of venturing out to experience new vistas, whereas Scorpio will want to explore every nook and cranny. They possess a great spirit for traveling, and both want to find meaning along their journey to new lands. Other cultures will be intriguing, and much will be learned to satisfy their curiosity. The impressive Grand Kabuki Theatre in Japan or the mystical land of Bali could be sights worth seeing. Since Scorpio has high expectations, they will do the serious planning to make sure all of the arrangements are secure, and Sagittarius will add the lighter touches with some fun-filled excursions. At times, Scorpio will be unimpressed with Sagittarius's risky travel plans, while Sagittarius may not be too thrilled with Scorpio's strong preoccupation to probe into every interesting place on the itinerary, leaving nothing unexplored. If they can find some common ground and appreciate what each other has to offer, their trip could be quite fulfilling with lasting memories.

Sagittarius/Sagittarius

When two dazzling fire signs come together, they harness their enthusiasm, relishing every moment as globetrotters. Their mutual curiosity will drive them to throw caution to the wind in exploring every facet of the planet they live on while traveling. They couldn't be more mentally stimulated than when they travel to uncharted territory that reeks of scenic beauty and history, such as Jackson Hole, Wyoming, and the captivating Grand Tetons. Although Sagittarius enjoys the entertainment they will find with Broadway shows or the likes of Las Vegas, they are much more intrigued with finding meaning in their traveling experiences and will be seeking art exhibitions, ancient artifacts, and philosophical findings. You might encounter this lively couple in a luxurious resort or sleeping under the luminous night sky as they camp out. It's through variety that these two truth-seeking signs will embrace the world, knowing there is always more to discover along the way. If something should go awry with their risk-taking antics, an argument could ensue. Their passion is likely to be rekindled as they resume their journey, being guided by their starry ambitions that inspire us all.

Sagittarius/Capricorn

When these two interesting signs pursue a traveling venture, they offer each other great support along the way. Capricorn will want to secure the reservations and itinerary, as Sagittarius designs a trip full of fun and adventure. If both respect the wishes of the other, Capricorn can learn to relax and be more outgoing, while Sagittarius can learn to follow some kind of an agenda to keep them on course in seeing all of the sights. Gallivanting through Europe offers ancient history, preferred by Capricorn, and yet its monuments, heralding wisdom, and beautiful, expansive terrain will intrigue Sagittarius. Desiring freedom and an exciting escapade, Sagittarius may need to prod Capricorn into leaving the house to experience a life-altering journey. Even in compromising, Capricorn will still prefer to stick to the agenda. Seeking out what discoveries can be made in any new community, Sagittarius enjoys the thrill of the moment. Capricorn, eager to learn about life by traveling the globe, offers a more structured means of doing so. When both combine their efforts and decide on a clear itinerary for their excursion, they will surely benefit.

Sagittarius/Aquarius

This thrill-seeking team will thoroughly delight in one another's company while traveling the Earth. Sagittarius is a natural traveler, while Aquarius likes the idea of venturing into areas of new discovery. The knowledgeable wit of Sagittarius will be accessed to formulate a fabulous excursion. Aquarius, however, will implement their own insightful vision of how to indulge in a travel experience. There will be perpetual excitement while on the road, and perhaps a little competition on whose unique itinerary will be used. You will find this friendly duo in every part of the world. Unexplored cultures will draw them into new lands with great intrigue. They will prefer flying to get to their destination as quickly and conveniently as possible. Without wasting precious time, they will have more fun relishing every moment. The beaches and nightlife in Acapulco as well as the majestic mountains in Aspen are alluring as long as they have their high-tech camera ready to go. The "connoisseurs of traveling" is an appropriate title for these two bold and ambitious signs.

Sagittarius/Pisces

Since Jupiter is the planet that excites travel, and is the ruler of Sagittarius and coruler of Pisces, it stands to reason that these two signs would find a unique way of having fun while traveling together. Pisces dreams of the perfect vacation as Sagittarius is quick on coming up with a fantastic excursion worthy of an experienced travel agency. The two in combination are bound to explore the reaches of the world, where there are no limits as to what can be seen. The more idyllic, the better the challenge. Since they are both fascinated with learning about the world around them, they may make their appearance at the Egyptian Sphinx and Pyramids of Giza or the Taj Mahal in India. Exploring other cultures and different languages has them thrilled with humanity itself. Being understanding, they will try to accommodate each other's needs and desires along the way. As excellent traveling companions, touring the planet is a real joy.

Capricorn/Aries

Although these are both very enterprising signs, Aries and Capricorn need to express their traveling intentions to avoid a trip that is moving in two different directions. Capricorn likes to plan and be prepared for all occasions, and Aries prefers to be spontaneous, winging it for the thrill of the moment. If they can put their two heads together, they will be able to arrange a successful trip that satisfies both parties. This can be accomplished only by opening up the dialogue between them. First-class accommodations are preferred while away from home; after all, they work hard for it. However, slower-paced Capricorn may have trouble keeping up with fast-paced Aries. Though they may seem like an odd couple, they can complement each other by introducing new experiences to their partner that make traveling fun and enjoyable. Their mutually driven strength will allow them to endure long, grueling trips, such as flying from San Francisco to Paris, taking the bullet train to Switzerland, and skiing the Alps for two weeks! A vacation that we all might envy.

Capricorn/Taurus

The result of two earth signs coming together equals a very successful trip, especially when it's Taurus and Capricorn. Efficient planning and packing is a must. Both have an agenda that needs to be met for the effort they're putting into their journey. This team is practical on all they say and do. They prefer traveling when the reservations and accommodations are secure, for only then can they relax. Since they both desire to be greatly moved by their journey, their itinerary will be scheduled to a "T." They also hope to take advantage of the best travel package. Bargain hunting will drive them. They will be most comfortable on a Mediterranean cruise or European tour, as they are able to thoroughly enjoy the highlights of various sites without being rushed. With such wonderful compatibility, this pair could eventually tour all of the corners of the world.

Capricorn/Gemini

Carefree Gemini and structured Capricorn may have some challenges while traveling together. This unlikely duo must be willing to compromise to make any journey a success. Capricorn will prefer following an outlined itinerary for the best results, whereas Gemini is more comfortable with being spontaneous and winging it. Here, Capricorn will need to be more flexible and recognize that while on vacation, you can break the rules and have fun. Although Gemini can appreciate Capricorn's structured and reliable manner, the easygoing spirit of Gemini thrives on new experiences so Capricorn needs to loosen up. Since they both want to accomplish getting to their destination, there is some mutual agreement, yet they may have varying ideas on which path to take. They will both like seeing the historical past, such as visiting the sites of Hungarian coronations, touring the Schonbrunn Palace in Vienna, and cruising on the Danube, which is bound to conjure up some great conversation. Capricorn will want to be in charge, but Gemini will add the final touches. As long as they are open to what each other has to offer, they will surely benefit while exploring the world.

Capricorn/Cancer

When Capricorn and Cancer travel together, opposites do attract. In this case, the strength of both signs creates a relationship foundation that succeeds at conquering any obstacle. This pair will agree on staying in a safe haven, like the charming Grand Hotel on the pristine, secluded Mackinac Island off the coast of Michigan. This summer hotel, built in 1887, offers Old World hospitality. Even in planning their trip, it will be a step-by-step process that leads to the accomplished goal, a sound and reliable trip. They will go out of their way to seize even the smallest reward. Spending days following up on a vintage stamp collection is not uncommon. Capricorn is driven to calculate their spending limit, prepare all of the accommodations and modes of travel, and double-check all tours on their journey's itinerary. Cancer never overlooks the necessities of home while traveling, bringing slippers, pajamas, whatever it takes to create a warm ambiance. Occasionally, Cancer's moodiness may interfere with Capricorn's structured manner or vice versa. Here, both need to respect the feelings and needs of the other to smooth over any rough spots. Regardless, these are two strong-minded signs that will endure any hardship to complete their exciting and well-planned journey.

Capricorn/Leo

When Capricorn and Leo tour the world, they put themselves and others at ease in securing comfortable accommodations, dining, and entertainment that feels like they've accomplished quite an endeavor. Capricorn will be keen on arranging the trip that Leo is sure to enjoy. Leo will acknowledge and respect Capricorn's wisdom for a job well done. Yes, with a little effort, Leo and Capricorn can unite in a strategy that proves rewarding while vacationing. This couple is a strong pair that can endure the wilds of nature, like touring the Tigris River or any daring adventure that calls them. Even though they can rough it, they do have a flair for style and will appreciate dining out in a chic restaurant, satisfying Capricorn's etiquette and Leo's flamboyance. Taking in a gala performance at the San Francisco Opera House would also be quite fulfilling. Capricorn's practical sense keeps them adhering to a budget, being on time, and aware of one's surroundings, keeping Leo in check. Leo encourages Capricorn to move beyond his or her conservative boundaries and enjoy what life has to offer when seeing the sights. This hardworking and appealing couple will be moved to find enchantment, whether they have to take the most challenging road to get there or not.

Capricorn/Virgo

This no-nonsense couple makes a great team when traveling together. They both approve of being functional and efficient, from making reservations to embarking on a spectacular expedition that includes the magically ornate structures of Saint Petersburg, Russia, and the ancient architecture that you will find in Saint Basil's Cathedral in Moscow. Practical to a "T," they like being organized with the proper traveling gear and attire. Virgo will like taking care of the details, while Capricorn wants to control how the journey will actually unfold. Their particular tastes may be demanding of others to make their trip as wonderful as can be. With the use of their intellectual brilliance, they will work hard to accomplish whatever goal they set out to acquire. Both will plan and coordinate their trip, looking for the best deal around. They will be intrigued with prearranged tours. Being economical is a strong priority, even in purchasing souvenirs. Little can come between this resourceful couple, who make excellent traveling companions.

Capricorn/Libra

This team will make the most secure trip as perfect as can be. Traveling plans aim for first class or at least close to it. Capricorn will want to address all of the traveling arrangements so everything is under control. Libra will put on the final touches, adding a more luxurious approach to accommodations and scheduling beautiful, scenic tours that you can behold on the Italian Riviera or the French Côte d'Azur. Capricorn will appreciate Libra's leisurely, romantic style while on their journey, making both feel at ease as they get the most out of their vacation. At times, however, Capricorn's rigid ways may be intentional to keep up with the itinerary, as Libra wants to relax, socialize, and spend more time enjoying a particular sight. As long as they both respect the wishes of the other, they can reach a compromise, which of course Libra would prefer. If friction exists, they may need some space to pursue separate itineraries during the trip so that both of them are happy as they discover new traveling vistas.

Capricorn/Scorpio

Capricorn and Scorpio are a winning team not only in business, but traveling as well. The efficient, structured side of Capricorn will want to build a solid trip that ensures a great journey. Scorpio will probe even deeper to make sure everything is in place. The individual strengths of these two signs are a remarkable testimony to a magnificent trip. They will both naturally encourage each other's growth toward a meaningful experience with ancient artifacts, historical architecture, and being among other cultures. Even though they appear sturdy and reliable, this duo may be careful, shy, and secretive at times with their plans. As long as they can have their privacy, their trip will be time well spent. Brief trips are just as significant as long ones. A fun-filled or weekend romantic rendezvous to Saint Thomas Island can be just as fulfilling as seeing the "Jewels of Alpine Europe," including Lake Geneva in Switzerland. As a couple, they are not known to be ardent travelers. However, when they get a chance to enjoy a change of scenery, their vacation will be nonetheless rewarding.

Capricorn/Sagittarius

When these two interesting signs pursue a traveling venture, they offer each other great support along the way. Capricorn will want to secure the reservations and itinerary as Sagittarius designs a trip full of fun and adventure. If both respect the wishes of the other, Capricorn can learn to relax and be more outgoing, while Sagittarius can learn to follow some kind of an agenda to keep them on course in seeing all of the sights. Gallivanting through Europe offers ancient history, preferred by Capricorn, and yet its monuments, heralding wisdom, and beautiful, expansive terrain will intrigue Sagittarius. Desiring freedom and an exciting escapade, Sagittarius may need to prod Capricorn into leaving the house to experience a life-altering journey. Even in compromising, Capricorn will still prefer to stick to the agenda. Seeking out what discoveries can be made in any new community, Sagittarius enjoys the thrill of the moment. Capricorn, eager to learn about life by traveling the globe, offers a more structured means of doing so. When both combine their efforts and decide on a clear itinerary for their excursion, they will surely benefit.

Capricorn/Capricorn

When two Capricorns travel together, they supervise events like an impresario for a Broadway show. Everything runs on time, and that is a reflection of their itinerary. The organizational skills of this duo will secure an excellent trip, and thus a terrific traveling experience. They orchestrate their agenda to accomplish seeing many sights in one day. Even if their expedition demands endurance, they are determined to reach their destination, no matter what is encountered along the way. The sea goat, the symbol for Capricorn, wants to climb the highest mountain and feel successful in enjoying the view at the top. The spectacular Grand Canyon may be a desirable site for them to see. These two earth signs need only to be careful of trying too hard to control each other and thus undermine the excursion taking place. Nevertheless, they will hold the strength of the Rock of Gibraltar, which ensures a well-built, synchronized vacation that has all the perks.

Capricorn/Aquarius

Although their outlook is very different, these two signs can bring out the finer qualities of one another while traveling. Aquarius will rely on Capricorn's sturdiness to plan an excellent vacation from beginning to end. Capricorn will be influenced and amazed by Aquarius's intuitive insight, which turns out to be a superb traveling guide. As long as Capricorn isn't too cautious and controlling and Aquarius isn't too whimsical and restless, they can appreciate what their partner has to offer to fully enjoy their trip. When Aquarius has wandered too far, Capricorn will be resourceful and bring them both back to safety. When Capricorn is too stagnant, Aquarius will be instrumental in lightening their load and seeking out adventures of discovery that replicate a wonderful journey, like touring Barcelona's unique architecture seen in La Sagrada Familia Cathedral, the Parque Guell, and La Pedrera. When not left to their own devices, Capricorn and Aquarius will gain tremendously from each other's expertise while traveling.

Capricorn/Pisces

Capricorn and Pisces are an unlikely pair who are able to capitalize upon their strengths to achieve a wonderful traveling experience, such as visiting the spectacular Castle of Hradčany or the 15th-century astronomical clock in Prague. Here the idyllic trip seen through Pisces can be realized through the efforts of Capricorn and enjoyed by them both. Capricorn, not a stranger to hard work, is keen on applying themselves to make sure they have a great time touring the planet. However, Pisces's evasiveness will not agree with Capricorn's realistic manner, and Capricorn may need to flow more with Pisces's imaginative vision of the magical places they wish to visit. While Pisces's persuasiveness encourages travel and exploring the corners of the world, they must have a strategy to convince Capricorn that it's economically feasible and worth their time and energy. Capricorn appreciates Pisces's compassion in devoting so much vitality toward the project. Together, they can respect each other's best and coordinate a fabulous journey.

Aquarius/Aries

This terrific team is sure to enjoy the auspices of traveling together. The spontaneity of Aries mixed with the inspiration of Aquarius creates great excitement on any journey. This "live wire" couple will pursue the most innovative trips. Whatever hasn't been explored will be. Taking in some delicious cuisine in Split, Croatia, and then touring the islands of Brac, Hvar, and Korcula will be of interest. Each sign has an effective way of motivating the other so that the fun just continues. If they had their way, they would never stop traveling. The vision of Aquarius will be eagerly pursued by the exhilaration of Aries. Although their opinions may differ on which vacation spot to visit or which site to see next, there is never a dull moment with this globetrotting duo. Their fascination with one another's outlook on their trip keeps them inspired along the way, especially while waiting through travel delays. Their enthusiasm while touring the world is contagious and motivates other worthy travelers. You may find this couple doing extreme skiing, whitewater rafting, or parachuting, since the better the thrill, the more the intrigue. Their slightly accident-prone nature will not deter them from experiencing every adventure known to humankind.

Aquarius/Taurus

When Aquarius and Taurus travel together, the "bull" and the "water bearer" join forces to create a great team while venturing out into the world. A well-orchestrated trip allows them both to have a fabulous time. Aquarius's intuitive know-how is used as a terrific travel guide as Taurus's pursuit of logic gives the trip a solid foundation that's hard to beat. Although Taurus looks for a bargain, they desire first class if it is available, whereas Aquarius is comfortable anywhere. As a couple, they prefer doing the unusual, like trekking through the magnificent pyramids in Mexico's Yucatan or venturing on a train through the Himalayas in Tibet. They prefer to see rare events in places few visit. Only their stubbornness will stall the great moments yet to be experienced on a trip. When they are ready to see each other's point of view, they can blend their ideas for a monumental journey.

Aquarius/Gemini

These two cerebral signs are a great match for traveling together. They are keen on motivating each other to enhance their insightful wit, especially while gallivanting throughout the world. There will never be a dull conversation between them, only a delightful rapport that lasts throughout the day. With Gemini's keen perceptiveness and Aquarius's grand intuition, they can plan an incredible vacation complete with all the perks. Since they both love their freedom, traveling by car or RV gives them the independence they need to carry out their own agenda. Jet-setting around the globe to distant lands such as Ecuador and the Galapagos Islands or the beautiful, Old World city of Prague, Czech Republic, will satisfy their thirst for intrigue. Since this pair needs excitement, you will not find them glued to one place for too long. They can easily wander in any direction, as they are adaptable to new surroundings. They are the best of friends, with Gemini arranging their travel itinerary and Aquarius steering them in the right direction. With such a great partnership, before a trip has ended they are already planning the awesome details of the next one.

Aquarius/Cancer

There is one element that draws these two signs together for a traveling experience: they are both incredibly intuitive and can rely on their intuition to steer them in the best direction with travel plans. Even though they seem to be miles apart, their sixth sense drives them right back to each other. They are humanitarians by nature, Cancer being more sensitive to conditions that affect humanity, and Aquarius being more intellectual about how to approach a widespread problem concerning the masses. Aquarius will certainly pursue an unconventional venue when it comes to traveling, while Cancer will feel emotionally motivated to stay at home. Through Aquarius's exciting manner, Cancer is inspired to pack their bags and travel with abandonment as long as their Aquarius partner is right beside them. Venturing out to Cape Cod and Martha's Vineyard will satisfy both signs. Cancer, more interested in setting up comfortable lodging quarters, will rely on impressive and sociable Aquarius to book the proper accommodations and travel arrangements for an exciting time. Whether it's on the road or in the air, these two unlikely signs find a way to complement each other and travel the world like no other two zodiac signs.

Aquarius/Leo

The foresight and creativity that this union emanates will generate a sparkling aura for all to see. In this case, opposites attract, displaying such a flair for socializing and excitement. This amazing duo can be seen running a bed-and-breakfast, being tour operators, or overseeing a travel agency. Their love for journeying the globe will keep them involved with some aspect of travel. Aquarius's insights and Leo's smarts are able to formulate the best vacation itinerary for their needs. As a team, their productive, humanitarian, and outgoing manner finds them volunteering for the Peace Corps or assisting abandoned children overseas. They are willing to tread through any country, purging their fears and learning from every incredible experience that beholds them. Easily adjusting to other cultures and languages, they are welcomed by the inhabitants of new lands as they enjoy the challenges that face them. Leo and Aquarius can be spotted counting the stars and appreciating the destiny behind each one of them. When all is said and done, this couple will wine and dine in style as Leo shows off their flashy attire and Aquarius invites publicity with their unique fashions. A weekend out in the Hamptons on Long Island is the pleasant, upscale environment they may seek. An occasional misstep may impede their trip, but this couple will still delight in all that can be attained.

Aquarius/Virgo

These two exceptionally bright signs are fine partners when it comes to traveling together. The natural intuitive wit of Aquarius combined with the practical intelligence of Virgo makes this a duo that is able to delve into the illuminating recesses of the mind to guide them both toward the most rewarding places to see while on their journey. They will be fascinated with exploring the many universes in our galaxy. Here on planet Earth, Virgo and Aquarius may want to visit the ornate Saint Stephen's Basilica in Budapest or delight in the unique architectural treasures of Istanbul. Virgo needs to appreciate Aquarius's intuitive insights, and Aquarius needs to appreciate Virgo's logic. Both can learn and gain from each other while experiencing the wonders of the world. If they allow their differing views to clash, their illustrious vacation will fall short of their expectations. Also, Virgo likes to be precise and on time, whereas Aquarius may be open-minded to exploring various options as they appear. Compromising is the key to keep this journey moving in a mentally intriguing direction.

Aquarius/Libra

These two lively air signs create a very stimulating energy for traveling. The harmonious ways of Libra combine with the exciting, intuitive manner of Aquarius for a motivating trip. They may be considered frequent travelers, ready to go at a moment's notice. Yet, Aquarius's restlessness and Libra's occasional indecision may clash at times. Even if there is a difference of opinion, they still complement each other nicely. Since they love their freedom, they both will enjoy gallivanting around the planet. Mentally inspiring places activate great conversation along the way. Their enjoyment of stargazing may take them to the Lowell Observatory in Flagstaff, Arizona—a popular destination for tourists who enjoy astronomy, and famous for its discovery of Pluto. Their accommodations and traveling plans are handled in a quick, easy manner so as not to waste precious time. They both are interested in learning a new language, especially if it will benefit their journey. Exploring new cultures, which prevail in the traditional customs of Japan or the long-standing pride of Greece, opens them both up to a fascinating world that continues to promote travel in the future.

Aquarius/Scorpio

This loyal pair is an interesting couple that can benefit from each other's acquired wisdom when traveling. Scorpio will be shrewd in carrying out the whimsical ideas of Aquarius in devising an itinerary for their journey. Both can connect on a higher intuitive level to work out the details. Aquarius will be intrigued with Scorpio's depth, as Scorpio will be enlightened by Aquarius's flash insights. However, Aquarius's flightiness may be mistaken for a lack of depth by Scorpio, and Scorpio's secretive manner and stubbornness may not win approval from Aquarius's openness. Hopefully, their intellectual status will lead them back to what's important while on their journey. Since they like their privacy and freedom, kayaking down the Nile River or venturing into the lost cities of ancient Peru and Machu Picchu would be quite fulfilling. They derive great pleasure in immersing themselves in nature. Trusting their mate, they may feel comfortable enough to briefly separate and rejoin their loved one at a specified location. In this way, both are satisfied with seeing certain highlights of their trip and sharing the jubilant results with their traveling companion.

Aquarius/Sagittarius

This thrill-seeking team will thoroughly delight in one another's company while traveling the Earth. Sagittarius is a natural traveler, as Aquarius likes the idea of venturing into areas of new discovery. The knowledgeable wit of Sagittarius will be accessed to formulate a fabulous excursion. Aquarius, however, will implement their own insightful vision of how to indulge in a travel experience. There will be perpetual excitement while on the road and perhaps a little competition on whose unique itinerary will be used. You will find this friendly duo in every part of the world. Unexplored cultures will draw them into new lands with great intrigue. They will prefer flying to get to their destination as quickly and conveniently as possible. Without wasting precious time, they will have more fun relishing every moment. The beaches and nightlife in Acapulco, as well as the majestic mountains in Aspen, are alluring as long as they have their high-tech camera ready to go. The "connoisseurs of traveling" is an appropriate title for these two bold and ambitious signs.

Aquarius/Capricorn

Although their outlook is very different, these two signs can bring out the finer qualities of one another while traveling. Aquarius will rely on Capricorn's sturdiness to plan an excellent vacation from beginning to end. Capricorn will be influenced and amazed by Aquarius's intuitive insight, which turns out to be a superb traveling guide. As long as Capricorn isn't too cautious and controlling and Aquarius isn't too whimsical and restless, they can appreciate what their partner has to offer to fully enjoy their trip. When Aquarius has wandered too far, Capricorn will be resourceful and bring them both back to safety. When Capricorn is too stagnant, Aquarius will be instrumental in lightening their load and seeking out adventures of discovery that replicate a wonderful journey, like touring Barcelona's unique architecture seen in La Sagrada Familia Cathedral, the Parque Guell, and La Pedrera. When not left to their own devices, Capricorn and Aquarius will gain tremendously from each other's expertise while traveling.

Aquarius/Aquarius

When two Aquarians travel together, fortunately their intuitive insights will act as a terrific travel guide, taking them in the right direction. Their intellectually quick minds will rapidly plan a travel itinerary, book it, and pursue it. What better way to address their need for personal freedom than to travel the world? This team's open-mindedness will take them north, south, east, and west—wherever their fancy lies. Although their agenda may change and be unpredictable, they love the idea of meeting up with the unexpected. Fellow travelers may perceive them as unstable, but they're just missing out on all of the fun. Journeying to the far corners of the Earth may take them to see the Seven Wonders of the World. As they create their own rules, they are reassured of the equal partnership they share while discovering unspoiled lands that embrace the planet.

Aquarius/Pisces

What a pair! Aquarius is intuitive intellectually and Pisces is intuitive emotionally, which makes for an innate understanding of what each other wants when planning a journey together. Without wasting a minute, Aquarius will be arranging the accommodations and tours that both are soon to enjoy. Pisces will insist their ideal trip be pursued for the most rewarding journey. Together, their imagination will design the "perfect" trip. Yet, this excursion out of town may not always be realized, since formulating the details will be discussed, but not always pursued. When they finally do travel, it may be a spontaneous venture that is filled with excitement. They will find conferences and retreats appealing, as what is gained expands their consciousness. More leisurely trips may involve a unique, creative venue, such as visiting the Louvre in France or the Picasso Museum in Catalonia, Spain. Whether they are on a mission or travel for pleasure, this couple is bound to capture the essence of sporting the globe to enhance their lives.

Pisces/Aries

The idyllic scenario of where to travel envisioned by Pisces is sure to arouse Aries's enthusiastic side. Pisces will want to be intrigued with their surroundings, and Aries will want to conquer the world. These two signs are able to assist one another throughout their trip to get the most out of it. Aries will persuade Pisces to tour one site after another, not allowing Pisces to become too immersed in one site for too long. Pisces will encourage Aries to slow down and appreciate the intricate wonders of our world, such as the majestic snowcaps of Alaska's Glacier Bay or the Eilean Donan Castle in the Scottish Highlands. Pisces's sometimes ambiguous approach will force Aries to take control and make sure all of the reservations are set and the right travel gear and attire are packed. As long as both are able to pursue their vacation preferences, they'll be happy on the road, in the air, or on the seas.

Pisces/Taurus

This calm duet is very compatible while traveling. The insightful compassion of Pisces is well received by the receptive and, in turn, nurturing Taurus. Pisces will dream up a wonderful vacation, while Taurus is busy weaving it all together. Pisces is convinced that a trip that includes a humanitarian effort will give their journey more meaning. Taurus, preferring a relaxing trip with no concerns, at the request of Pisces will learn to explore their philanthropic side while away from home. Together, they can bring goodwill into the world. Basic accommodations and necessities may not fare as well for Taurus as it does for Pisces, so there may have to be a compromise here. Their travels may take them to the Peace Corps efforts in Kenya or the Hawaiian Islands, paradise on earth. Their romantic expectations can be easily satisfied by a glorious sunset overlooking the ocean. Both can enhance each other's view of the world by appreciating what each other has to offer when exploring new lands.

Pisces/Gemini

These two will enhance each other's best qualities while traveling together. Gemini's wittiness is sure to realize Pisces's dream vacation. The result is that both are happily satisfied while on their fabulously planned journey. Gemini, needing mental stimulation, will want to move quickly from place to place, while Pisces may be happy with just enjoying the impact of their immediate surroundings. Both may find satisfaction touring the legendary ruins of Pompeii or trekking through the Scandinavian countries. They may prefer their own transportation with travel gear it tow. Food can always be found along the way, with an interesting variety for anyone's palate. Their ability to be flexible and adapt to any new environment is a plus. However, there will be times when they are both wondering which way to go, and end up delayed or not going at all. It's best to decide their itinerary early on, before embarking on their anticipated journey. Once a trip is finalized, they can delight in the wonders of the world.

Pisces/Cancer

When Pisces and Cancer tour the world together, these two water signs are an excellent match that will hold up through the years. The compassionate gestures of Pisces will be highly supportive of Cancer's emotional need for stability. Catering to Cancer's needs, Pisces will bring all sorts of goodies to make any journey, short or long, a truly comfortable one. Pisces can be easily diverted to embark on any traveling excursion, whereas reclusive Cancer will engage in traveling only when they are both financially and emotionally ready to explore new sites. Cancer may need to be gently persuaded and also have sound reassurance from their sometimes evasive Pisces traveling companion. Journeying through the Napa Valley vineyards on an elegant dining train and wine tasting in their grandiose wineries may easily satisfy both zodiac signs. Their intuitive qualities will allow them to succeed at planning a wonderful trip with little effort. As long as they have each other, they are ready to travel cross-country in a sporty convertible or discover new terrain in a foreign country, just for fun.

Pisces/Leo

Tremendous creative energy will make this couple very appealing, even though their styles are different. The compassionate and introspective Pisces is happy to go along with their partner, as Leo's strong persona will dominate by organizing the trip and packing their bags. They both may plan many more vacations than what they actually take, for it is thinking up the possibilities that excites them. Looking through travel magazines or browsing the internet for vacation deals is a great way for this couple to pass the time. Since Leo and Pisces are both dreamers, when traveling they will shoot for the perfect trip and then dream away. Leo will direct them both through amazing jungles or the wild streets of civilized societies. They may enjoy the magnificent, romantic Eiffel Tower just as much as a panoramic view of Vancouver Island. Pisces will be supportive of their partner and definitely fascinated by it all, looking up to Leo with gratitude. Being a great host and hostess, Leo and Pisces may look for friends or traveling companions to display their social skills and artistic prowess. As long as Leo allows Pisces's perceptiveness to assist with the plans and doesn't dominate or show a lack of appreciation for what Pisces has to offer, and Pisces doesn't become too evasive with their itinerary, these two signs can happily travel the Earth together.

Pisces/Virgo

These two opposites combine their unique qualities to enhance their journey together. The practicality of Virgo blends with the creativity and vision of Pisces to create wonderful traveling excursions. Virgo is keen on making sure everything is in order with their itinerary, right down to the smallest detail. Pisces visualizes the entire journey and relays this to Virgo. Pisces will appreciate the specific information that Virgo has researched on every place they visit. Virgo will enjoy Pisces's relaxed and dreamy approach, so they both can experience a great vacation. What Virgo lacks, Pisces makes up for, and what Pisces lacks, Virgo makes up for, which creates an excellent balance while traveling. Here, they are able to strike a nice balance that meets each other's needs while touring the globe. Their compassion and willingness to be of service to others draw them to remote and underprivileged areas, where they are rewarded with the satisfaction of helping others. You may find them trekking through the provinces of Africa, Asia, or South America. Collecting artifacts from other countries, they decorate their home as a memorandum of their travels. In discovering more about people and other cultures, they are continually fascinated with the world around them.

Pisces/Libra

The romanticism of Libra and the idealism of Pisces creates an imaginary world of traveling that is very appealing. You may find these two signs at the awe-inspiring canals of Venice or the Taj Mahal. They may also experience great pleasure in taking a voyage across the ocean, which instills fun and romance. Libra may be particular about their travel arrangements, and Pisces is likely to go along with the plan. Their mutual compassion and sensitivity draw them closer together as they jaunt from place to place, taking in the wonders of the world. Since Libra likes one-on-one communication and Pisces prefers another "fish" to swim with, they both gravitate toward each other, expressing their views and forming tighter bonds along their journey. As long as the vagueness of Pisces and the indecision of Libra are held in check, this unlikely duo can embrace every traveling experience for the fabulous expedition that it is.

Pisces/Scorpio

Two water signs linking up for a traveling experience is an excellent match. Since they are both emotionally intuitive, they will sometimes communicate on a telepathic level and have an in-depth understanding of one another. Pisces's dream trip can be researched by intense Scorpio so that it's not only scenic, but holds great meaning. Scorpio is grateful for Pisces's vision, and Pisces is happy that Scorpio can be attentive to the details that are involved in creating a fabulous expedition. Scorpio will be tolerant of Pisces's vagueness from time to time, as Pisces will accept Scorpio's desire to be secretive. Whether they are traveling first class or camping out under the stars, they do prefer their privacy. While on their journey, Scorpio will want to investigate every fascinating site. Both will be captivated by the unforgettable impression of the luscious Costa Rican rainforests, with the most beautiful waterfalls in the world. Capturing a rare moment in silence is what is most rewarding when traveling together. Overall, this pair is an excellent partnership, walking hand in hand in exploring the planet they live on and appreciating its grandeur.

Pisces/Sagittarius

Since Jupiter is the planet that excites travel, and is the ruler of Sagittarius and coruler of Pisces, it stands to reason that these two signs would find a unique way of having fun while traveling together. Pisces dreams of the perfect vacation as Sagittarius is quick on coming up with a fantastic excursion worthy of an experienced travel agency. The two in combination are bound to explore the reaches of the world, where there are no limits as to what can be seen. The more idyllic, the better the challenge.

Since they are both fascinated with learning about the world around them, they may make their appearance at the Egyptian Sphinx and Pyramids of Giza or the Taj Mahal in India. Exploring other cultures and different languages has them thrilled with humanity itself. Being understanding, they will try to accommodate each other's needs and desires along the way. As excellent traveling companions, touring the planet is a real joy.

Pisces/Capricorn

Pisces and Capricorn are an unlikely pair that is able to capitalize upon their strengths to achieve a wonderful traveling experience, such as visiting the spectacular Castle of Hradčany or the 15th-century astronomical clock in Prague. Here, the idyllic trip seen through Pisces can be realized through the efforts of Capricorn and enjoyed by them both. Capricorn, not a stranger to hard work, is keen on applying themselves to make sure they have a great time touring the planet. However, Pisces's evasiveness will not agree with Capricorn's realistic manner, and Capricorn may need to flow more with Pisces's imaginative vision of the magical places they wish to visit. While Pisces's persuasiveness encourages travel and exploring the corners of the world, they must have a strategy to convince Capricorn that it's economically feasible and worth their time and energy. Capricorn appreciates Pisces's compassion in devoting so much vitality toward the project. Together, they can respect each other's best and coordinate a fabulous journey.

Pisces/Aquarius

What a pair! Aquarius is intuitive intellectually and Pisces is intuitive emotionally, which makes for an innate understanding of what each other wants when planning a journey together. Without wasting a minute, Aquarius will be arranging the accommodations and tours that both are soon to enjoy. Pisces will insist their ideal trip be pursued for the most rewarding journey. Together, their imagination will design the "perfect" trip. Yet, this excursion out of town may not always be realized, since formulating the details will be discussed, but not always pursued. When they finally do travel, it may be a spontaneous venture that is filled with excitement. They will find conferences and retreats appealing, as what is gained expands their consciousness. More leisurely trips may involve a unique, creative venue, such as visiting the Louvre in France or the Picasso Museum in Catalonia, Spain. Whether they are on a mission or travel for pleasure, this couple is bound to capture the essence of sporting the globe to enhance their lives.

Pisces/Pisces

This idealistic twosome favors any expedition that will resemble escaping from reality and experiencing happy times together. Their emotional compatibility promotes sensitivity to each other's wishes that creates a compassionate bond. Although they dream of the "perfect" vacation, not all trips will be pursued, as some of their ideas drift into the wind to return at a later date. Once they isolate their perceptive thoughts, they are capable of organizing a trip of their liking. Nevertheless, the fantasy continues and will encourage travel to distant places around the globe. Journeying to Auckland, Australia, City of Sails, or the magical Luxor Temple and its archeological treasures will be inviting. Their compassionate side will encourage trips of a humanitarian nature to help the less fortunate. Whatever the reason, they will pursue their ideals with vigor until they are realized, and they are blessed with the fact they are in the company of someone who knows them as well as they know themselves.

Chapter 7

THE PLANETARY CELESTIAL BODIES

There are 10 planets, including the Moon, that are used in astrology: the Sun, the Moon, Mercury, Venus, Mars, Jupiter, Saturn, Uranus, Neptune, and Pluto. Each planet has a different effect on us that influences the direction of our life and our experiences.

Sun

The Sun represents the self, one's will, vitality, strength, and one's goals or purpose in life. It indicates where you become aware of your purpose in the world and are encouraged toward greater achievements. Honoring integrity, you recognize your importance and are able to express your fullest potential. Your will is your greatest asset. The Sun in favorable aspect to Jupiter supports travel. The Sun in adverse aspect to Mars, Saturn, Uranus, Neptune, or Pluto may cause difficulty with your traveling experiences.

Moon

The Moon represents emotions, feelings, sensitivity, instincts, the mother, and all female associations. Emotional responses emanated from the Moon may explain your mood swings, which can be set off in a positive or adverse manner by the other planets. Your inner being will display behavioral patterns that describe conditions from early childhood. Feeling out circumstances, you learn to adapt to new conditions and find emotional stability. Traveling when the Moon is in favorable aspect to any planet allows our emotions to be more stable. We encounter emotional instability when the Moon is in adverse aspect to Mars, which may cause accidents, as well as to Saturn, Uranus, Neptune, and Pluto.

Mercury

Mercury represents communication, understanding, the intellect, learning, and analysis. Through the process of gathering information, you learn to analyze your ideas and develop a communicative rapport with others. Reasoning skills allow you to accumulate data that will increase your versatility and allow your plans to run smoothly. Since how we communicate will greatly affect our traveling experiences, Mercury in positive aspect to Jupiter promotes travel and excellent communications. Mercury in adverse aspect to Mars, Saturn, Uranus, Neptune, and Pluto may cause serious difficulty with traveling. I do not advise traveling under these unfavorable Mercury aspects.

Venus

Venus represents love and affection, attraction, self-esteem, beauty, comfort, femininity, values, and financial prosperity. It is through the power of love that you learn to establish meaningful values, especially in learning to love and appreciate yourself as well as those around you. The magnetic appeal that Venus displays allows you to attract opportunity. You are prone to seek harmony and beautify your surroundings. Wherever Venus is, there is comfort and love. Venus in positive influence to any planet, especially Jupiter, will help appease a situation. When Venus is in adverse aspect to Saturn, Uranus, Neptune, or Pluto, feelings of love, attraction, and financial security are repressed, erratic, vague, or challenged, thus curtailing our traveling experiences in some manner.

Mars

Mars represents desire, energy, passion, independence, aggression, and masculinity. Here, energy can be used constructively or destructively. Mars can create much damage when misdirected. When it is properly channeled, you are driven to establish your identity by seeking out your independence and personal goals. Your desire nature will invoke intense passions that can be directed toward a love interest or an important ambition. Mars in favorable aspect to any of the planets can be productive, especially Jupiter, which will motivate Mars toward excellent traveling experiences. When Mars is in adverse aspect to Mars, Saturn, Uranus, Neptune, or Pluto, challenging and dangerous situations could erupt, causing disastrous results while traveling.

Jupiter

Jupiter represents expansion, opportunity, abundance, good fortune, optimism, travel, philosophy, religion, and wealth. It indicates where you look for opportunity to attract the good fortune that life has to offer. Always broadening our consciousness, you will look to expand mentally, socially, spiritually, physically, and emotionally. Jupiter instills an optimistic and confident persona that invites benefits. As long as you don't overextend yourself, expanding your experiences will lead to fulfillment. Since Jupiter is the planet that rules over travel and optimistic circumstances, when it is in positive aspect to any of the planets, you can expect favorable travel experiences. However, when Jupiter is in adverse aspect to Mars, Saturn, Uranus, Neptune, or Pluto, our travel experiences are possible yet challenging.

Saturn

Saturn represents limitation, reality, control, discipline, responsibility, maturity, and authority. Here, you must confront reality and recognize your limitations. You will learn how to consolidate your goals by structuring yourself appropriately. You may encounter hard times that test your patience and fortitude. Applying discipline and hard work in some capacity will be required, but you will develop integrity and gain respect from others. Saturn's calculating manner reaps solid results. What you come to realize is that it is only through earning your way that you will truly appreciate life. Saturn in positive aspect to any planet is still challenging because of the limitations Saturn puts on a person. Saturn in adverse aspect to Mars, Saturn, Uranus, Neptune, or Pluto could attract devastating results while traveling. It is best to avoid this influence.

Uranus

Uranus represents sudden change, the unpredictable, progress, the future, excitement, uniqueness, the unconventional, and one's individuality while traveling. There is much encouragement to be your unique self, capitalizing upon your individuality. Due to its erratic, out-of-control tendency, circumstances are unpredictable and prone to sudden changes. There will be a breaking away of any limiting conditions that are hampering your progress, so you realize your fullest potential. There is a desire to be free and escape the status quo. You enhance your existence as you continue on the path of self-discovery. Uranus in auspicious aspect to any planet opens doors to progress and self-discovery. When Uranus is in adverse influence to any planet, the Sun, the Moon, Mercury, Venus, especially Mars, Jupiter, Saturn,

Uranus, Neptune, or Pluto, the unexpected could occur, causing much upset in your life while traveling.

Neptune

Neptune represents illusion, idealism, creativity, compassion, spirituality, nebulousness, deception, and dissolution. You may pursue your greatest hopes and dreams, which inspire the imagination. Creative aims and spiritual quests that embrace a sympathetic understanding of humanity are highlighted. However, due to vague and deceptive encounters, you could meet up with disappointment. You will learn to cultivate perceptiveness to take advantage of the idealistic means of Neptune and to avoid the undermining world of illusion. Neptune in favorable aspect to any planet inspires our creativity, idealism, and compassion. When Neptune influences a planet in adverse aspect, a disappointment is likely while traveling. A possible disaster may occur while traveling when Neptune is adversely affecting any planet, especially Mercury, Mars, Saturn, Uranus, Neptune, or Pluto.

Pluto

Pluto represents intense involvement, power, transformation, regeneration, partnership, joint finances, sex, endings yet new beginnings, obsession, manipulation, elimination, regeneration, and death and rebirth experiences. The process of transformation involves dramatic change that allows for a new phase to begin. Through Pluto, you encounter the heights and the depths of an experience. Partnerships and sex are explored. Dominating or manipulative behavior can lead to devious and evil actions. Powerful, explosive circumstances occur under Pluto transits. Pluto in positive aspect to any planet will bring depth and meaning into your travel experiences. In adverse aspect, Pluto creates intense, manipulative, coercive, and powerfully destructive encounters while traveling. Malefic Pluto influences are present under nefarious actions noted in sabotage, conspiracies, and terrorism.

Chapter 8

OPTIMAL TRAVEL CHARTS

Learn the perfect timing for your trip. This chapter provides examples of astrological charts for optimal travel. Here, several aspects of the travel strategy proposed throughout this book are described in detail.

Cindy's Chart for Favorable Summer Vacation Travel

During summer vacation, "Cindy" was on a trip to visit friends and relatives. Her trip was reassured by the Moon in favorable sextile aspect to Jupiter, Mercury conjunct Jupiter, and Moon sextile Mercury. Upon leaving her home, a safe and easy ride to the airport followed. However, at check-in, "Cindy" finds out that her plane is grounded and that she may have to switch planes. Here, Saturn semisquare Mercury is causing a temporary setback. However, despite an hour delay, the situation was quickly remedied and the itinerary actually changed for the better. Hearing good news and supporting a positive traveling experience, Mercury conjunct Jupiter and the wide Sun conjunct Jupiter came through, and "Cindy" thoroughly enjoyed her flight. The rest of her trip was excellent, especially her long-anticipated visit with her mother, Moon sextile Jupiter, which left her with special memories. Due to such a meaningful traveling experience (Moon/Jupiter/Mercury/Pluto midpoint), she now looks forward to her next trip. Neptune in trine aspect with her ninth sector of travel added extra inspiration while traveling. Any personal issues (Sun sesquiquadrate Pluto) or restlessness (Sun inconjunct Uranus) were easily resolved by the persuasive Jupiter influences. Extra compromising smoothed over any social tensions that were foreseen with Venus in sesquiquadrate aspect to Mars. The positives far outweighed the negatives, resulting in a favorable journey. Travel was after the Full Moon, approaching the New Moon. The Moon was not void of course, and there were no adverse Moon/Mars influences.

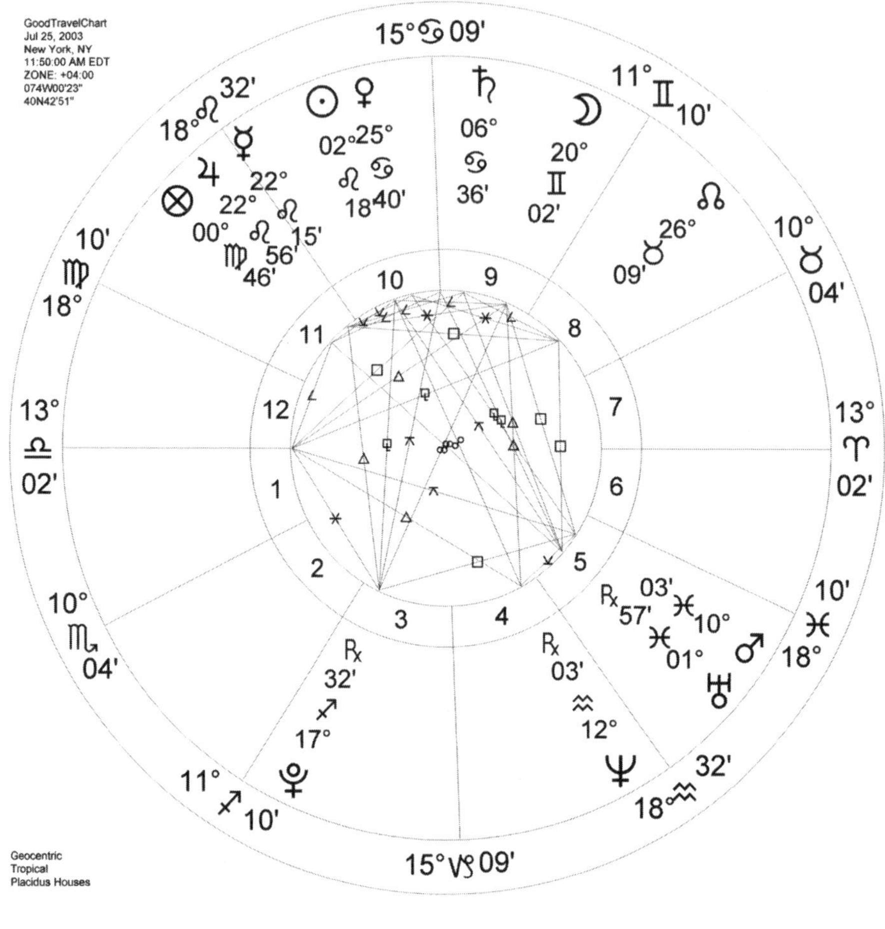

Rachel's Chart for Favorable Holiday Travel

Traveling home for the holidays is always something to look forward to, especially if you live 3,000 miles away. The terrific aspect of Jupiter trine Pluto was bound to encourage an uplifting trip for "Rachel," bolstering her confidence and attracting goodwill her way. Jupiter conjunct Moon and Jupiter in sesquiquadrate aspect to the Sun only augmented the joy surrounding this festive time. As long as she did not make too many demands (Sun semisquare Mars), the Venus/Jupiter influences to the Sun and to each other brought unexpected social favors that complemented the overall journey. Saturn in trine aspect to Uranus stabilized the trip, and Venus square Jupiter attracted some lovely Christmas surprises her way. Although "Rachel" experienced some tension in cooperating with others, a lively yet relaxing atmosphere also added to the events. Neptune in trine aspect to the North Node in the fourth sector of home and family enhanced "Rachel's" trip, adding to her dreamlike experience. The Mars/Sun and Mars/Jupiter influences contributed in a great way to her passion for sports, particularly aggressive skiing. Social charm (Venus conjunct Mars) was displayed in the evening hours. In most respects, the Jupiter influences, especially the Jupiter trine Pluto, encouraged personal strength, protection, and a compromising attitude that helped Rachel win over any audience while on her special journey. Mars was in trine aspect to her Ascendant, getting the trip off to a good start. The Moon was not void of course, travel was after the Full Moon, and there were no adverse Moon/Mars influences.

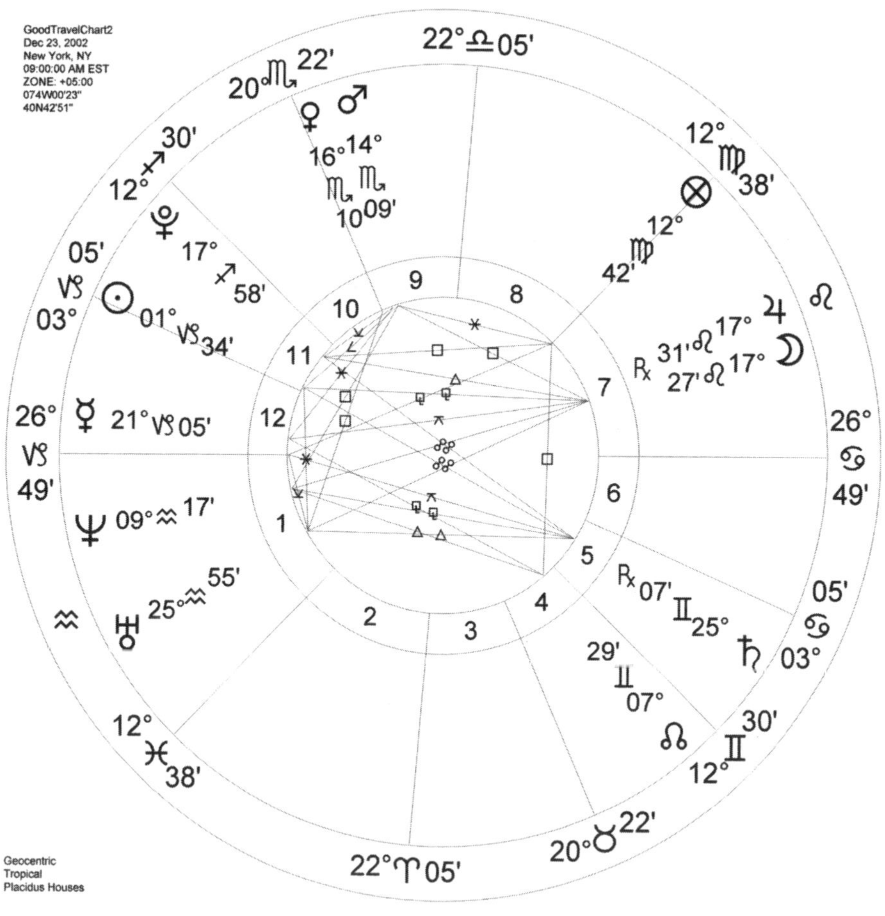

Chapter 9

HAZARDOUS TRAVEL PATTERNS: ACCIDENTS, CRASHES, AND TERRORISM

You can avoid the unthinkable and steer your journey in a favorable direction when you are equipped to accurately predict accidents, hijackings, bombings, and more. In a world of uncertainties, applying the travel strategy will allow you to rest assured and enjoy a safe traveling experience, knowing the stars are here to guide you safely to your destination. Knowledge is power when you are equipped with the proper tools. In preparation for this book, my analysis of countless charts of impactful events has led to predictable astrological patterns that can be harnessed and shield you and your loved ones from tragic occurrences and calamities. The following charts clearly show the significant patterns and provide you with a better understanding on how to ensure your safety and security while traveling.

Alaska Airlines Flight 261

Although air travel is supposed to be the safest way to travel, that was unfortunately not the case on January 31, 2000, at 4:19 p.m. PST, when Alaska Plane 261 crashed in Point Mugu, California, killing 88 people on board. A probable cause was the loss of airplane pitch control, which eventually caused the plane to lose altitude, spin erratically, and crash into the Pacific. There was an exact Moon at 21 degrees Sagittarius square Mars aspect at 21 degrees Pisces, which clearly indicates that this was an accident. Neptune was in midpoint aspect by 6 degrees to Saturn and the Sun, describing the deteriorating situation. Pluto was also in sextile to the Sun and inconjunct to Saturn on that ill-fated afternoon.

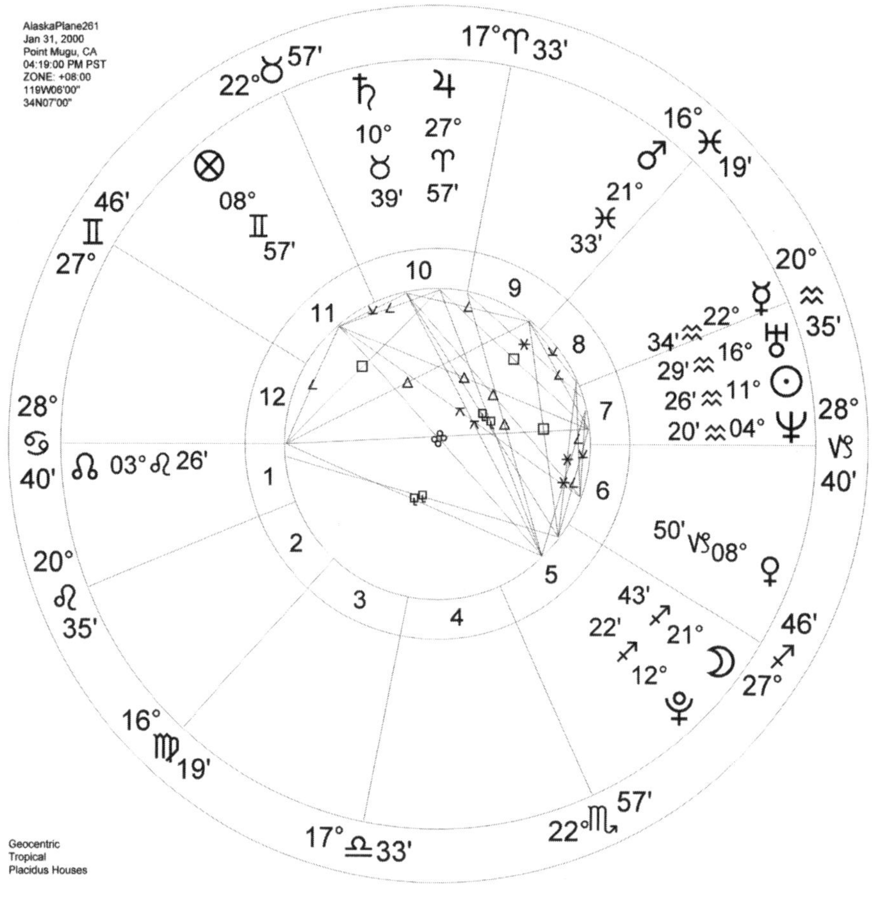

Korean Air Flight 801

On August 6, 1997, at 1:42 a.m., in Asan, Guam, Korean Air Flight 801 crashed onto a steep hillside 1 mile from the airport. Guam is known as a tropical vacation island, but there was nothing exemplifying paradise that day when the airplane's nightmare accident occurred. Crashing into the lush jungle ravine on Nimitz Hill, Flight 801 killed 229 people, with 25 survivors. The astrological chart of the horrible crash clearly displays a malefic Moon/Mercury midpoint semisquare aspect to Mars. The Moon is at 8 degrees Virgo, Mars is at semisquare 9 degrees Virgo, and Mercury is at 10 degrees Virgo. Also evident is a midpoint T-square involving Neptune to a Mars/Saturn opposition. Saturn was at 20 degrees, Mars was at 24 degrees, and Neptune was at 28 degrees in cardinal signs Aries, Libra, and Capricorn. When Mars and Saturn influence one another, a destructive incident may occur. The adverse angle involving Neptune only added to an already collapsing situation that ultimately led to the complete failure and crash of Flight 801.

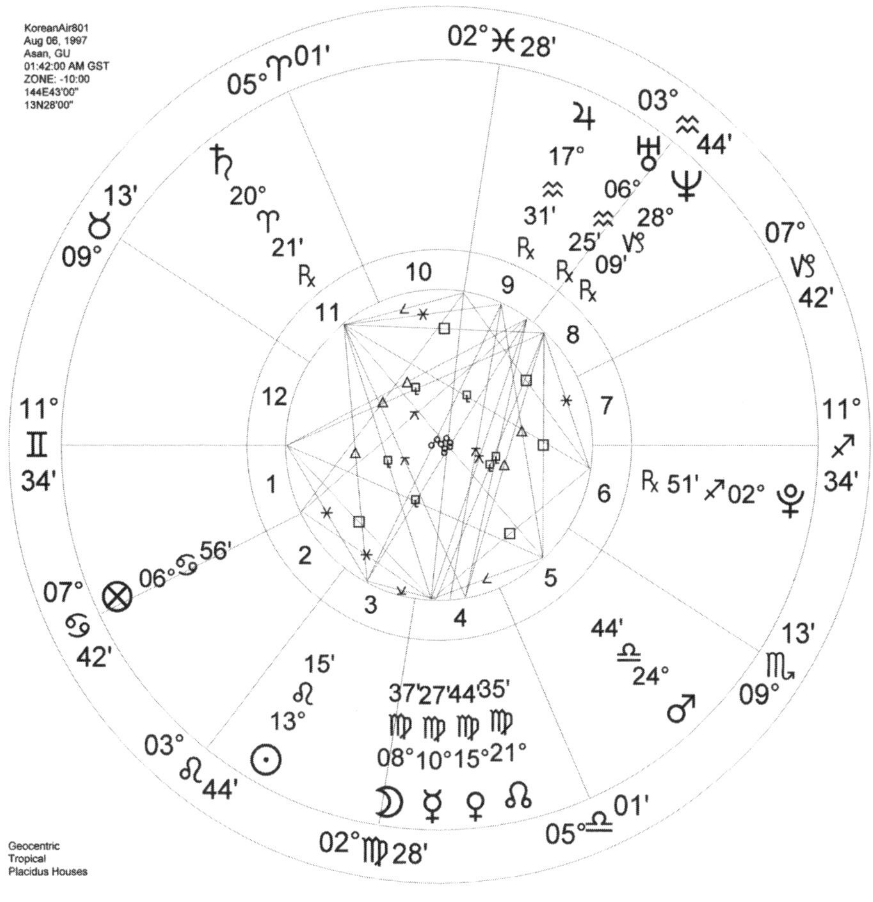

Mozambique Train Collision

On May 25, 2002, at 5:00 a.m. EET in Maputo, South Africa, two trains collided with each other, killing 192 people. It was alleged that a passenger train was towing a goods train and was unable to climb a hill and had to be separated. After leaving, the front train started rolling back at high speed and crashed into the cargo goods train, killing many on impact. Once again, a 2 degree midpoint planetary influence involving Neptune, Mars, and the Moon caused this deadly accident. The Moon in

Scorpio, the sign of death, is in detrimental midpoint sesquiquadrate aspect to Mars, denoting conflict and destruction, and semisquare aspect to Neptune, indicative of mishap and disillusionment. Mars is also in the sign of Gemini, representing the two trains. Emphasizing the impact of the disaster, note how the Moon, Mars, and Neptune midpoint is also part of the fixed angular cusps 1st, 4th, 7th, and 10th. The exact Saturn/Pluto opposition with Pluto in its ruling eighth house of death also lends itself to a destructive event of major proportion. Could this horrific scene have been avoided? Yes, if the trains had not been traveling during that time on that day.

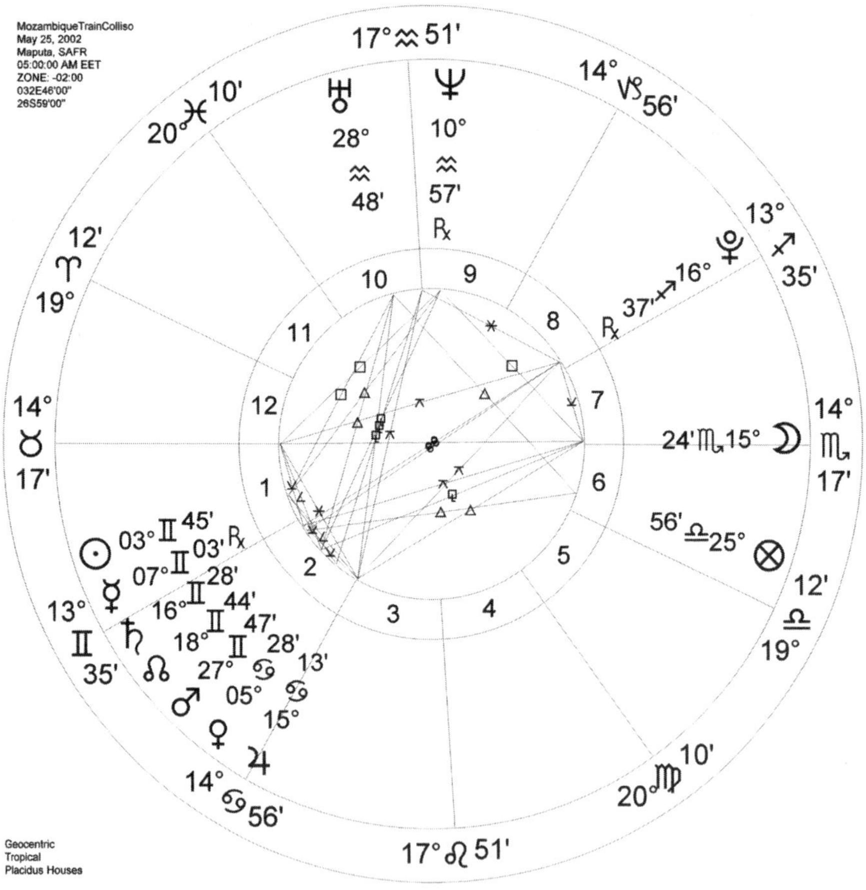

Simultaneous Train Bombings in Madrid

On March 11, 2004, starting at 7:39 a.m. CET in Madrid, Spain, 191 people were killed on a commuter train. Ten backpacks were filled with explosives that went off in a 15-minute period. Pluto near the midheaven in malefic square aspect to the Sun and Ascendant and inconjunct Mars greatly impacted the disaster and indicates terrorism at work. Pluto is the ruler of the ninth house of travel, Scorpio. A Sun, Ascendant, Uranus, and Pluto midpoint further accentuated an underhanded plot. Although the Moon was in wide aspect to Mars, it was not an exact midpoint aspect, which is what you would typically see in an accident. Terrorism is a planned attack, *not* an accident. Saturn is 2 degrees away from a malefic semisquare with Mars, indicating destruction and evil actions, and there is an adverse 2 degree midpoint

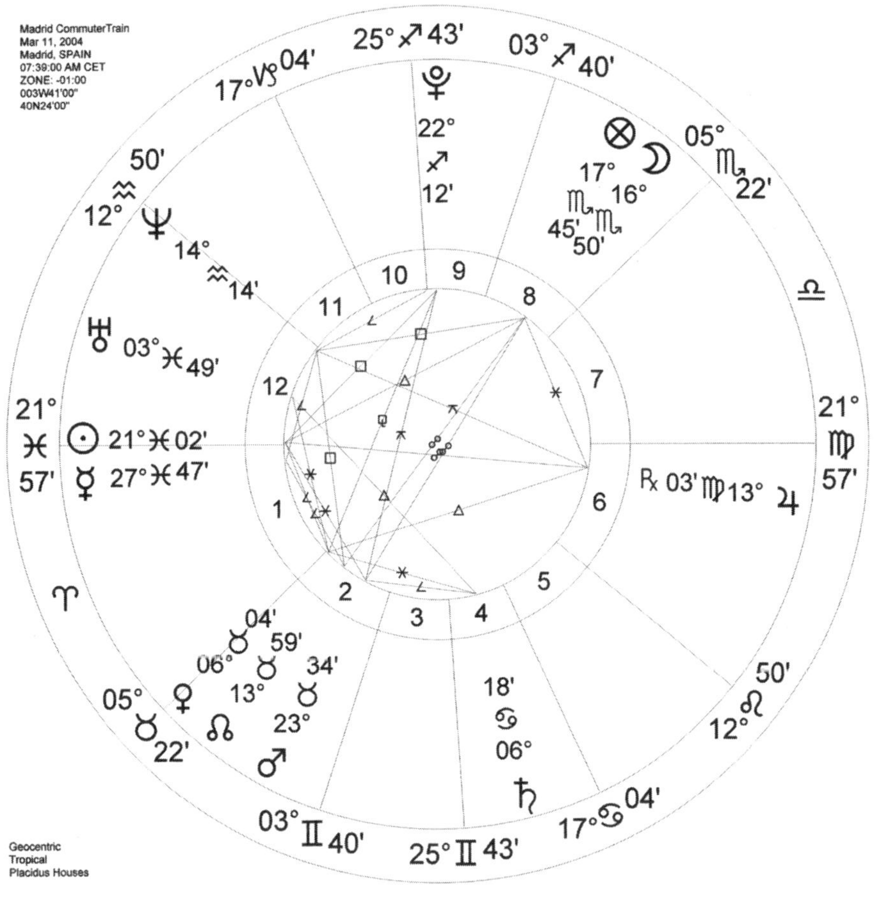

aspect between the $12^{th}/6^{th}$ house sector cusps, Neptune, and the Moon, which denotes disillusionment. Here, the far reaches of evil are pronounced in great capacity, as terrorists invoke fear and death to the people of Spain and beyond.

Terrorists Crash American Airlines Flight 11

On September 11, 2001, at 8:45 a.m. EDT in New York City, American Airlines Flight 11 crashed. Terrorists who had hijacked a plane crashed it into tower 1 of the World Trade Center. The world has never been the same. New Yorkers and the nation spent years rebuilding all that was lost in the wake of this unthinkable act. Sabotage is clearly displayed in the astrology chart of this tragic event. At 2 degree intervals, the Sun at 18 degrees is in adverse T-square aspect to Saturn at 14 degrees Gemini, opposing Pluto at 12 degrees Sagittarius. Any adverse angle with Pluto or Scorpio to the Sun will suggest sabotage. In this case, malefic Sun, Saturn, and Pluto angles invoked a conspiracy—the hijackings and death of 2,749 people on that ill-fated day. Saturn and Pluto were in opposition, indicating destructive intent resulting in absolute devastation. In the chart, the Ascendant is at 14 degrees Libra, and Saturn is in trine aspect to the Ascendant and Mercury. The Moon is void of course and 3 degrees from an opposition to Mars. An exact degree aspect of the Moon to Mars would indicate an accident, which this certainly was not! The Moon in Gemini, noting two planes crashing into the WTC, is also approaching an adverse, midpoint sesquiquadrate aspect to Uranus and Neptune in Aquarius. The v/c Moon and detrimental angles to Uranus and Neptune indicate a situation out of control. Mars exalted in Capricorn is also adversely aspecting Neptune and Uranus on 5-degree intervals. Mars on the semisquare would be 16 degrees Aquarius, 10 degrees away from Neptune and 5 degrees away from Uranus. Another indication revealed of a totally deceptive catastrophe, as it was that horrific, unforgettable morning in New York City.

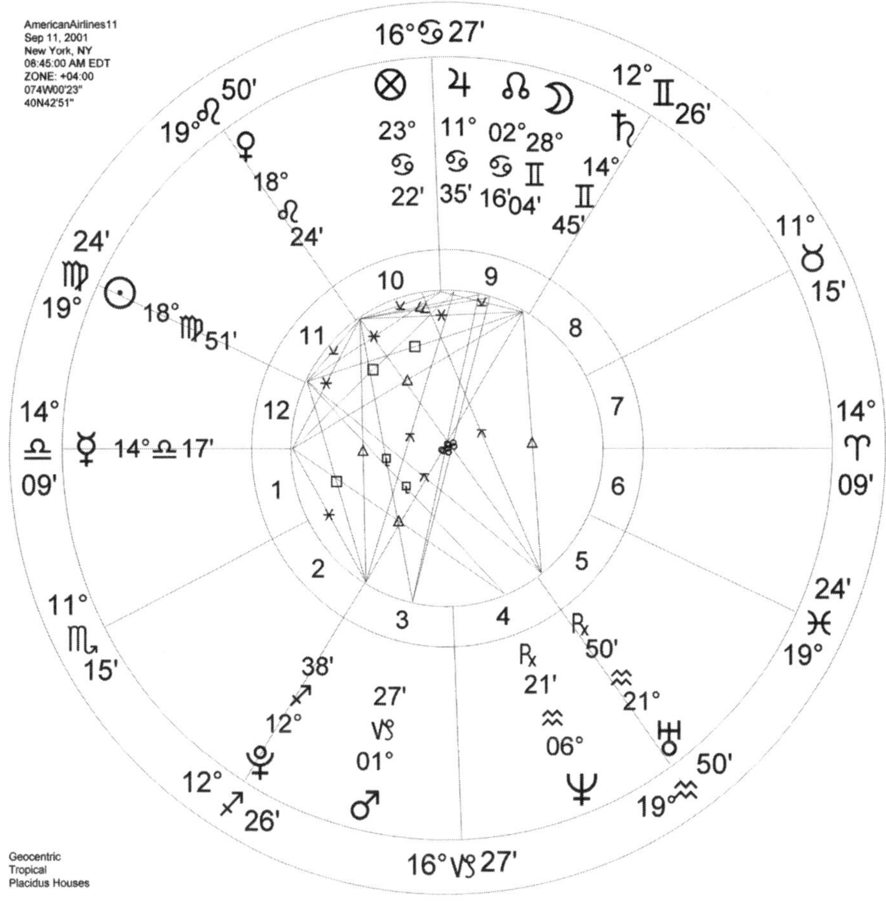

Terrorists Crash United Airlines Flight 175

On September 11, 2001, at 9:03 a.m. EDT in New York City, hijacked Flight 175 crashed into the World Trade Center tower number 2. This horrific moment shocked onlookers and indicated to all that two planes crashing into both towers was not an accident. The United States was unquestionably under attack. As in the first deliberate crash, the Sun continues to form an adverse, midpoint angle to Saturn and Pluto at 2 degree intervals, indicating terrorist activity. Mars is also in negative midpoint aspect by 5 degree intervals to Neptune and Uranus, denoting a deceptive, sudden, and chaotic tragedy, and the Moon, void of course, still approaching an adverse, midpoint aspect to Neptune and Uranus, indicating crazy, unpredictable behavior. The Moon is also in wide opposition to Mars. The midheaven at 19 degrees and 59 minutes, almost 20 degrees, is at a 3 degree adverse square to the Ascendant at 17 degrees and Mercury at 14 degrees. In fact, they are only 0 degrees and 9 to 10 minutes apart at that 3-degree interval. Close enough for me! Saturn continues to trine Mercury, which rules the ninth sector of travel. The devastating conclusion speaks for itself.

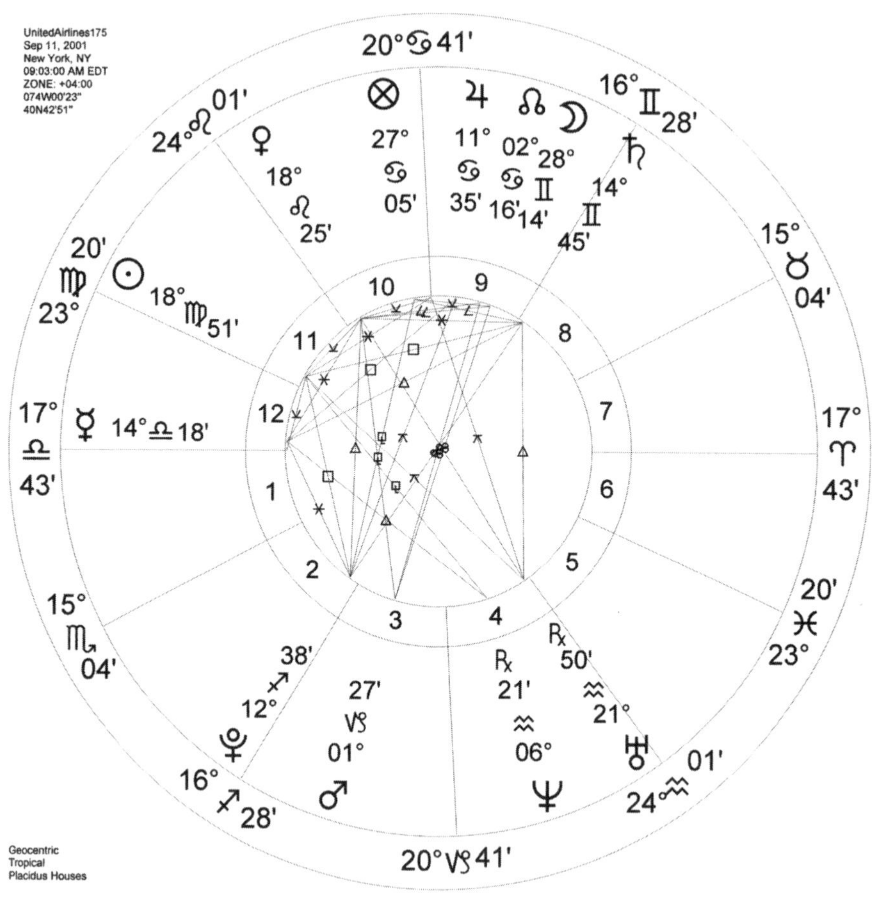

Terrorist Bombings in Tula and Rostov-Na-Donu

On August 24, 2004, at 10:56 p.m. BGT in Tula, Russia, and 11:00 p.m. BGT in Rostov-Na-Donu, Russia, two planes crashed minutes apart, caused by a planned terrorist attack. Altogether, 89 people lost their lives. An adverse Mars midpoint aspect involving the Sun, Saturn, Uranus, and Pluto was behind these hideous acts. A strong Mercury, Mars, and Uranus midpoint opposition had a tremendous impact on this scenario as well. Saturn was ruling over the ninth house sector of travel and semisquaring Mars to contribute to the destructive incident. Gemini on the Ascendant indicates two planes. There is also a midpoint Venus, Pluto/Moon, Saturn inconjunct aspect. The sudden, destructive situation that evolved from the takeoff chart of the plane that crashed in Tula, Russia, had a Mars/Uranus opposition in Virgo/Pisces in malefic, midpoint T-square aspect to the 6 degree Gemini, 49 minute Ascendant. Since there is a Sun/Pluto midpoint involving other planets and no Moon/Mars aspect (which would indicate an accident), the Sun/Pluto connection clearly indicates terrorism.

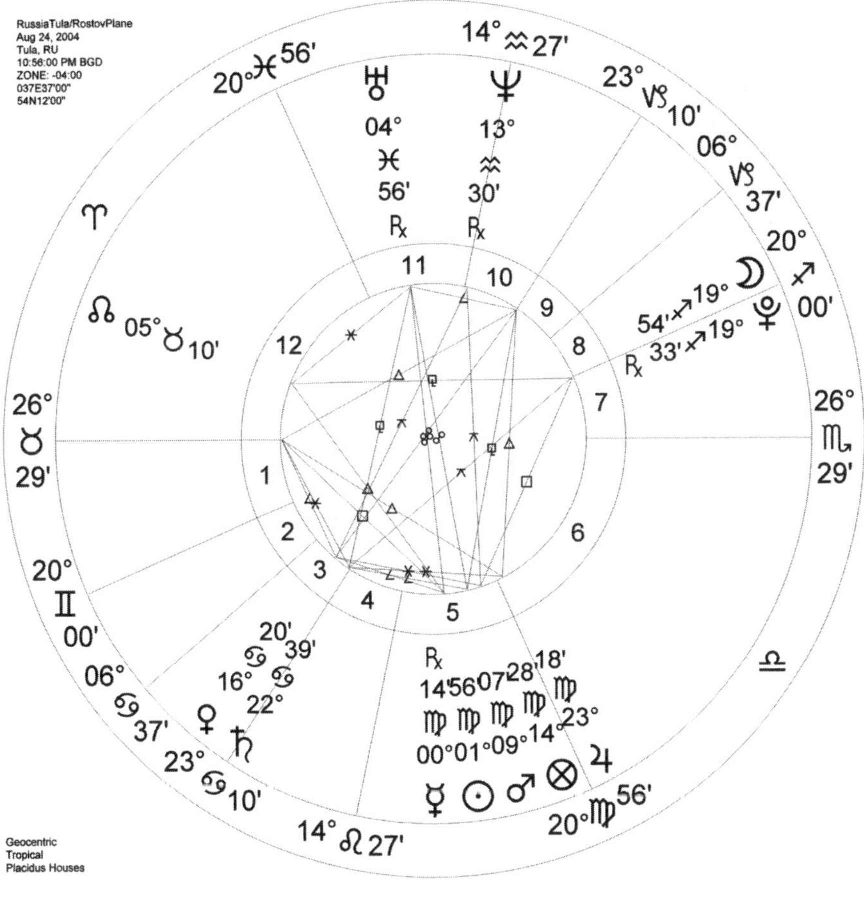

Pan Am Flight 103 Explodes

On December 21, 1988, at 7:03 p.m. GMT over Lockerbie, Scotland, Pan Am Flight 103 disappeared from the radar after exploding in midair. Pieces of the wreckage fell over Lockerbie, killing 11 people on the ground and 259 people on board the Boeing 747. Later, it was discovered that a terrorist from Libya had orchestrated the bombing of Flight 103. After much debate and grueling court appeals the families of the victims were compensated for the deaths of their loved ones. The absence of an adverse Moon/Mars aspect indicates that this was not an accident, and the presence of adverse Pluto influences to the Sun indicates that this plane had been clearly sabotaged. There is a malefic, midpoint semisquare aspect between Pluto

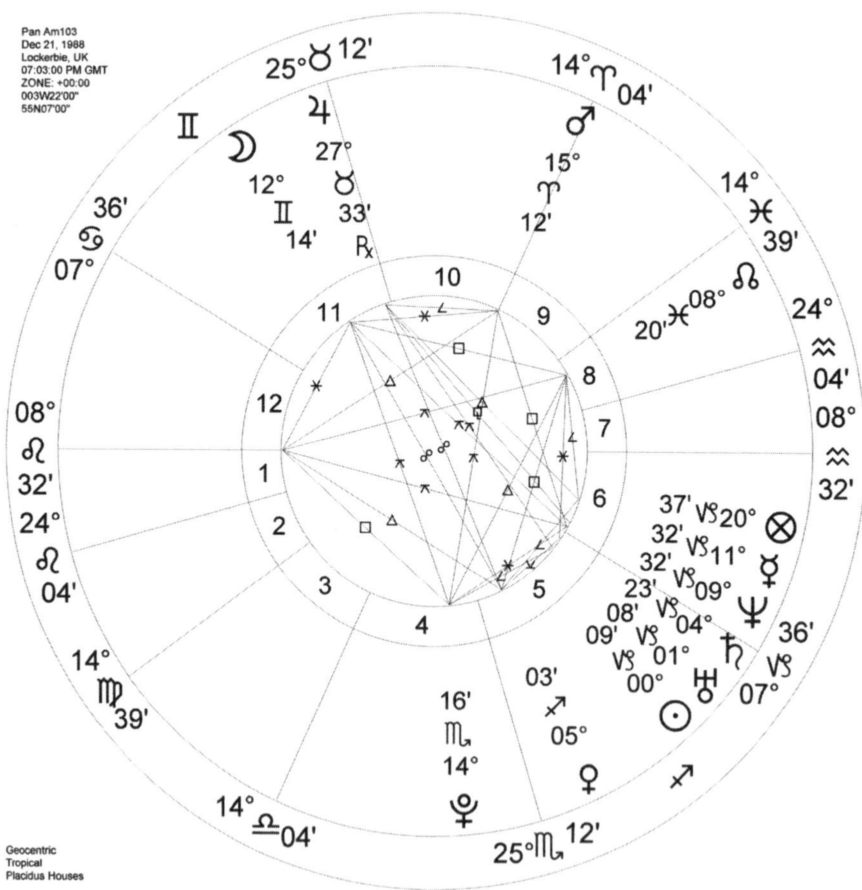

and the Sun and Uranus, all 1 degree apart by aspect. Pluto is also in its ruling sign of Scorpio, only further pronouncing the conspiracy when in aspect to the Sun. In addition, there is an adverse, midpoint semisquare angle between Pluto, Saturn, and Neptune, all 5 degrees apart, which describes the capacity for violence, destruction, death, and evil. Here, one is crushed by overwhelming odds. The Moon/Mars sextile is 3 degrees apart, which is too wide in aspect to be an accident. Pluto is also inconjunct Mars in its ruling sign of Aries and in the 9th house of long-distance travel, producing a negative combustion that lends itself to explosions. The combination of these many horrific influences led to the terrorist plotting and destruction of Pan Am Flight 103.

TWA Flight 800 Explodes

On July 17, 1996 at 8:31 p.m., off the coast of East Moriches in Long Island, New York, TWA 800 disappeared from radar as it exploded at 13,700 feet above sea level. The big question concerning this flight is: Was TWA 800 shot down by a military missile? In looking at the astrology chart of this aviation disaster, the Moon is in adverse sesquiquadrate aspect to Saturn in Aries, which indicates a difficult situation, compounded by the fact that Aries is a military sign. As Saturn is in Aries, a military regiment or situation is at hand here. Over 154 eyewitnesses, some quite reputable, described seeing a missile heading through the sky, and the convergence point was where the jumbo jet exploded. In the astrology chart of Flight 800, there are negative aspects to Pluto, which rules over Scorpio, located on the cusp of the 9th house sector of distant travel. This is significant, as the plane was on its way to Paris, France. The intense conditions would play out at 8:31pm EDT over Long Island. The Sun is in opposition to Neptune in Capricorn, indicating a debilitating situation and deception. And both the Sun and Neptune are in malefic T-square aspect to Pluto, which describes the hellish scenario that occurred in the air, as well as a possible conspiracy at hand. In a disaster such as this, Sun/Pluto malefic aspects represent sabotage. The exact opposition of Mercury and Uranus in Aquarius, which represents aviation, forms a detrimental T-square angle to Mars, planet of war and destruction. The US National Transportation Safety Board claims that this was an accident caused by a spark that ignited a center fuel tank, but astrology suggests otherwise. Detrimental Moon/Mars aspects within 1 degree cause accidents, which are not present in the chart of this horrible incident. The Moon in sextile to Mars at 3 degrees is too wide of an angle, thus indicating that this disaster may not have been an ill-fated accident. The downing of TWA Flight 800 was a catastrophic, unexplained act that claimed the lives of 230 people in the explosion that occurred.

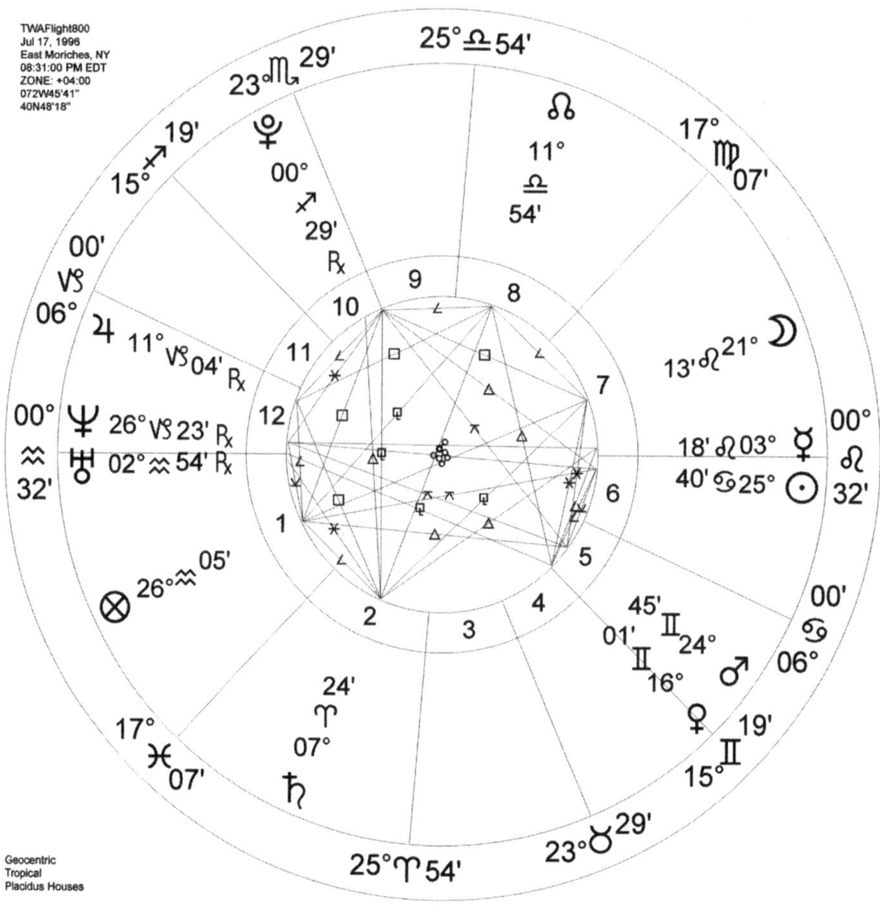

TWAFlight800
Jul 17, 1996
East Moriches, NY
08:31:00 PM EDT
ZONE: +04:00
072W45'41"
40N48'18"
25°♎54'
23°♏29'
17°♍07'
15°♐19'
00'♑06°
00°♒32'
00°♌32'
00'♋06°
17°♓07'
15°♊19'
25°♈54'
23°♉29'
♇ 00° ♐ 29' ℞
☊ 11° ♎ 54'
♃ 11° ♑ 04' ℞
♆ 26° ♑ 23' ℞
♅ 02° ♒ 54' ℞
☽ 21° ♌ 13'
☿ 03° ♌ 18'
☉ 25° ♋ 40'
⊗ 26° ♒ 05'
♂ 24° ♊ 45'
♀ 16° ♊ 01'
♄ 07° ♈ 24'
1
2
3
4
5
6
7
8
9
10
11
12
Geocentric
Tropical
Placidus Houses

Chapter 10

TRAVEL TIMING

What makes the difference in having a good trip or not can also be dependent on the time that we leave for a trip. The alignment and position of the planets at the time of departure can affect the ultimate outcome of your journey. Therefore, the specific time that one takes off for a trip will indicate the conditions of the overall trip and what one can expect to encounter along the way.

It's also important to remember that the time you leave your house is just as important as the time your transportation leaves. As a double precaution, when I plan a trip, I take into consideration not only the time I leave my place, but also the time the car, bus, train, boat, or plane leaves. I take into account potential delays in taking off as well, for not all travel schedules leave on time. If all looks good, it's a go.

For trip timing, you can draw up an event chart to determine the best time to leave your place, and also include an event chart for the time the car, bus, train, boat, or plane departs. Many factors need to be taken into consideration when you compose a trip-timing astrology chart. Usually, when the Sun, Mercury, Venus, or Jupiter are moving through the travel sectors, third and ninth houses, and/or the fifth house sector of leisure life, travel is encouraged. Sometimes Uranus, Neptune, or Pluto may also emphasize your traveling experiences one way or another. One rarely travels when Saturn is transiting the third or ninth travel sectors, or when there are adverse aspects to planets in your third or ninth sector. When planets in the third, fifth, or ninth house sectors are aspecting the Ascendant or other favorable planets such as Venus or Jupiter on a positive angle, your journey will be enjoyed and may also guarantee safe passage. You would not want to leave on your trip when Uranus was in malefic, square aspect to the Ascendant or Mars, thus indicating the possibility of accidents, traveling detours, and reversals of activity occurring. The specifics of trip timing may be time consuming, but so are the problems you may encounter before or during your journey if you have not planned your trip carefully. Here, planning ahead takes on a whole new meaning.

To emphasize this point, below are the charts of the *Columbia* space shuttle takeoff and breakup, and the departure, iceberg collision, and sinking of the *Titanic*. Strong, malefic midpoint aspects of Mars and other planets to the Moon indicate how these two tragedies were accidents of the worst kind.

The *Columbia* Space Shuttle Take-off

In the astrology chart of the *Columbia* space shuttle, the exact takeoff time from Cape Canaveral clearly depicts a disaster ahead. On January 16, 2003, at 10:39 a.m. EST in Cape Canaveral, Florida, the *Columbia* space shuttle took off for an exploratory mission for two weeks. The shuttle's astrology chart details the tragic destiny of its flight. There is an exact, adverse midpoint planetary aspect between the Moon, Mars, and Neptune, indicating plans going awry in the worst way. Mars is in Scorpio and

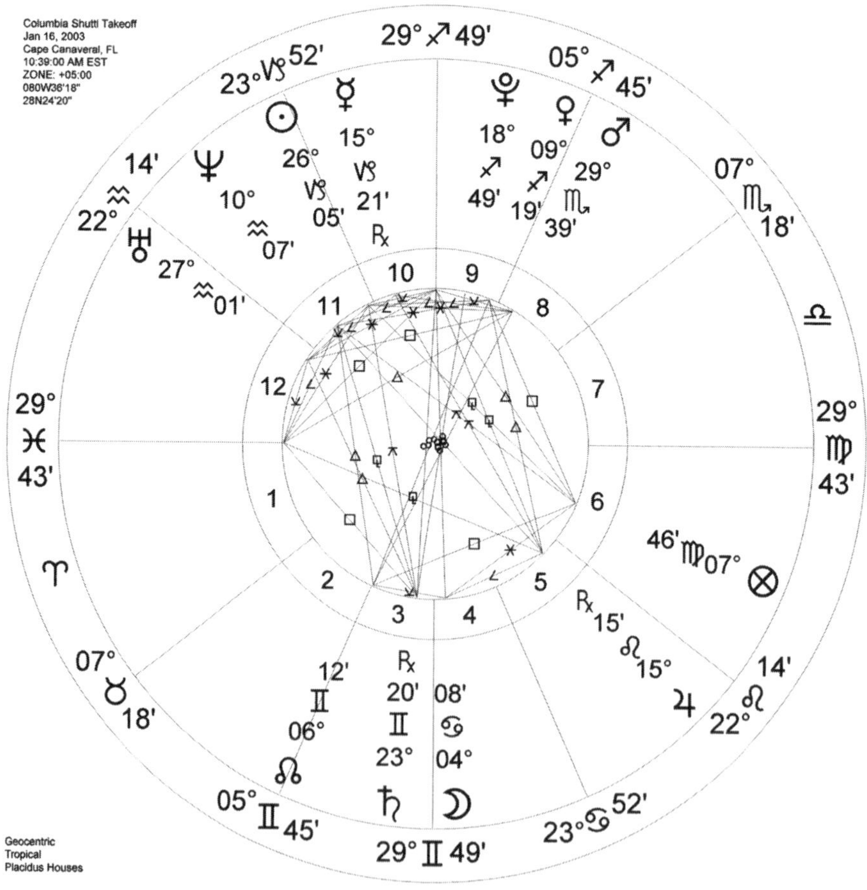

in the eighth house of death experiences. Mercury was also retrograde and in malefic semisquare aspect to Mars and Uranus, and Mars and Uranus, an accident-prone aspect, are squaring each other. Everything was aligned for a terrible disaster to occur, which took place on February 1, 2003, when the shuttle reentered the Earth's atmosphere.

The *Columbia* Space Shuttle Breakup

On February 1, 2003, at 8:58 a.m. MST in Lubbock, Texas, the *Columbia* space shuttle had already entered the Earth's atmosphere and was flying over Texas when pieces started to fall away from the spacecraft. Two minutes later, the shuttle disintegrated. This horrible event was witnessed by several people videotaping the shuttle in flight. The Moon, the Sun, and Neptune in Aquarius are in midpoint aspect to Mars and

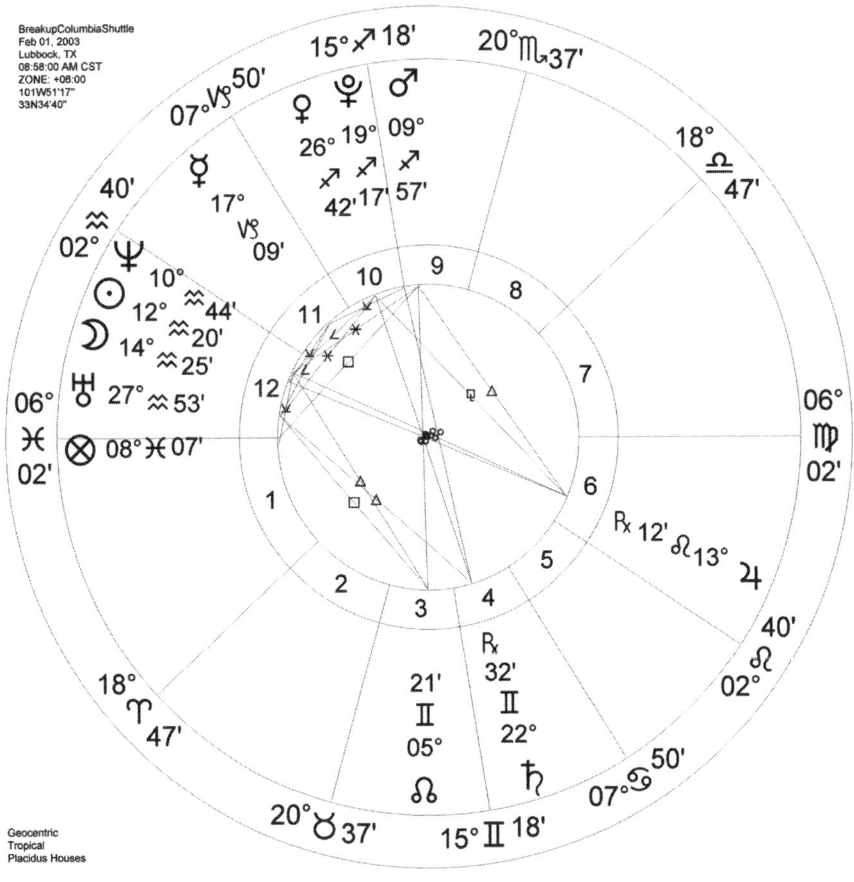

Pluto in Sagittarius. There is a Mars and Saturn midpoint opposition to Pluto and Venus, indicating a recipe for a major disaster—an intense, difficult, and possibly deadly situation. Although the shuttle breakup chart indicates this horrific event happening, the takeoff chart describes this catastrophe as well. The time of departure played a critical role in the *Columbia* space shuttle's demise.

The Titanic Leaves Southampton

On April 10, 1912, the *Titanic* left port at Southampton, England, at 1:30 p.m., after an hour and a half delay caused by another ship that broke from its pier and almost hit the *Titanic*. With two scheduled stops, the *Titanic* made its last stop at Queenstown, Ireland. The starboard anchor was raised, and at 1:30 p.m. on April 11, 1912, the *Titanic* departed for its first transatlantic crossing, bound for New York City. It's

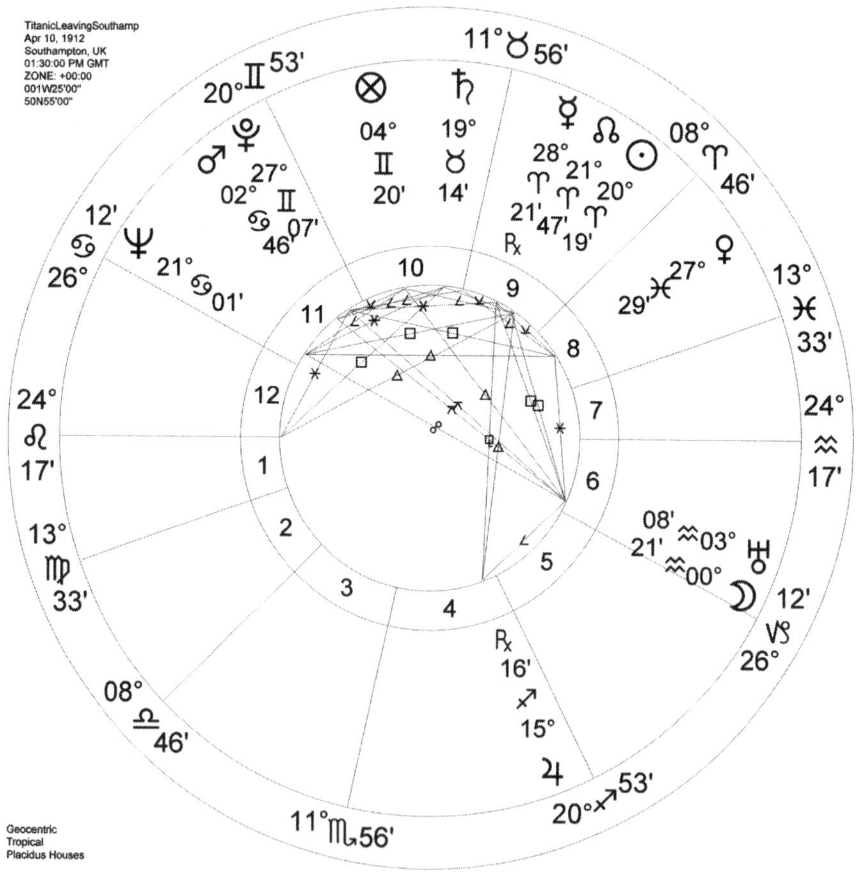

interesting to note how the departure time from Southampton and Queenstown are similar in nature and clearly describe the tragedy that lay ahead. In both charts, Mercury is retrograde, Neptune is in adverse square aspect to an Aries Sun and the North Node, and Mars is inconjunct Uranus in Aquarius. The Mars/Uranus inconjunct is forming adverse midpoint angles on a 3 degree interval to the Moon in Aquarius and Pluto in both charts as well! The 3 degree midpoint interval is in tighter orb in the Southampton chart, but in the Queenstown chart, the Mars/Uranus inconjunct is more exact, and Mars is only 1 degree away from the semisquare to Saturn, which would indicate, along with the Moon, Mars, Uranus, and Pluto configuration, that great damage could occur.

The Titanic Hits the Iceberg

On April 14, 1912, at 11:40 p.m. AST near Halifax, Nova Scotia, the world's largest ship (at that time) hit an iceberg on its maiden voyage to New York City. The devastation that followed has been profoundly recorded in history, as it should be. In the astrology chart of the *Titanic* hitting the iceberg, we find the Moon and Venus in the area of travel, the third house, and in midpoint 2 and 6 degree intervals, squaring Mars and Pluto. Even Uranus in semisquare aspect to the Moon is on an 8 degree interval, a derivative of 2. The Moon and Pluto are in exact square aspect by a half degree. Neptune is in exact, adverse square aspect to the North Node and also squaring the Sun and Mercury, which just happens to be retrograde. Travel during a Mercury retrograde can be risky unless the trip is planned well. Even then, with Neptune squaring a Mercury retrograde, too much confusion and missed information led to the demise of the ship. There is also a damaging Mars/Saturn semisquare that helped destroy the *Titanic* completely. The *Titanic* sank at 2:20 a.m., with only 702 survivors, and 1,500 passengers dying in the frigid waters of the Atlantic. The erratic influence of Uranus semisquaring the Ascendant and Pluto in an 8 degree opposition as Mars is in a 16 degree midpoint opposition to Uranus, which further added to the horrible tragedy that unfolded that day.

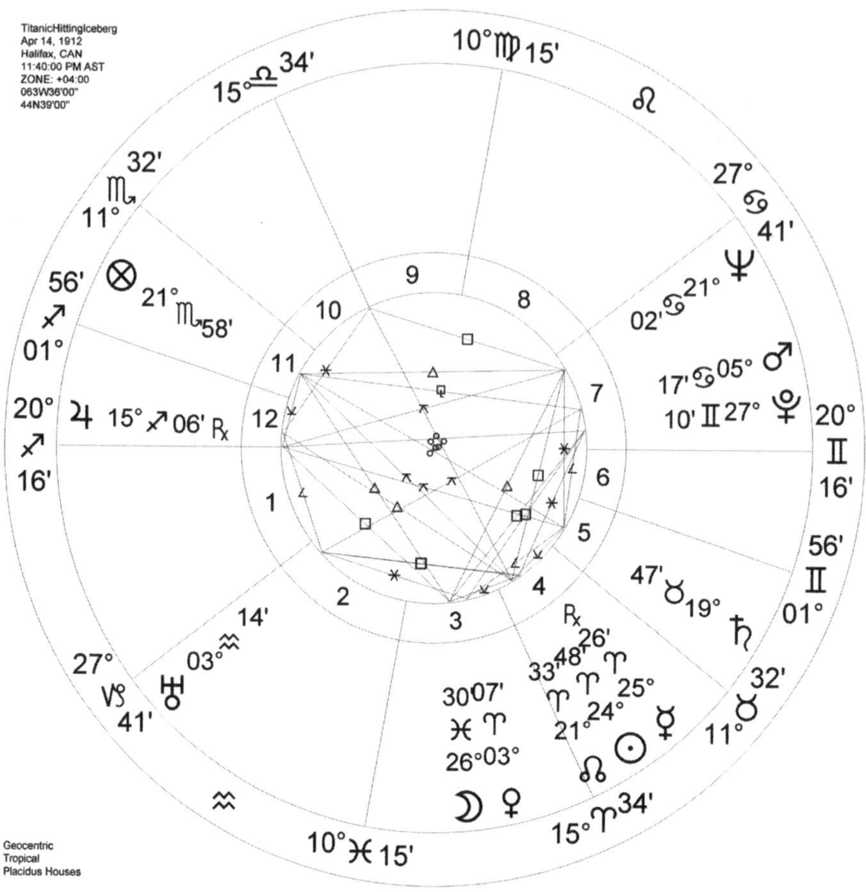
TitanicHittingIceberg
Apr 14, 1912
Halifax, CAN
11:40:00 PM AST
ZONE: +04:00
063W36'00"
44N39'00"
Geocentric
Tropical
Placidus Houses

The Significance of Midpoint Aspects in Traveling

The significance of midpoint aspects can clearly be seen by the several charts discussed throughout this book. Adverse midpoint aspects are also common in charts foreseeing hijackings, bombings, and terrorism. This could set off a chain reaction that could lead to great damage. A very obvious midpoint example can be found in the chart of the horrible subway fire in Daegu, South Korea, on February 18, 2003, at around 9:53 a.m. Over 192 people died in the tragedy, which was the work of an arsonist who had planned to commit suicide and ended up killing everyone around him. The worst combination of planets was involved, a Mars/Pluto/Saturn midpoint aspect including Mercury, Saturn, Neptune, and Pluto. Saturn is at 22 degrees Gemini; Mars is at 20 degrees, 30 minutes Sagittarius; and Pluto is at 19 degrees and 39 minutes, respectively. The outcome was absolutely disastrous.

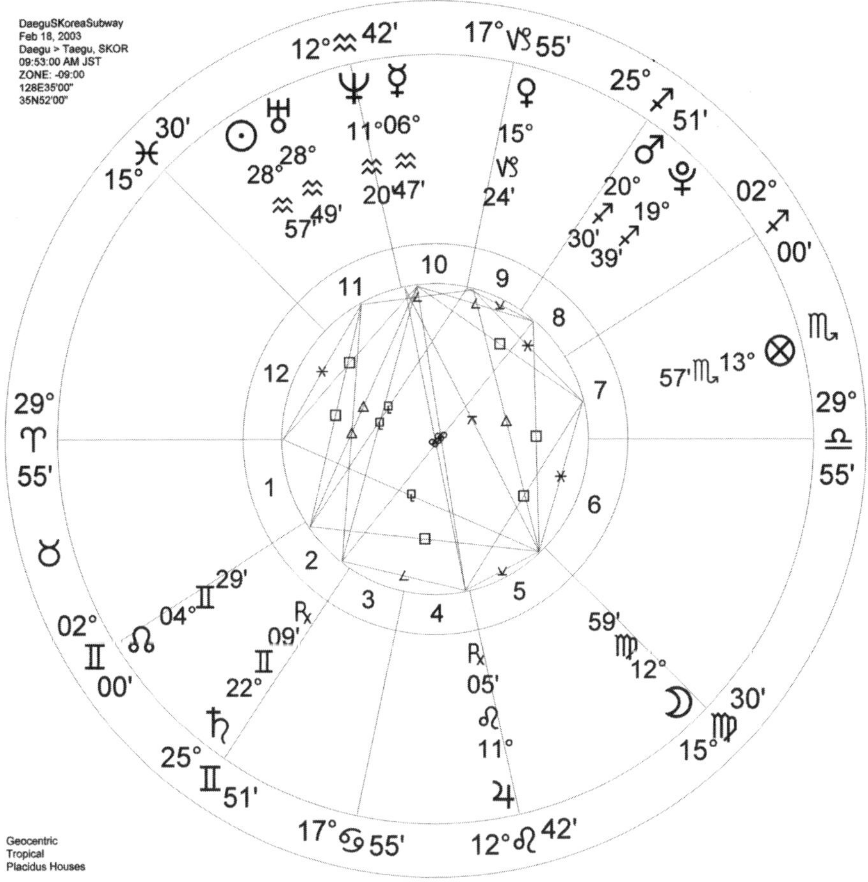

Chapter 11

AVOIDING SABOTAGE AND TERRORISM

Nefarious Planetary Influences

In astrology, we find that secret, nefarious operations take place under Plutonian and/or Scorpion influences for Pluto and Scorpio rule over the underworld that harnesses corruption and evil. If Pluto or a planet in Scorpio, such as Mercury in Scorpio, is in adverse aspect to another planet, especially Mars, Saturn, Uranus, Neptune, or Pluto, the likelihood of sabotage and destruction is present. Hijackings, bombings, suicides, and terrorism occur under Plutonian and Scorpion influences, usually in adverse aspect. Plotting these aspects in an astrology chart is, in most cases, obvious, where one can do so from a visual assessment. A Sun in Scorpio in opposition to Mars in Taurus, or a Sun in Scorpio in adverse aspect to any planet, especially Mars, Uranus, Neptune, and especially Pluto—is to be avoided.

Another element to further our analysis is that we need to look for Mars and the Moon not in exact aspect with each other or within 1 degree of orb. A Moon/Mars exact aspect indicates an accident has occurred, which is also to be avoided. However, when the Moon and Mars are not in exact aspect yet it exists, and the Scorpion or Plutonian aspects are strongly noted, the conditions are right for a possible sabotage to occur. You may also find other malefic influences, such as Mercury square/oppose Neptune, Mars square/oppose Neptune, Mars square/oppose Pluto, or Saturn square/oppose Pluto, adding to an already disastrous situation unfolding.

Travel during a Pandemic

Even pandemics can take the form of an unwelcomed sabotage, as the human body is attacked by an unrelenting virus. When a pandemic is occurring and one has to travel, can you protect yourself from acquiring a virus? Using the travel strategy outlined in this book, it will surely help in protecting you, but hygienic protocols need to be in place.

Favorable planetary influences involving Jupiter offer some protection, whereas Saturn influences may deplete your vitality, lowering your immune system and therefore making you susceptible to any virus, especially the common cold.

When you look back in time at the periods when pandemics struck the world, you will find a common planetary thread, Saturn and Pluto are in aspect along with other adverse planetary influences. Tremendous hardship occurs under Saturn/Pluto aspects, and if there are also other challenging influences going on, especially Mars influencing Saturn and Pluto, and Saturn/Neptune aspects, then you need to be especially careful. These planetary influences may breed pandemics.

During the black plague that started in 1347, Saturn was in Pisces, a very debilitating placement and in adverse aspect to Uranus. The plague peaked in 1348, and by 1349 Saturn and Pluto were both in the sign of Aries, guaranteeing a serious loss of life, millions of people.

The Spanish flu, which occurred in 1918, was influenced by a Saturn/Neptune conjunction, a very debilitating planetary aspect. Within six months, Saturn came into semisquare aspect with Pluto, opposition to Uranus, and was in adverse square aspect to Mars, further escalating the pandemic. Once again, millions perished.

With the COVID-19 virus, a Saturn/Pluto conjunction is clearly indicated. This influence started to form a conjunction in November 2019 as it was adversely aspecting Mars. Saturn was also in sextile aspect to Neptune, which tends to be debilitating. Then the pandemic gradually escalated by March 2020, as Mars joined Saturn and Pluto in Capricorn. As a pandemic is true to its nature, all countries were affected.

In all three cases, there was an undermining Saturn/Neptune or Saturn in Pisces influence. Saturn and/or Neptune was in adverse aspect to Uranus, and an impactful Saturn/Pluto aspect was occurring or would gradually occur, encouraging the pandemic.

However, avoiding these nefarious influences while traveling will safeguard your trip, and adding positive Jupiter influences, especially to your Sun, Moon, Mercury, Venus, Mars, and Jupiter, will offer some further protection against viruses. Regardless of the planetary aspects, when traveling during a pandemic, caution is always to be exercised.

Refer to chapter 12, Adverse Travel Times, for more information.

Chapter 12

ADVERSE TRAVEL TIMES

Adverse Travel Time Influences

Difficult travel times are what you will need to avoid in order to have a good, safe, and productive trip. The following sections detail the specific adverse travel connections that could spell havoc on your trip. These aspects refer to the transiting planets; however, transits to natal, progressions, and solar arc directions have a similar and sometimes more intense effect. When consulting an astrological chart, all the aspects discussed herein should be tight, within 1 degree of influencing each other.

Moon conjunct Mars

I strongly suggest that you do not start your trip on any Moon/Mars aspects, and if you encounter them on your journey, keep a low profile and your wits about you. Stress may occur from family members or a woman. Any adverse aspect of Mars to the Moon indicates the probability of an accident occurring. Although there will be a desire to use the energy of this influence constructively, it could just as easily backfire on you. If this aspect involves other outer planets making unfavorable angles, a nasty situation could result. The conjunction of the Moon and Mars does not always play out in an accident scenario; however, accidents have occurred under this aspect.

Moon square Mars

Acting out in an aggressive manner will only garner the same response in return. Under this influence, the chance of accidents is high, tempers flare, quarrels occur with those around you, and family or a woman being difficult add to the tense scenario. Here a moody, impulsive restlessness may play out in a major accident if traveling under this influence. Even though you are trying to be constructive, everything may seem to be out of control, including how your trip is going. I strongly suggest that you plan your trip for another day. On October 31, 2000, at 11:17 p.m. CCT in Taipei, Taiwan, Singapore Airlines Flight 006 crashed on the runway. There was a Moon square Mars within 1 degree of aspect, both inconjunct to Saturn at the time of takeoff.

Moon opposition Mars

You may find yourself busier than usual and involved with vigorous activities. Yet, this type of opposition with the Moon and Mars spells trouble. It will take a lot of patience to smooth over difficult situations that arise. Under this influence, women and family situations may be difficult, as tempers flare and quarrels with those around you add to the tense scenario. Here, volatile mood swings may play out, as well as a major accident if you are traveling under this influence. Consider planning your trip for another day.

Moon inconjunct Mars

The inconjunct of any two planets gives you the impression that you have things under control, and then suddenly things go awry. There is an inconsistency with this energy that is not to be tested when the Moon and Mars are involved. Under this influence, a moody restlessness may play out as women and family may be difficult, tempers might flare, and quarrels with those around you add to the tense scenario. A major accident could occur if traveling under this influence. On April 18, 2000, a plane crashed in Davao, in the Philippines. Air Philippines Flight 541 was preparing to land and at 7:00 a.m. slammed into a plantation on an island hill near the airport, killing all 131 people aboard. Mars in Taurus at 18 degrees was in exact inconjunct to the Moon in Libra at 18 degrees. Saturn was conjoining Mars, and both were in square aspect to Uranus.

Moon conjunct Saturn

Moon/Saturn influences are not known to cause accidents unless they are tied into Mars, Uranus, and/or Pluto. Your energy will be low, and you could feel lonely, sad, overworked, and exhausted and may have insufficient funds for a good travel experience. You may encounter problems with children or family members. There is a chance of experiencing an upset stomach. Tedious tasks may need to be addressed. Beginning your trip under this aspect is not recommended, since it lacks enthusiasm and excitement. Mars in aspect to a Moon/Saturn conjunction could cause accidents.

Moon square Saturn

Your energy level will be very depleted, and you will be feeling antisocial. You will be concerned with and run into difficult problems with children and family members that require your utmost attention. Watch what you eat, as an upset stomach is likely. You could feel lonely, sad, overworked, and exhausted and may have insufficient funds for a good traveling experience. Your life at this time seems to be full of responsibilities. Since this aspect offers you only a gloomy outlook and lacks any joy or excitement, it is not recommended to begin your trip under this aspect. Mars aspecting a Moon square Saturn influence could cause accidents.

Moon opposition Saturn

Your vitality will be very depleted, and you may feel antisocial. You will be overly concerned and/or run into problems with children and family members. Watch what you eat, as an upset stomach is likely. You could feel lonely, sad, overworked, and exhausted and may have insufficient funds for a good traveling experience. Your life at this time seems to be full of responsibilities. Since this aspect offers you only a gloomy outlook and lacks any excitement, it is not recommended to begin your trip under this aspect. The presence of Mars involved with this aspect could cause accidents.

Moon inconjunct Saturn

Your energy level will be depleted, and you will be feeling somewhat antisocial. You may run into problems with children and family members. Watch what you eat, as an upset stomach could occur. You could feel lonely and overworked and not possess the funds you need for a positive traveling experience. It is not recommended to begin your trip under this aspect, as it lacks joy and excitement. The presence of Mars involved with this aspect could cause accidents.

Moon conjunct Uranus

Your planned activities throughout the day will fluctuate and be difficult to keep up with as the Moon aspects Uranus. Since Uranus is known for the unexpected, when in aspect to the Moon, just that can happen. Usually you can get through the day relatively unscathed, unless the Moon conjunct Uranus influence is being aspected by Mars. The combination of the Moon, Mars, and Uranus will set off a chain reaction that makes having an accident more likely, especially if traveling. A change of schedule is also noted.

Moon square Uranus

Your planned activities will surely fluctuate, and you may experience changes that will be difficult to handle. You may be forced to adjust to a new traveling itinerary. Be ready to switch your route with planes, trains, boats, or cars, which could produce undue stress. An erratic disposition is likely to follow you. Unstable situations with women and family may arise. Due to the sudden, unexpected situations one might encounter under this planetary connection, accidents could occur while traveling, especially when aspecting Mars.

Moon opposition Uranus

All of your planned activities will surely fluctuate and experience changes that will be difficult to handle. You will need to be flexible in adjusting to a new traveling itinerary, whether traveling by plane, train, boat, or car. If you're feeling stressful, an erratic disposition is likely to overtake you. Unstable situations with women and family may arise. Due to the sudden, unexpected situations one might encounter under this planetary connection, accidents could occur, but are more often foreseen under adverse Moon/Uranus influences aspecting Mars.

Moon inconjunct Uranus

You will encounter an inconsistent restlessness that also causes all of your planned activities to fluctuate. Be flexible with your plans, as your traveling itinerary is subject to change. An erratic disposition is likely to follow you, as unstable situations with women and family may unfold. Due to the sudden, unexpected situations one might encounter under this planetary connection, accidents could occur with Mars involved.

Moon conjunct Neptune

Usually under this Moon/Neptune aspect, family outings, reunions, or spiritual gatherings are indicated. However, it may be such that a family member or close friend doesn't show up, causing you to feel some slight anxiety. You can dream of the ideal trip, but only if you have planned well. In most instances, those around you will offer sympathy and compassion. If you are feeling out of sorts, don't dwell on negative scenarios that could play out. A Moon/Neptune conjunction aspecting Mars may cause accidents.

Moon square Neptune

You will need to act carefully with vaguely disappointing situations. Family members may be of concern or not around. Your travel itinerary doesn't seem to come together as planned. Although you may dream of running away to an exotic island or experiencing a romantic rendezvous, your ideal vacation cannot be realized at this time. Overemotionalism and rejection may not help the situation. Try being sensitive to others to relieve some of your anxiety, especially if you are feeling out of sorts. Adverse Moon/Neptune aspects involving Mars may cause accidents.

Moon opposition Neptune

Vaguely disappointing situations with family and friends will require your attention. You will also be dissatisfied with your travel itinerary, which doesn't seem to be panning out. Although you may dream of running away to an exotic island or experiencing a romantic rendezvous, your ideal vacation cannot be realized at this time. Even if you are feeling overemotional, rejected, and not yourself, try being sensitive to others to relieve some of your anxiety. Don't dwell on negative scenarios that could play out. Adverse Moon/Neptune aspects involving Mars may cause accidents.

Moon inconjunct Neptune

The inconsistency of family and friends will cause vague disappointments. Feeling a moody sensitivity, you will vacillate between which travel plans to pursue or being dissatisfied with your travel itinerary. You may want to escape to a fantasy island or partake in a romantic rendezvous, but your ideal vacation may not be realized at this time. Even if you are feeling overemotional and not yourself, try being sensitive to others. Make the best of negative scenarios. This might be a time to appreciate your solitude. Adverse Moon/Neptune aspects involving Mars may cause accidents.

Moon conjunct Pluto

Intense emotions will either keep you interested in planning and beginning your trip on time or overwhelm you with decision-making. A powerful woman could be influential in outlining your agenda. A deep experience may be thought provoking. This is definitely a time to transcend personal issues from the past by involving a psychological approach. The worst-case scenario is an emotional upheaval occurring with family and/or friends. A revision in the home or moving is also possible. Accidents may occur with the Moon/Pluto conjunction aspecting Mars.

Moon square Pluto

The intense emotions you will feel when planning and pursuing a trip will be very overwhelming, especially in the decision-making process. Dependents will be demanding and manipulative, especially a strong woman. Deep psychological connections can develop that may leave you feeling drained. Although you could make some progress transcending personal issues from the past, departing from a loved one needs to be carefully considered. A revision in the home or moving is possible. This is not the journey you want to take on the road. I suggest waiting for a better time to travel. Adverse Moon/Pluto aspects involving Mars may cause accidents to occur.

Moon opposition Pluto

Although the intense emotions you feel in planning and pursuing a trip may be overwhelming, you may also feel the need for a deeper, more meaningful experience in your life. A woman could have manipulative tendencies or a powerful influence over you in deciding your agenda. Deep psychological connections are both fulfilling and draining. Unhappy experiences from the past may surface and need to be confronted. Dependents are demanding of your time. A revision in the home or moving is possible. This is not the journey you want to take on the road. As emotional upheavals are foreseen with family and friends, it may be best to postpone your trip for another day. Adverse Moon/Pluto aspects involving Mars may cause accidents to occur.

Moon inconjunct Pluto

Intense, fluctuating emotions may cause resistance or manipulative tactics to surface that leave you feeling drained, especially in any decision-making process about traveling. You may be open to a more meaningful experience yet feel forcibly persuaded to change your travel agenda by a powerful female figure. Dependents will also be demanding of your time and energy. Emotional upheavals could occur with family and friends, so be prepared to resolve any conflicts that surface. If any psychological issues present themselves, write down your thoughts and pursue them at another appropriate time. Mars aspecting a Moon inconjunct Pluto influence could cause accidents to occur.

Mercury conjunct Mars

You will be taking a direct approach in getting tasks finished, especially when booking that flight or beginning a traveling excursion. However, not everyone around you will be so punctual, which you may find quite irritating. It's best to avoid impulsive decisions, especially in confronting someone who may want to resolve a situation through physical means. Expressing your many thoughts in an intellectual manner will channel this vocal influence without getting you into trouble. Accidents are likely if the Moon is involved with Mercury conjunct Mars.

Mercury square Mars

You will be aggressive in taking a direct approach to get tasks finished, especially when booking that flight or beginning an excursion. However, you will be quite irritated by others' lack of punctuality or moodiness. Since travel requires patience, you may want to consider starting your journey on another day, as impulsive decisions may cause arguing or an aggressive confrontation with a bystander or your traveling companion. You may find yourself feeling rejected or insulted, as others will not like what you have to say. Keep your thoughts to yourself, unless you can handle more than an aggressive debate. You may later come to regret the actions you take. Keep your wits about you. Fast driving could easily land you a ticket. Accidents are likely with the Moon aspecting Mercury square Mars.

Mercury opposition Mars

Although you will be keen on taking a direct approach in getting tasks finished, especially booking that flight or beginning a trip, your impulsive reasoning puts you at odds with others. Since travel requires patience, you may want to consider another day to start your journey. You may find yourself feeling rejected or insulted, as others will not like what you have to say. A hostile confrontation may occur with your traveling companion or a bystander. Keep a handle on your thoughts, as you may later regret the actions you take. Any reckless driving is sure to attract a ticket. Accidents are likely under this influence if the Moon is involved.

Mercury inconjunct Mars

You will prefer taking a direct approach for accomplishing tasks, especially when booking that flight or beginning a trip. However, your impulsive reasoning puts you at odds, and you will be irritated by your traveling companion or a bystander. Since travel requires patience, you may want to consider another day to start your journey.

Otherwise, avoid impulsive haste to the plane, train, boat, or car. Still, you may find yourself feeling rejected or insulted, as others will not like what you have to say. Keep a handle on your thoughts, as you later may regret the actions you take. Any reckless driving could easily attract a ticket. Accidents are likely if the Moon is involved with this aspect, especially when you think everything is moving along smoothly.

Mercury conjunct Saturn

Although you will not be operating at your social best, this is still a decent time to organize your plans and financial status. Travel experiences, however, may seem tedious and worrisome. Delays are inevitable. Others can be depressing and critical. Your ideal vacation may have to wait for a more optimistic period of time. Build a solid foundation at work and home before you venture out.

Mercury square Saturn

You will feel antisocial and pessimistic. Your popularity will dwindle fast, as most people will not care to be in your company. Travel experiences are tedious, worrisome, or plagued with delays or don't happen at all. Others are depressing and critical. Important connections are delayed or disappointing. Avoid planning your ideal vacation until a more optimistic time. Your judgment is marred, and travel will only be met with obstacles. If this Mercury/Saturn influence involves Mars and the Moon in tight aspect, accidents are possible.

Mercury opposition Saturn

Feeling antisocial and pessimistic. Your popularity will dwindle, as most people will not care to be in your company. Travel experiences are tedious, worrisome, or plagued with delays or don't happen at all. News and communications may be disappointing. Others are depressing and critical. Important connections are met with delays. As travel looks bleak, avoid planning your ideal vacation until a more optimistic time. Decisions encounter obstacles, and your judgment is marred. Secure your needs at home and work before embarking on your journey. If this Mercury/Saturn influence involves Mars and the Moon in tight aspect, accidents are possible.

Mercury inconjunct Saturn

You may feel mentally pressured and not be operating at your social best. Yet, this is still a decent time to organize your plans and financial status. Travel experiences, however, may seem tedious and worrisome or not happen at all. Delays are inevitable. Any news you hear may be disappointing. Others as well can be depressing and critical. Your ideal vacation may have to wait for a better period of time. Build a solid foundation at home before you venture out. If this Mercury/Saturn influence involves Mars and the Moon in tight aspect, accidents are possible.

Mercury conjunct Uranus

New information will be stimulating toward a traveling experience. Your mind is mentally sharp yet at times indecisive. Sudden changes to your traveling agenda are possible. Call ahead to make sure your reservations are secure. If the unexpected occurs, be prepared to come up with an original strategy to accommodate your needs. Nervous tension may cause restlessness and lack of sleep.

Mercury square Uranus

Unexpected information can be stimulating or upsetting. You will have a difficult time sorting things out, as you are undecided about which course of action to pursue. Unexpected changes to your traveling itinerary will have you mentally stressed out. Your traveling companion may be nervous or detached, making communication difficult. Since sudden changes are possible, call ahead to secure your reservations. As the unexpected is likely to occur, be prepared to come up with an original strategy to accommodate your needs. Nervous tension may cause restlessness and lack of sleep, especially when needed. Being innovative with your thinking will channel mental impulsiveness. If a Mercury/Uranus square involves Mars and the Moon in tight aspect, accidents are highly probable.

Mercury opposition Uranus

Unexpected situations and surprising news can be stimulating or upsetting. You will have a difficult time sorting things out as you are undecided about which course of action to pursue. Sudden changes to your traveling itinerary will have you mentally stressed out. Those around you are unreliable, and your traveling companion may be nervous or detached, making communication difficult. Since erratic changes are possible, call ahead to secure your reservations. Try to prepare for the unexpected by coming up with an original strategy to accommodate your needs. Nervous tension may cause restlessness, lack of sleep when needed, and, in extreme cases, hysteria. Being innovative with your thinking will channel mental impulsiveness. If a Mercury/Uranus opposition involves Mars and the Moon in tight aspect, accidents are highly probable.

Mercury inconjunct Uranus

New information and unexpected situations will be stimulating or upsetting toward a traveling experience. Your mind may fluctuate between being mentally sharp yet at times indecisive. Sudden changes to your traveling agenda are possible. Those around you may not be so reliable. Call ahead to make sure your reservations are secure. If the unexpected occurs, be prepared to come up with an original strategy to accommodate your needs. Nervous tension may cause restlessness and lack of sleep when needed. Being innovative with your thinking will channel mental impulsiveness. If a Mercury/Uranus inconjunct involves Mars and the Moon, accidents are probable.

Mercury conjunct Neptune

Although you will dream about the ideal traveling experience, you may be lacking mental focus to put the right itinerary together to accomplish your goals. Drifting thoughts will make you feel isolated from the rest of the world and cause you to be prone to deceptive tactics. Economically speaking, this is an unfavorable time to pursue any traveling, as you may find your funds slipping through your fingers to pay for tickets, gas, accommodations, and/or overall expenses when away from home. Relax, see an amusing movie, enjoy a symphony or creative pursuit, or seek out meditative silence.

Mercury square Neptune

You will dream about escaping your everyday world for the ideal traveling experience but be seriously lacking mental focus in order to plan appropriately. Others may not understand you. Drifting thoughts will make you feel isolated from the rest of the world and cause you to be prone to deceptive tactics. You could forget your passport, money, or directions to your destination. Communication may be elusive and frustrating. No matter what you do, you may not be able to succeed at acquiring the right travel itinerary for you. What you do end up planning will seem vaguely disappointing and leave you feeling drained. As your funds will be slipping through your fingers to pay for tickets, gas, accommodations, and/or overall expenses when away from home, this is a bad time to travel. Show compassion to others in need, involve yourself with creative or spiritual pursuits, or watch a mysterious movie to pass the time. The *Titanic* left port and sank under a Mercury retrograde square Neptune influence on April 14, 1912.

Mercury opposition Neptune

You must attempt to bring clarity back into your life to secure the right traveling itinerary, even though you prefer to dream about the perfect trip. Drifting thoughts will make you feel isolated from the rest of the world and cause you to be prone to deceptive tactics. Someone may cancel on you or let you down with great disappointment. This is an unfavorable time to travel, as your money to pay for overall expenses will be subject to outrageous prices. Communication will be elusive and frustrating, making it difficult for others to understand you. Drifting thoughts will make you feel isolated from the rest of the world and cause you to be prone to deceptive tactics. You could forget your passport, money, or directions to your destination. No matter what you do, you may not be able to succeed at acquiring the right travel itinerary for you. What you do end up planning will seem vaguely disappointing and leave you feeling drained. As you are vulnerable to confusion and scandalous dealings, this is a bad time to travel. Either pass the time with a movie or a creative or spiritual interest or show compassion to those in need.

Mercury inconjunct Neptune

You may be struggling with a wavering lack of clarity that has you daydreaming about the perfect trip, yet wondering how you will be able to book it. If you're feeling isolated from the rest of the world, your thoughts may drift like the tides and cause you to be prone to deceptive tactics. Your traveling companions and people in general may let you down, causing disappointment. Even though you are attempting to cut through elusive communications, others will find it hard to understand your point of view. This is an unfavorable time to travel, as your money to pay for overall expenses will be subject to outrageous prices. Not only could you forget your passport, money, or directions to your destination, but you are vulnerable to scandalous dealings. When you finally think you have it under control, you may still not be able to succeed at acquiring the right travel itinerary. What you do end up planning will seem vaguely disappointing and leave you feeling drained. Involve yourself with creative or spiritual pursuits or a movie, or show compassion to those in need.

Mercury conjunct Pluto

In and of itself, Mercury conjunct Pluto could cause some difficulty with coerced decision-making and stressed-out thinking and communication, yet this doesn't provoke accidents. However, you may find that some intense soul-searching takes place that will help you resolve a frustrating issue. Unless Jupiter or Sagittarius is involved to enhance a profound and optimistic experience while traveling, I suggest you appreciate this influence by exploring your emotions in private, a therapy session, or deep mystery.

Mercury square Pluto

You will encounter stress and obstacles with trying to persuade others to agree on a mutual approach. Feeling drained with these uncooperative individuals, you will be forced to make your own decisions. However, your mental judgment will vacillate with repetitious thought. Feeling isolated and frustrated, it is hard to make yourself understood by others. Your traveling companion may have hidden motives that, upon coming to the surface, shock you. A broken relationship may be the result. Since you are better off being alone and exploring your solitude, I don't recommend traveling under this influence. Your traveling agenda may fall apart, leaving you tense and exhausted. Spend time with yourself exploring your emotions, or read a great mystery or books that dwell on self-analysis.

Mercury opposition Pluto

As others are not being cooperative, you will be compelled to make critical decisions on your own or may find that you are being coerced into doing things their way. If you're feeling mentally drained and manipulated, your judgment will vacillate with repetitious thought. It is difficult to make yourself understood by others. Even your traveling companion may have hidden motives that, upon coming to the surface, shock you. If you are forced to give an ultimatum, be prepared for the result. With a sense of solitude and isolation, it may be necessary for you to do some serious soul-searching and purge old, worn-out thoughts and desires that don't serve you anymore. Traveling under this influence would leave you tense and exhausted. You may be required to adjust to changes with your traveling itinerary, and bad news could happen at any time. Opinionated views will only bring resistance from others. Try to cooperate where you can.

Mercury inconjunct Pluto

You may find yourself encountering inconsistent news, causing much stress. Not everyone is willing to cooperate, and some may attempt to persuade you to follow their lead. With patience, you might be able to get others to agree on a mutual approach so you are not forced to make your own decisions. Still, your mental judgment will vacillate with repetitious thought, trying to figure out how to make yourself understood by others, which can be rather frustrating when trying to secure your traveling itinerary. You may even feel stressed out by communicating with your traveling companion. Consider this a good time to explore your solitude. Although you may have some profound experiences in discussing or thinking about the psychological you, traveling under this influence will be challenging. You benefit by becoming involved with an intense mystery book or one covering self-analysis.

Mars conjunct Mars

Although you may be driven to accomplish many goals at once, such as packing, attending to the chores around the house, and following up on reservations, this same motivation could lead to angry criticism, frustration, and a possible fight. Impulsive decisions are not advised. Make sure you have plenty of time to channel this energy properly so the worst doesn't occur. Old resentments may need to be brought out into the open and directly confronted so they don't follow you on your trip! Turn this energetic influence into a constructive activity like sports or a passionate rendezvous to be more agreeable. Still, accidents are likely if this influence is aspecting the Moon and Uranus.

Mars square Mars

You will encounter trauma, hostility, criticism, and rejection. Feeling uptight, you are prone to lashing out at someone irritating you. Any impatient actions could easily turn into angry criticism or a brawl. Acting quickly may help avoid an explosive situation or accident. As you may be feeling irritable and exhausted, traveling under this influence will only add to your stress. Using tools, handling repairs, and hard physical labor will direct this energy toward constructive goals. Competitive sports, lusty passion, or an action movie can also help channel this challenging aspect. If this influence is also in tight aspect to the Moon and Uranus, accidents are likely.

Mars opposition Mars

Feeling highly restless, your tendency may be to be critical of someone irritating you. You may also encounter in your environment a critical rejection, argument, trauma, or hostility that you would rather avoid. You may need to take quick action to sidestep a volatile situation or accident. Traveling under this influence is not recommended, as it creates more stress. Performing hard labor at home or work, participating in competitive sports, or watching a passionate or action movie can help channel this challenging aspect. If this influence is also in tight aspect to the Moon and Uranus, accidents are likely.

Mars inconjunct Mars

Feeling restless and overwhelmed with accomplishing many goals at once, you may strike out at someone irritating you. Encountering a critical rejection, argument, or hostility will put you on the defensive. Quick action will help avoid a precarious and volatile situation or accident. Any old resentments may need to be dealt with directly to clear the air. Traveling under this aspect will require great restraint. Otherwise, you will find yourself warding off anger, criticism, or a fight. Being industrious at your home or job will ease the potential stress. Engaging in competitive sports, lusty passion, or an action movie will be far more constructive than risking a frustrating journey. Impulsive decisions are not advised. If this influence is in tight aspect to the Moon and Uranus, accidents are likely.

Mars conjunct Jupiter

As you are motivated to travel to new lands with a restless spirit, this influence could cause you to overexert yourself. Impulsive actions may desire a robust adventure without counting the cost. Avoiding rash spending and overindulgence is advised. Overexerting yourself may cause stress, a fever, or a depleted sense of vitality. Both excitement and stress could be experienced under this influence. A passionate rendezvous is likely. Regardless, you may be willing to take the risk to enjoy your freedom, no matter what the cost. Still, accidents are possible with the Moon in aspect to a Mars/Jupiter conjunction.

Mars square Jupiter

Feeling energized to travel the world, you are restless and willing to take risks that could lead to you overexerting yourself. Still, a passionate rendezvous is possible. However, stress, a fever, or a depleted vitality may be the result. Whether you are buying, selling, or spending, don't act on impulse or you will be taken for a ride. A cautious approach will save you time and money. Overindulgence is costly. If you are careless, there is danger of loss or theft. No one wants to lose their pocketbook while traveling, so watch your possessions at all times. Although your adventuresome spirit will persuade you to travel, this is a risky influence because of financial loss and overexertion that could leave you feeling exhausted. Accidents are possible with the Moon aspecting Mars square Jupiter.

Mars opposition Jupiter

Restless, optimistic energy will cause you to want to roam the Earth, willing to risk it all. If your freedom has been restrained, you will impulsively go to extremes in seeking out adventure without counting the cost. A passionate rendezvous is possible. Yet, overexerting yourself could cause stress, fever, or a depleted vitality. Avoiding rash spending and extravagance is advised. Calculated risks will save you time and money. Overindulgence is costly. Carelessness will lead to loss or theft. Keep an eye on your possessions, as cash, traveler's checks, and credit cards will lure a thief. Traveling under this influence is risky business; however, you are highly motivated to take a gamble, regardless of the abundant cost or exhaustion that follows. Accidents are possible with the Moon aspecting a Mars/Jupiter opposition.

Mars inconjunct Jupiter

Although you are motivated to travel to new lands, a restless spirit will cause you to scatter your energy and be unproductive. Impulsive actions may desire a robust adventure without counting the cost. Avoiding rash spending and overindulgence is advised. Carelessness with your possessions will attract a cunning thief interested in your cash or credit cards. Overexerting yourself could cause stress, a fever, and a depleted vitality. Both excitement and stress could be experienced under this influence, as well as a possible passionate rendezvous. Regardless, you may be willing to take the risk to enjoy your freedom, no matter what the cost. Accidents are possible with the Moon involved.

Mars conjunct Saturn

You will want to take constructive action in planning a practical travel itinerary. However, you will also find several blocks to your desires that demand hard work and courage to get you through the day. A direct and hard-driving style will not agree with those around you. Yet, you will feel determined to accomplish your agenda. In your immediate environment, you may encounter competition, hostility, or rejection, even from your traveling companion. There is a chance of physical injury, pain, and criticism. You will end up feeling resentful and angry. Traveling is not advised under this difficult influence. Not only are accidents foreseen with the Moon involved, but aches and pain are noted as well.

Mars square Saturn

As people will be cold or mean spirited, you will have to do everything you can to secure a practical travel itinerary. No matter what you do, there will be serious blocks to your desires that demand tremendous hard work and extra hours. Your own directness will be very unpopular with those around you. You are bound to encounter exhausting competition, hostility, or rejection, even from your traveling companion. Try to exercise control and self-discipline; otherwise, you will be defeated. There is a chance of danger, physical injury, pain, and criticism. You must put yourself in survival mode or you will end up feeling resentful and angry. Traveling is absolutely not advised under this difficult influence, especially if the Moon is involved in tight aspect. Aches, pains, and accidents are likely under this influence. Personal items may also be damaged.

Mars opposition Saturn

Self-control will be required, as you will clash with people who are cold or mean spirited. You will meet up with several obstacles in trying to secure a practical travel itinerary. No matter what you do, there will be frustrating blocks to your desires. You could make a situation worse by being too direct and becoming unpopular with those around you. Not only will you have to work very hard to accomplish any goal, but you are bound to encounter exhausting competition, hostility, or rejection, even from your traveling companion. It will take great courage to overcome serious setbacks and delays. There is a chance of danger, physical injury, pain, and criticism. You must put yourself in survival mode or you will end up feeling resentful and angry. Traveling is absolutely not advised under this difficult influence, especially if the Moon is in tight aspect. Aches, pains, and accidents are likely under this influence. Personal items may be damaged.

Mars inconjunct Saturn

You will be able to use your energy constructively as long as you don't clash with people who are cold or rude. Even so, obstacles will need to be conquered to secure a solid travel itinerary. At times, no matter how hard you try, there will be frustrating blocks to your desires. It will take long hours and tedious work to acquire any goal. You may still meet up with exhausting competition, hostility, or rejection, even from your traveling companion. Although you might be feeling resentful and angry, you must find the courage to overcome serious setbacks and delays. Even if you feel that you are in control, there is a chance of danger, physical injury, pain, and criticism in your immediate environment. Traveling is not advised under this influence, especially if the Moon is in aspect.

Mars conjunct Uranus

This erratic influence will set off nervous tension and incite possible clashes with others. Your independent nature may not agree with those in your company and must be channeled toward new avenues of discovery that excite everyone. Since you are apt to set people off, invoking sudden hostility, keep your guard up. Spontaneous anger could come from your close confidant or a stranger. You could cut off a worn-out relationship or confront your partner directly to work things out. New individuals that you want to establish a connection with, especially those with a romantic interest, will not endure. When traveling, unexpected accidents are likely if the Moon is aspecting Mars conjunct Uranus.

Mars square Uranus

Unexpected situations arouse an impatient temper or explosive restlessness that could incite aggressive clashes. Still, you are willing to take foolish risks that cause sudden hostility in others. An independent streak could bring out spontaneous anger either from yourself, a close confidant, or a stranger. You are pushed to break off a worn-out relationship with impersonal impunity. New, intriguing individuals whom you want to establish a connection with, especially those with a romantic interest, will not endure. Most people are unreliable, so do not count on anyone or take advice. Reversals of activity will make it difficult to get through this period of time. Sudden changes could seriously affect your travel itinerary and be very frustrating. Directing your independence toward new avenues of discovery is a constructive approach. Traveling is not advised under this influence, so be very cautious as unexpected accidents are highly probable, especially if the Moon is involved with Mars square Uranus.

Mars opposition Uranus

You will be severely challenged with unexpected situations that arouse an impatient temper or explosive restlessness that incites aggressive clashes. Still, you are willing to take foolish risks that cause sudden hostility in others. Matters you have counted on may not come through as expected, due to reversals of activity. Most people are unreliable, so do not count on anyone or take advice. Being too independent may incite anger from those around you. Feeling detached, you could easily break off a worn-out relationship. New, exciting relationships, whether romantic or friendly, will not endure. You may be required to adjust to sudden changes that could affect your travel itinerary. Pursuing original ideas and new avenues of discovery constructively may direct this influence. Be very cautious if traveling; unexpected accidents are highly probable, especially if the Moon is involved with Mars oppose Uranus.

Mars inconjunct Uranus

Although you will attempt to be flexible with unexpected situations, an impatient temper may cause aggressive clashes with others. You may need to curb an independent streak that invokes anger in those around you. Reversals of activity have you moving in different directions to accommodate your needs. This is not the time to count on anyone, as most people are unreliable. Impersonal feelings may lead to breaking off a worn-out relationship. New relationships, although exciting, are not guaranteed to endure. You may be required to adjust to sudden changes that could affect your travel itinerary. Pursuing new avenues of discovery constructively directs this influence. Be cautious if traveling; unexpected accidents are highly probable if the Moon is aspecting Mars and Uranus.

Mars conjunct Neptune

Although your creative imagination may wander, you could be easily deceived by sinister individuals in your environment. Steer clear of dramatic conspiracies. Aim toward compassionate ideals that benefit humanity. If you don't have all the facts, it's better to postpone decisions. Travel could be both intriguing and disappointing, so you may need to be flexible. Don't have a lot of expectations. Be as realistic as you can in pursuing your aims. Since you could be disillusioned by new romantic encounters, do exercise caution. Romance with the right person will be ideal. Accidents are likely with the Moon in aspect with this influence.

Mars square Neptune

A strange restlessness and anxiety are compounded by situations not materializing as planned. Major disappointments could leave you brooding and exhausted. Any travel plans may encounter serious delays or problems that are difficult to resolve. Beware of complex schemes that deceive your better interests. Alcohol or stimulants could have a dramatic effect on you. Romantic encounters are sure to disappoint. Put your faith in humanitarian ideals. Advice from others may not be reliable at this time. Analyze all information carefully. This aspect indicates that action meets with deception; thus an accident is likely if the Moon is involved in tight aspect. Even though we may plan well, sometimes our course of action does not lead us to the desired result. This influence is not recommended for travel, as you will most likely be very disappointed.

Mars opposition Neptune

A vague restlessness and anxiety will detract from your daily progress. A certain matter may fall through, leaving you drained and dissatisfied with the result. Major disappointments with your traveling itinerary are difficult to resolve. Multifaceted schemes may drown you in a maze of deceit. As advice from others is not reliable, don't count on it. Be realistic with any information received. You could easily be deceived by starry-eyed romantic experiences that are castles in the sky. Do limit your alcohol or stimulant consumption, as this could have an exaggerated effect on you. This aspect indicates that action meets with deception; thus an accident is likely if the Moon is in tight aspect with this influence. Even with well-thought-out plans, the desired result is most likely unattainable. Travel is not recommended under this aspect, as you are apt to be disappointed.

Mars inconjunct Neptune

An inconsistent restlessness may cause much confusion with where you stand on a particular situation. A certain matter may seem to be dissolving, regardless of how much effort you make to turn it around. You will encounter disappointments with your traveling agenda that are more complicated than originally thought. Vague schemes could draw you into a world of illusion and deceit. You are better off trusting your own instincts, as advice from others is not reliable. Be realistic with romantic prospects, as they will surely dissipate into the ether like pipe dreams. Limiting your alcohol or stimulant consumption is recommended, as this could have an exaggerated effect on you. Even with solid planning, disappointments and accidents are likely under this influence with the Moon in tight aspect.

Mars conjunct Pluto

Due to stressful situations, you will be persuaded to shift your direction toward a specific goal. Pressure will mount as others try to resist and/or manipulate the outcome of your plans. You may be forced to take a stand and call the shots. A driven determination will see you through to acquire any objective. A personal transformation can occur under this influence, where you purge yourself of worn-out issues. In group situations, everyone needs to cooperate for all to benefit. If this influence involves the Moon, accidents are likely.

Mars square Pluto

A personal transformation may require some solitude to take on a positive effect. Yet, others will interfere, causing much stress. A rebellious, jealous, or hostile attitude will emanate from you or someone in your company that demands cooperation but receives resistance. Angry, compulsive actions will work against you. You may feel forced to compromise your position by manipulative individuals. Ultimatums will bring a situation to a close. A strong determination can benefit you and the group, as long as your desires are directed toward constructive avenues. Accidents are likely under this influence, especially if the Moon is involved.

Mars opposition Pluto

You may feel compelled to pursue a personal transformation that changes the direction of your life. However, interference from those around you will be frustrating, especially when they attempt to manipulate you to their point of view. A jealous, rebellious, or hostile attitude will emanate from you or someone in your company that demands cooperation but receives resistance. Critical ultimatums or rash anger could work against you. Although you will not want to compromise your position by manipulative individuals, it may be the only way to keep unity. If you are determined to work toward constructive projects, you not only benefit yourself, but those around you. You achieve the most through group activities. Accidents are likely under this influence, especially if the Moon is a participant.

Mars inconjunct Pluto

There may be an inconsistent sense of direction of what you need to pursue to experience a personal transformation. Interference from those around you will not help in your indecisiveness, especially when they attempt to manipulate you to their point of view. Any jealous, rebellious, or hostile tendencies from you or another will need to be curbed. Resistance, critical ultimatums, or rash anger could work against you. Compromise when and where you can, working around the persuasiveness of manipulative persons. If you are determined to work toward constructive projects, you not only benefit yourself, but those around you. Although you can achieve the most by cooperating with the group, secret motives may still be evident from one individual. Accidents are likely under this influence, especially if the Moon is involved.

Jupiter conjunct Saturn

Although restrictions on your freedom will make it challenging to travel under this influence, you may decide to go anyway. Personal and work obligations may interfere with travel plans. Progress could be slow and money tight. Your trip may become a laborious one. Investments or legal proceedings will involve some time and energy. If you find yourself overwhelmed with extra responsibilities, worry, or poverty, then traveling under this influence is not recommended.

Jupiter square Saturn

Although Jupiter is known as the planet that rules over travel, in aspect to Saturn, the planet of reality, your trip may become a laborious one. One may be attending to personal obligations or a pressured business meeting, making your journey a rather somber experience. You may also be limited financially in how much you are able to extend yourself. Unless you are willing to take on extra responsibilities, travel is not recommended under this aspect, even though it is not known to be an accident-prone influence.

Jupiter opposition Saturn

Restrictions on your freedom will make it difficult to travel under this influence. You are subject to extra duties or personal obligations that limit your experience. Progress is slow with work matters, and money is tight. Your trip may become a laborious one. This is an unfavorable time for purchases, investments, or legal proceedings. If you are overwhelmed with extra responsibilities, worry, or poverty, then traveling under this influence is not recommended. Pay your dues now and plan for the ideal trip later. This is not known to be an accident-prone influence.

Jupiter inconjunct Saturn

Inconsistent restrictions on your freedom will make it difficult to travel under this influence. Although you are handicapped by personal and work obligations, you will be torn between pursuing travel plans or being responsible with work. Progress is slow and money is tight. Your trip may become a laborious one. Investments or legal proceedings will involve time and energy. If you find yourself overwhelmed with responsibilities, worry, or poverty, then traveling under this influence is not recommended.

Jupiter square Uranus

The changes you hope to make are out of sync with your expectations. Unexpected situations push you to come up with an original strategy concerning your travels. An overwhelming independent streak encourages you to expand your perception of the world. Although you can trust yourself with newly implemented plans, you may question other people's reliability. Trips domestic or abroad are exciting yet are met with scheduling changes and erratic circumstances that challenge you every step of the way. The timing is not supportive of your need for freedom and exploration. You might want to indulge yourself in unusual subjects such as philosophy, religion, or the occult. Even these topics may seem too far-fetched for your interests. Economic and business transactions tend to be overrated. Someone you meet may have a flamboyant style that is appealing yet unstable. Gather your insights together, as this is a time of preparation.

Jupiter opposition Uranus

You may feel the need to start a new cycle in your life, which may involve travel, but the freedom you desire is hindered by unstable situations that require more time to be resolved. Expectations of your future are overrated. The timing is premature for you to move too quickly into a new direction or plan that great trip. Advances made now could be disruptive to your normal routine. You may need to curb your demand for more freedom and growth until things settle down. Erratic situations can cause much tension. Expenditures as well are unwise at this time and are apt to be expensive. Any gifts or favors may come with stressful obligations. A new individual, although interesting, may be too eccentric for your style. Original ideas may need to wait for a better time.

Jupiter inconjunct Uranus

You may vacillate between expressing your need for freedom and feeling inhibited. Not sure whom you can trust, you may question other people's reliability. Trips domestic or abroad are exciting yet meet up with scheduling changes and erratic circumstances that challenge you. The timing is not supportive of your desire for freedom and exploration. Unexpected situations can cause much tension. Expenditures as well are unwise at this time and are apt to be expensive. Any gifts or favors may come with stressful obligations. A new individual, although interesting, may be too eccentric for your style. Keep your original ideas intact, as they might serve you in the near future.

Jupiter square Neptune

Even though this could be a vague period of expansion, you will be prone to dreaming of pursuing the ideal traveling experience. As you desire more adventure and freedom, you may need to be more realistic with your expectations, since you may not have a sense of direction and may be disappointed when your traveling agenda is not up to par. You could be easily taken with a financial scheme that guarantees a splendid trip. If you are careful with those who might squander your money, you can relax with ease, enjoying your adventure and perhaps a sunny day at the beach. Take everything in stride. This is not known to be an accident-prone influence, yet you could be promised more than can be delivered.

Jupiter opposition Neptune

As this is indicated to be a vague period of expansion, your ideal traveling experience may not be attainable at this time. You may need to be more realistic with your expectations, so you don't encounter disappointments. As you are vulnerable, you could be easily misled about the rate of return on your trip. Double-check any promises, financial schemes, or legal matters for their validity. Your trip or vacation may encounter delays, deception, and/or monetary loss. Since you are longing for a dream trip, be careful in squandering your money away in spite of your desires. Once you are situated, relaxing and enjoying your adventure will bring some peace. This is not known to be an accident-prone influence, yet you could be promised more than can be delivered.

Jupiter inconjunct Neptune

You will be vacillating with a desire for more hunger and freedom, yet a vague sense of direction. Your ideal traveling experience is difficult to attain. You will encounter less disappointment if you are realistic with your expectations. As you are vulnerable, you could be easily misled about the rate of return on your trip. Carefully weigh promises, financial schemes, or legal matters for their validity. If your trip or vacation meets up with delays, deception, and/or monetary loss, be flexible with your plans. Although you are longing for the ideal dream trip, travel will still have its problems, and how you handle everything could make the trip a positive experience or negative one. Once you are situated, relaxing and enjoying your adventure will bring great peace. This is not known to be an accident-prone influence.

Jupiter square Pluto

You will be required to cooperate in order to maintain the continuance of your agenda. Still, obstacles will be encountered from a coercive situation. If need be, any upsetting element can be eliminated from the group to help keep the peace and further the expansion of your aims. Tolerate what you can, but be aware of manipulative scenarios that test your faith. You will be inclined to expand your horizons and travel under this influence; however, stressful conditions will have to be addressed.

Jupiter opposition Pluto

Cooperating with others will gradually gain their trust and provide mutual benefits. Still, obstacles will be encountered from a coercive situation. Only with compromise can you expand your position. In group activities it is wise to be agreeable and optimistic. As you desire growth and expansion, travel is on the agenda. Even as others try to persuade you, trust yourself and have faith in your philosophy and goals. Beware of those who wish to manipulate your ideas and claim them as their own. You will want to seek adventure and travel under this influence; however, demanding conditions may need to be addressed.

Jupiter inconjunct Pluto

You will vacillate between cooperating with others to gain their trust and pursuing your freedom. However, you will quickly find that only with compromise will you advance your position. Still, obstacles will be encountered from a coercive situation. Being agreeable and optimistic in group situations will work in your favor. As you desire adventure and personal growth, travel is on the agenda. You must have faith in your philosophy and goals, as you will be tested when you least expect. Subtle manipulation by others will not be appreciated and will force you to take a stand when and where it's called for. Travel can be enjoyed under this influence as long as you are willing to make adjustments to unanticipated conditions.

Chapter 13

YOUR PARTNER'S PLANETS IN YOUR THIRD AND NINTH HOUSE TRAVEL SECTORS

Before embarking on a personal or business trip, or significant excursion with another individual, you can easily find out how you will get along by comparing your astrological birth chart to your traveling companion's. If any of your natal planets fall in their natal third or ninth house travel sectors, read up on how it will significantly influence your trip. Venus or Jupiter landing there will offer pleasantly supportive or happily inspiring traveling experiences, whereas with Pluto in your third or ninth house sector, you may encounter a deep, life-changing experience. Taking these astrological influences into account will give both of you better insight into your traveling adventures and how they can be thoroughly enjoyed.

Your Partner's Sun in Your Third House Travel Sector

When your partner's Sun falls in or aspects your third house travel sector, there is an emphasis on interacting in your environment, gathering new information, and traveling. You are mentally stimulated, formulating and exchanging ideas that open up your perspective and allow you to appreciate the art of conversing and listening attentively. Your Solar mate encourages you to take command and draw up a well-orchestrated traveling itinerary. This mental exchange promotes camaraderie.

Under afflicted aspects, the Sun person will expect you to comprehend and accept their ideas about traveling without a response. More often than not, misunderstandings occur along with clashes of opinions, such as which country to visit.

Although your partner will expect you to be able to tackle any problems, determine an agenda, or make plans for traveling, they will provide the intellectual insight to help you achieve success.

Your Partner's Sun in Your Ninth House Travel Sector

When your partner's Sun falls in or aspects your ninth house, you are inspired to travel to influence your life direction as you embrace a new philosophy. This is a significant placement for being guided by a guru, and therefore your travels could easily take you abroad. Your Solar partner may instill in you their own beliefs about traveling that will enhance the mental exchange between you both. The Sun in the house of Jupiter will enlighten your intellectual rapport and offer expansive opportunities for growth.

Afflicted aspects will persuade the Sun person to expect you to comprehend and accept their concepts and ideas about traveling without a rebuttal. Beware of the religious fanatic who may entice you into a cult. More often than not, misunderstandings occur along with clashes of opinion, such as which country to visit.

Travel may continue to be a theme in the relationship, especially if you have met this way. Improving on a travel agenda is noted, as you are exposed to other cultures by your Solar partner.

Under favorable aspects to the Sun, a subjective understanding will be communicated that benefits both parties. Fulfillment is attained by moving beyond the confines of your surroundings and pursuing higher ideals.

Your Partner's Moon in Your Third House Travel Sector

When your partner's Moon falls in or aspects your third house, they are inclined to promote your communicative potentials, which will enhance the travel rapport between you. Your partner will be intrigued with your mental abilities, including problem-solving techniques when things go awry on the road. They will also be actively involved. When one's intellectual prowess is augmented, both parties gain.

Discordant aspects to the Moon may make it difficult to comprehend one's point of view. Your Lunar mate may become emotionally touchy when you fail to be a good listener and mistakes are made when taking a trip. Whatever ideas you do prefer to express may not be heard, due to a moody disposition or lack of interest.

Harmonious aspects to the Moon favor educational interests, such as traveling to historical sites, where you are mentally stimulated to expand your cerebral point of view. Your mate's objective will be to open up your mind to exploring new concepts about the world and to help you converse more effectively. If your partner is looked upon as a mentor, this placement is excellent for increasing the rapport between teacher and student. What can be gained through traveling may also be introduced by your Lunar partner. Brief trips to connect with siblings or relatives are encouraged.

Learning to appreciate what your partner has to say will expand your intellectual horizons. The instinctual feel on how to relate to your partner will cause the communicative exchange to flourish, cultivating a strong friendship.

Your Partner's Moon in Your Ninth House Travel Sector

When your partner's Moon falls in or aspects your ninth house, you will be intuitively guided by your Lunar mate to expand your horizons through travel, educational pursuits, and experiencing other cultures. Your partner may feel they comprehend your beliefs and philosophy about life, but may want to add to your ideas to reshape your theories. Traveling to foreign countries is highly encouraged, as your Lunar mate, with their dreamy imagination, will want to explore all facets of the world.

Afflictions to the Moon indicate a lack of understanding of your beliefs or your philosophical outlook on life. Travel and educational goals may be limited or not pursued at all, denying you the opportunity to better yourself. The mental rapport you and your partner desire may be unsatisfying and disagreeable, making travel plans difficult.

Favorable influences give your Lunar mate an innate ability to expand upon your travel itinerary and philosophy, thus benefiting the both of you. The discovery of what can be learned from different cultural backgrounds will enhance your sympathetic understanding of the world around you. This emotional perceptiveness will enrich you intellectually. Appreciating your partner's viewpoint will allow you to be more sensitive to humanity. The result is a shared, higher-minded affinity that enriches you both.

Your Partner's Mercury in Your Third House Travel Sector

When your partner's Mercury falls in or aspects your third house, you are motivated to share in the intellectual exchange of ideas and opinions that could enhance your travel plans. Your Mercurial mate will feel at ease maintaining an open dialogue with you.

If Mercury is ill aspected, restricted communications lead to misunderstandings that are difficult to resolve, causing further complications while on a trip. Your ideas may clash with your partner, causing arguments.

Under well-aspected influences, knowledge is acquired through the discussion of new and interesting concepts, including brief excursions out of town. Ideas flow easily, engendering a successful rapport. Your partner may put you in touch with the neighborhood and siblings alike. Travel plans are encouraged.

We are constantly learning through our interactions with each other. It's advantageous to aim toward a communicative exchange that benefits you and your partner.

Your Partner's Mercury in Your Ninth House Travel Sector

When your partner's Mercury falls in or aspects your ninth house, you will be inclined to relate to your partner on a higher intellectual level that includes the study of other cultures, yet discussing everyday events may also be a part of the conversation. When traveling together, you will be exposed to exciting new sights that may change your outlook on life.

Unfavorable aspects indicate that you may be at odds in conversing with your Mercurial partner. Differences of opinion, such as which vacation site to see, may lead to arguments.

Under favorable influences, Mercury in the house of Jupiter will promote the expansion of your mental horizons. Excellent one-on-one communication is developed, involving different cultures and one's beliefs and philosophy about life. Your view of life will be enriched through your partner's cerebral inspiration.

Your Partner's Venus in Your Third House Travel Sector

When your partner's Venus falls in or aspects your third house, a smooth communicative rapport is developed that enhances the bond between you. Your Venusian partner's warm reception will motivate you to express your thoughts and feelings in a pleasing manner, thus enjoying brief trips that are pursued. Being your charming self, you will take advantage of the many ideas that intellectually inspire you. Your partner will also share their compromising perspective, making them a delight to be around while traveling.

Unfavorable aspects to Venus block the natural course of conversation. Your partner may have an uncooperative attitude about your travel itinerary, causing a strained rapport.

Favorable influences indicate an effortless rapport, where both of you will share your ideas, thoroughly enjoying your traveling experiences. A mutual understanding instigates a harmonious exchange.

Your Partner's Venus in Your Ninth House Travel Sector

When your partner's Venus falls in or aspects your ninth house, you will establish a congenial rapport that improves the flow of ideas toward traveling, especially abroad, your beliefs, and your philosophy of life. You are encouraged to embody a more relaxed and agreeable disposition when planning your vacation itinerary. Your Venusian partner will show you how to travel in comfort to make the most of any trip.

Discordant influences perpetuate a disagreeable manner where your partner is uncooperative in supporting your ideas, especially while pursuing a trip. Their philosophy is enforced, without consideration.

Under positive aspects, you are intrigued with your partner's philosophy about life, wanting to emulate their example. An understanding rapport attracts an agreeable environment where everyone is friendly, whether traveling domestic or international.

Your Partner's Mars in Your Third House Travel Sector

When your partner's Mars falls in or aspects your third house, they will motivate you to express your ideas and opinions that you may benefit socially, especially when on the road traveling. You will find your partner quick witted and intellectually stimulating. Challenging debates, possibly concerning which brief excursions to pursue, may ensue that entice you to get involved. Your Martian mate may expect you to courageously say what's on your mind, even if it causes conflict with others—although telling off an airline attendee will not get you on the next flight any faster.

Inauspicious influences will cause your partner to aggressively disagree when conversing with you, not wanting to comprehend your opinion even when you are lost out in the middle of nowhere. Nasty arguments could lead to animosity.

When auspicious aspects are present, you learn not to be swayed by another's point of view so that you base your own ideas on the information that you have derived. Your partner's insistence on opening up your mental perspective may lead to greater traveling experiences, as well as intellectual accomplishments.

Your Partner's Mars in Your Ninth House Travel Sector

When your partner's Mars falls in or aspects your ninth house, you are intellectually stimulated by your mate to formulate new ideas and philosophies to assist you in expressing yourself and exploring other cultures. At your partner's request, you are encouraged to travel to broaden your outlook. In assimilating new information, you are challenged to speak your mind, not backing down from any opposition, which will not fare well with flight security. Your partner will rely on your mental resourcefulness, expecting you to possess knowledge on every subject, especially when traveling from place to place. They will want you to be a good listener while your mate verbalizes what has been already decided upon prior to the conversation.

Discordant influences indicate disagreeable beliefs and philosophies that erode the communications between you. Arguments may ensue about your traveling agenda.

Under harmonious influences, vigorous communicative exchanges are highlighted that expand your perspective and desire to see the world.

Your Partner's Jupiter in Your Third House Travel Sector

When your partner's Jupiter falls in or aspects your third house, conversation is intellectually stimulating and traveling is a joy. You will feel enthusiastic about communicating your thoughts, building a wonderful rapport that can last for hours. The enjoyment of being in each other's company and journeying from place to place seems to never fail. Your Jupiterian partner will encourage you to pursue avenues of learning and new traveling experiences that further your wisdom.

Adverse aspects to Jupiter may cause your partner to dominate the conversation, at times mentally exhausting you. Travel can be overdone. Nevertheless, you will continue to feel motivated to express your ideas and opinions.

When Jupiter is well aspected, your partner is interested in expanding your knowledge, inspiring excellent communications and short trips where both parties benefit.

Your Partner's Jupiter in Your Ninth House Travel Sector

When your partner's Jupiter falls in or aspects the ninth house, its ruling position, expansive opportunities such as traveling enlighten your personal, spiritual, social, and physical experience. You will find your partner's enthusiasm to communicate ideas and explore the world mentally intriguing. You may develop a newfound confidence in your life direction as your philosophy and outlook inspire hope. Since Jupiter represents the teacher, the priest, and the guru, you will discover insights that may change your beliefs, especially as you explore new traveling vistas. Your partner will persuade you to further your education and travel opportunities and accumulate as much knowledge as you can to enlarge your experience in this lifetime.

When discordant aspects are present, your Jupiterian mate may expect you to gather information and be your own teacher, when you thought you could depend on them for guidance. The advice received may not be appropriate for you and could cause unproductive traveling situations.

Under positive aspects, your partner may rely on their own wisdom to enlarge your perspective of the planet Jupiter in its own house. Representing benefics in aspect, this can attest to great mental growth that has the capacity to change your life forever.

Your Partner's Saturn in Your Third House Travel Sector

When your partner's Saturn falls in or aspects your third house, you may address the areas of communication, travel, and learning in a serious, disciplined manner. Your partner will teach you strategies to firmly express yourself, which will help when planning a voyage overseas. Critical thinking will enable you to concentrate on the important issues so you develop a focused way of communicating. Trivial topics will be bypassed for more in-depth, comprehensive subjects, such as visiting historical sites when journeying through Old Europe.

If Saturn is afflicted, your partner may limit your ability to communicate effectively. Conversation may be frustrating and boring, as it lacks any kind of excitement. Your mate may cause the rapport with your neighbors to sour as well. Any advice on travel plans or furthering your education may not suit your purposes and experience setbacks and delays. Even attending to errands for your partner will be tedious.

When Saturn is well aspected, thought-provoking, meaningful subject matter inspires conversation between you, especially when touring the globe. Your partner will be able to intellectually guide you to make the most of your communicative capabilities.

Your Partner's Saturn in Your Ninth House Travel Sector

When your partner's Saturn falls in or aspects your ninth house, they will want you to be practical about travel plans, your beliefs in life, and considering a solid education. Your partner will act as your mentor as well, offering realistic guidance that has you reshaping your personal philosophy, as well as your spiritual or religious understanding. Your Saturnian mate will insist on effective, direct communication that impresses your listener, which will be an asset when making reservations for a trip. You will gain from a serious attitude that strengthens your conviction in acquiring your objectives.

Discordant influences to Saturn will cause you and your partner to have differing opinions, which could cause great upset while on a journey together. Your philosophies or religious beliefs may clash, causing much dissension. Since your ideas are not in agreement, it will be difficult to make plans for the future. You will feel frustrated in not being able to carry on a progressive conversation with your partner. Travel plans may be hindered or discouraged, limiting your mobility.

Harmonious aspects depict a planned strategy that enables you to accomplish your goals as well as formulate a travel strategy that is best for you. As you restructure your beliefs and philosophies, life takes on a realistic perspective that allows you to broaden your cultural horizons.

Your Partner's Uranus in Your Third House Travel Sector

When your partner's Uranus falls in or aspects your third house, you are mentally stimulated to express yourself and look for new avenues to explore, due to the enthusiasm conjured up by your partner. Since travel is highlighted, this is an activity that can be enjoyed together. You may visit thrilling places you have never seen before.

Your Uranian partner will inspire you to learn and gather new information that stimulates your intellectual growth. You may alter your perspective in lieu of innovative concepts that you find intriguing.

When Uranus is afflicted, your partner's ideas may drastically clash with your own, especially causing unexpected problems with a planned trip. Their concepts may be so outrageous that you are inclined to reject any suggestions. Nevertheless, you will be exposed to opening your mind to another's unusual views.

Under harmonious influences, you may benefit from unconventional methods of learning, such as discovering what's going on in an exotic country. You will relish each other's company with exciting, intellectual experiences. Uranus in the house of Mercury allows you to look at life from different perspectives that you and your relationship may truly benefit, especially when vacationing around the planet.

Your Partner's Uranus in Your Ninth House Travel Sector

When your partner's Uranus falls in or aspects your ninth house, you are challenged to alter your views on life and pursue journeying to different lands. Your beliefs and philosophy will be enlightened by other cultures, as well as by the persuasion of your partner. Expansive thoughts will stimulate your mind, possibly changing your outlook forever.

When Uranus is afflicted, the direction of your life may drastically change and any traveling excursions will be completely erratic, causing much trepidation. You will be confronted by your partner with radical ideas that may be too bizarre for your tastes.

When Uranus is well aspected, your partner will inspire you to take an interest in foreign dealings and travel abroad. You will form new opinions about your beliefs. Life will take on an entirely new meaning as you integrate original concepts into your philosophy.

Your Partner's Neptune in Your Third House Travel Sector

When your partner's Neptune falls in or aspects your third house, you will be inclined to go beyond everyday reality and develop your intuition when interacting with your mate or those around you. Learning through osmosis, you will cultivate an imagination that visualizes the perfect places to travel. Glamorizing your educational aims will make them more intriguing as well.

Discordant aspects to Neptune in the house of Mercury depict a complete breakdown in communication. You are two ships passing in the night, as nebulous ideas never seem to reach each other. Major misunderstandings will be the unfortunate result. If you cannot communicate with your partner, you do not have much of a relationship. The wrong information will seriously stymie learning experiences and travel plans.

When Neptune is well aspected, you will embellish your communicative thoughts, expressing yourself in a colorful manner. Using your vivid imagination will enable you to be entertaining in the company of others. Your Neptunian partner will persuade you with fascinating traveling adventures that revitalize your mind and spirit.

Your Partner's Neptune in Your Ninth House Travel Sector

When your partner's Neptune falls in or aspects your ninth house, you are persuaded to open up your mind to otherworldly avenues of communication as well as travel. Developing a spiritual understanding will change your outlook on life. A more compassionate approach to your beliefs and embracing the ideas of other cultures will broaden your understanding. As you cultivate an interest in unusual avenues of learning, you may find that being creative brings out the intellectual genius in you, which is especially helpful when touring the planet.

Discordant aspects may cause your mate to mislead you in the assimilation of intriguing ideas. Travel plans are not to be trusted and may collapse right when you are ready to embark on your journey. You may be led into religions or philosophies that do not agree with your beliefs. Phony concepts will disrupt your direction, making you feel disillusioned about learning in any capacity.

When Neptune is well aspected, your partner's imagination will redefine your own outlook and stimulate you to travel to new, colorful sites that you can only envision. Your Neptunian partner will motivate you to gather knowledge from many different sources, where you can reach new horizons and develop faith in a higher cause. Sometimes we must go beyond ourselves to have a more meaningful existence.

Your Partner's Pluto in Your Third House Travel Sector

When your partner's Pluto falls in or aspects your third house, you will explore the world of ideas and recognize that the vat of life's knowledge is ever filling. Your partner will strongly influence your opinions, questioning your every thought so that you may find deeper meaning, especially when traveling. You will be deeply intent on making the right reservations and following them through on your journey. As you modify your manner of thinking, you will demonstrate a powerful persona when communicating with others.

Discordant aspects may cause your partner to coerce you into following their pattern of thinking. They may want to manipulate you in conversation, which will cause much difficulty when trying to pursue travel plans.

Under harmonious aspects, you will apply depth of understanding to your thoughts, how you communicate, and all traveling experiences. Your mate's persuasion to probe your intellectual abilities will only add to your wisdom.

Your Partner's Pluto in Your Ninth House Travel Sector

When your partner's Pluto falls in or aspects your ninth house, you are swayed by your partner to change your beliefs, philosophy, and outlook on your existence. To do so, they will be intent on pushing you to go beyond your horizons and see the world. Your Plutonian partner will be instrumental in having you become involved with deeper aspects of your direction in life. You may be confronted to explore your own concepts and spiritual or religious values involving other cultures, finally concluding that you may need to totally alter your perspective. Understanding what lies behind a certain attitude or motivation will bring greater clarity.

When Pluto is ill aspected, your partner will try to persuade you to follow their beliefs and philosophy, which will cause major disagreements between you, especially if you are attempting to put together a traveling itinerary.

When Pluto is well aspected, you have an opportunity to examine your beliefs and perspective on life, discarding worn-out concepts and broadening your outlook, which may include traveling to foreign countries and experiencing other cultures. You may discover a deep interest in reaching for new possibilities that bring a profound, new experience.

Chapter 14

Relocation and Astrocartography

It's nice when you can get all of the planets lined up for a successful trip, but why not know if the place you are traveling to is supportive of your actions as well. The knowledge of astrocartography and relocation can assure you that the area you would be traveling to is conducive to a favorable experience. For every location that you are considering traveling to, you can erect an astrology chart that will specifically indicate what your travel outcome would be in a particular area of the world. By profiling the planets and stars, we can find more fulfillment by traveling to the places that best support us.

There has been considerable discussion on which is more informative to use—relocation or astrocartography. Both are important and provide us with a very clear understanding of what cosmic influences are affecting us in various locations throughout the world. In using relocation or astromapping techniques, a point to consider is: What are you ultimately looking for—a great traveling experience, a business opportunity, love and romance, spiritual growth, or just happiness?

In traveling to various places around the globe, you will be affected by the influences of the different planets in those areas. There is either a positive planetary influence or a challenging, karmic influence affecting these locations. Although you might think you would be more comfortable with a prominent Jupiter or Venus influence, which would attract happiness, love, and abundance, you may also feel right at home with Saturn, Uranus, Neptune, or Pluto, but usually on positive angles. Sometimes a person is drawn to a particular area where they need to experience a certain planetary influence, due to the karma that may need to be resolved. Usually with the outer planets, Jupiter is involved.

When you use relocation, the planets and signs remain the same, but the planets in the houses and the cusps will change. Especially the third and ninth house travel sector cusps will change, indicating whether a positive or adverse experience will occur while traveling to this particular area. Astrocartography explains the difference between one area and another, emphasizing the use of planetary angles on the first, fourth, seventh, and tenth house cusps. With relocation, you can change your chart by traveling away from your birthplace or the place where you are currently living, whereas with astrocartography, your cosmic map is stationary, based on your birth date, time, and place. Both need to be taken into consideration when traveling.

Angular Power Points

There are four power points, known as the *angles*, in astrology. When we are in touch with our planetary power points, we experience more of life—for this allows us to utilize our fullest potential. The angles that are represented by the Ascendant, or first house cusp, refer to your persona, personality, and physicality; what you are projecting out into the world; and your approach to goals. The IC, or fourth house cusp, refers to your home and family, the emotional home, and your roots and ancestry. The Descendent, or seventh house cusp, refers to marriage and defines your relationships with other people. The MC, or cusp of the 10th house, refers to your career, reputation, and social status. These angles hold great weight and are considered the most powerful points in a chart. Wherever you are traveling to will emphasize one or more of these angles, depending on the planets affecting the angles. If you were born with planets near these angular power points, you will project the qualities represented by those planets. An example would be that if you have Mars near your Midheaven, you will be very assertive with your career, or if Venus is on the Ascendant, you will be quite charming, artistic, and social. The same effect occurs in the place that you are traveling to on your journey.

When we are working with time and space, the birth time is important, as it locks in an astromap or relocation chart utilizing time and space in the most effective manner. *For we cannot travel through time, but we can travel through space and select a location that emphasizes your happiness throughout the chart and strengthens your potential.*

Your astrocartography as well as your relocation chart indicate the angles, the Ascendant, Descendent, MC, and IC, that are the power points in your chart at your time of birth. These can be mapped out and experienced according to the planet that rides over these angles wherever you will be traveling to, to bring out the potential of a certain area.

When we are traveling for pleasure or business, we need to examine in your relocation chart of a certain area what planets are affecting the third and ninth house sectors and cusps. For instance, if Jupiter is in the third or ninth travel sector or favorably aspecting the third or ninth house cusp, then this would bring enjoyment into your trip, as well as improve upon the communications of your journey. Thus, you would have a great time traveling in this area. If Saturn is in the third or ninth travel sector or adversely aspecting the third or ninth house cusp, you may experience a difficult time in this particular area. Knowing the influences to the third and ninth house travel sectors can make a world of difference with your trip.

When we travel or move, we are always hoping that our fate will be met with good fortune. Through understanding the relocation chart and astrocartography, some of our luck can be calculated, so what we experience is what we want to be happening. We must also remember that traveling or moving to a new area will not necessarily change or get rid of any deeply rooted problems—that's for your therapist. However, with time, even this may improve slightly.

Usually we seek out happiness in love, social life, work, and money. Following your astrocartography can lead to success in love or work or money. In other words, according to your astromap, you may find success with love but not with your work, or vice versa. Knowing this, the place you travel to or live in may be the reason why you are successful (or not) in your life.

So how can we change this scenario or balance this out so we can be happy in all areas of our lives? We want to look for and identify the areas or planetary power points as well as aspects to all of the cusps that will bring more happiness and prosperity into our travel experiences.

Taking a Planet Out of Context

In astrocartography, we tend to concentrate on one or two planets in a specified area; thus, taking the planet out of context. *Just because a certain planet, such as Venus, is in a particular area on the latitude line does not mean that this is all that is going on in that location.* All of the other planetary positions need to be taken into consideration, and not just the angles. So don't just rely on the planets themselves, but look at the aspects as well. Jupiter might be on the Ascendant, but if it is in square aspect to Saturn, the experience will be more challenging than opportune. Although you can read this planetary charting from the astromap, it's more elaborate in the relocation chart as we utilize the houses and signs. The planets in astrocartography, however, do not refer to signs or deal with houses and cusps, whereas the relocation chart does.

So, if you have traveled or moved to a Jupiter line and nothing exceptional is happening, check all of the aspects and transiting and progressed planets in the houses. This will give you an entire picture of what is happening here. You may have a Jupiter line affecting your relationship sector, but if Neptune is in semisquare aspect to your relationship sector, the Descendent, this may not bring you the desired result you want to experience. Sometimes it is difficult to be in the perfect place, for the ideal place is not accessible, such as being out in the middle of the ocean. So, we simply take the next-best place.

Now, in calculating the astromap or relocation chart, you may find a particular natal aspect, such as Saturn in opposition to Pluto, in someone's chart. You cannot change this configuration, but perhaps you can alleviate it to some degree. That is the objective.

In some cases, people experiencing Saturn or Pluto get stuck under the influence. Just as you can become comfortable in a dissatisfying or troublesome relationship, you can become comfortable with a negative planetary influence as well.

Although Pluto is difficult and brings up very intense situations on adverse angles, karmic connections, spirituality, and transformation can be experienced on favorable angles. Neptune may rule over nebulous experiences, but it could also mean living near water, pursuing a spiritual quest or a creative goal, or offering your time to humanitarian causes. Given that these are outer planets, there could be some important lessons learned.

Parans and Midpoints

So far, we have been discussing the singleton planets, one planet on an angle. Sometimes two planets are in conjunction with each other on an angle at a particular location. In astrocartography this is called a *paran*, which is a crossing of a planetary pair with an angular point. There are 45 possible crossings. Some are in the polar areas and therefore not useful. Paran crossings don't have to be in the foreground or in angular houses if you are interpreting a relocation chart. The crossing can be rising or setting, east or west, but within a 1–2 degree orb to be highly effective, or 15 degrees above or below the angle for astrocartography. For relocation, the crossing can be near the angular cusps or in the third, sixth, ninth, twelfth, but within a 6-degree orb of the angular cusps. When dealing with paran crossings, usually west is better. To change your Ascendant, you can go north or south of the latitude line, just as you can going east or west.

Now let's say you have a Mercury/Jupiter crossing on the same line of latitude. Anywhere on that same latitude line or parallel to it will resume the Mercury/Jupiter paran-crossing influence. If there are more crossings at a given latitude, all need to be considered. Depending on the planets involved, paran crossings can be negative or positive. If you can, try to utilize a positive paran crossing like Sun/Jupiter.

Midpoints are also very significant, as they not only can be used in the relocation chart but are also very visible in the astromap. In relocation, we calculate a midpoint by the middle point of the degree of two planets. In astrocartography, this is calculated by miles or degrees of orb. For instance, let's say you would like to visit or live in New York City, and in your astromap, you don't have any lines affecting that area. Then you find that a Venus line is 250 miles away, going east, and a Sun line is also 250 miles away, going west. Therefore, the New York area becomes a midpoint location for the Sun and Venus, making this a very nice place for social alliances and marriage, especially if Venus is on the Descendent.

Important Points for Astrocartography and Relocation

Whether it be the astromap or relocation chart, all angles are emphasized and hold the same chart meaning. A planet crossing these power points can either create challenges or support you in this location, depending on its influence and aspects to the planet. Jupiter may be on your MC (Midheaven), but if Saturn is in square aspect to it, many demands will be put upon you in your career. Queen Elizabeth has Jupiter conjunct her Ascendant and in square aspect to her MC and Saturn, which conjuncts her MC.

Lines near or crossing a particular location indicate the type of activity that will occur. Jupiter brings opportunity. Venus brings social benefits, love, and possible marriage. For example, Jackie Kennedy Onassis has Venus conjunct her fourth house cusp in her chart of Athens, Greece, and found marriage, comfort, and security there.

A location may be near lines of personal desire. For instance, you may be drawn to Montana for deep, spiritual reasons, which happens to have a Jupiter and a Pluto line on the Ascendant. Here the individual may experience a personal transformation, the desire of the individual.

A lack of planetary lines in a particular location doesn't necessarily mean that it is an insignificant location. In your relocation chart, these are like the areas or houses that don't have any planets, so we refer to the cusp sign for more information. *This is why the relocation chart is so important: because it can give us the total picture, whether you have planets in the houses or on the cusps or not.*

When analyzing and interpreting the astromap, refer back to the natal or relocation chart to check out all of the aspects. If there is a Uranus square to Mars, this adversity will influence the scenario in a stressful way, especially if one of these planetary lines is crossing a power point angle.

In the astromap, lines crossing through distant locations may influence you by the people from that area. In other words, the area's potential is activated no matter where you reside. Mars crossing through a distant location could bring out agitation, leadership ability, or, in the case of some presidents, war. In relocation charts, you can easily see if a planet is in an angular house, the first, fourth, seventh, or tenth, or in a cadent house, the third, sixth, ninth, or twelfth. In astrocartography, the area west of a line will describe the planet in an angular house, and the area east of a line describes a planet in a cadent house.

Any paran crossing of two lines in an astromap affects not only that location in which they cross, but also the entire latitude line where the crossing occurs. This has a tight orb of 1 degree, or approximately 80 miles, on either side of the line.

ORBS

In relocation, the orb can be up to 6 degrees. In astrocartography, it is calculated differently, 700 miles on either side of the line, which is about 1/4 of an inch on the map. With crossings, the orb is 1/16 of an inch on either side of the line. Some people encourage the use of a 400-mile area, which is almost 5 degrees of zodiac line.

ASPECTS

In astrocartography, aspects other than the conjunction, square, or opposition, such as the sextile, trine, semisquare, and inconjunct, do not show up. In addition, the Ascendant, Descendent, MC, and IC are the strong angles. The influence as well as the experience is intense. Therefore, you never want an outer planet, such as Neptune, right on an angle. For instance, 5 or 6 degrees away would be tolerable, and, better yet, preferably in a background position—the third, sixth, ninth, or twelfth houses.

TRANSITS, PROGRESSIONS, AND SOLAR ARCS

Transits, progressions, and solar-arc directions are what can give us a certain timing toward our future. You can apply all three to both the relocation chart and the astromap. In using transits, progressions, and solar arcs in the relocation chart, we are going to acquire more information because we have the houses and the signs to refer to along with the planets. Whereas in the astromap, you have only the planets; however, this is very objective information because of the declination and the curve of the line, which makes it clearer. *Again, for the best results, we must combine the use of relocation with astrocartography.*

In the relocation chart, we see how the transits, progressions, and solar arcs are affecting the entire chart, with the planets situated in various houses, which helps tell the full story. In astromapping, we are concentrating on the angles, the Ascendant, the Descendent, MC, and IC. Therefore, when a transiting, progressed, or solar-arc planet aspects a planet in the astromap, there is quite an impact. In some cases, it could change the direction of a person's life.

A station to these power points or a retrograde planet is highly significant, and the effect could last for years. The experience depends on the planetary influence at hand. A Pluto transit, which moves approximately 3 degrees a year, could remain in the same area for a couple of years. The individual could experience some major difficulties or perhaps a total transformation, which usually involves endings as well as new beginnings.

The effect of a transiting retrograde planet, Mercury through Pluto, is much quicker, as the planet (even on a retrograde) is moving in most cases faster than its respective progressed partner. However, a progressed Mercury or Venus retrograde could last for years. *You do not want to be traveling to an area where you are under an adverse Mars, Saturn, Uranus, Neptune, or Pluto transit, progression, or solar arc.*

Any transit, progression, or solar arc to a relocation chart or an astromap will bring up a situation or issue that needs to be addressed, especially if the planet in a location has not been activated. Sometimes one is not able to utilize the planet because it's retrograde, or a singleton planet, or in a background position, or intercepted, or you may be resisting the influence. Here is where a transit, progression, or solar arc to the astromap can be especially important.

THE CHARTS OF FRANK SINATRA AND PRINCESS DIANA

In the astrocartography and relocation chart of Frank Sinatra, you can easily see why he had such great success in Lake Tahoe, California, as a performer at the casino resorts. He was born with the Sun in square aspect to Jupiter, and in his relocation chart for Tahoe, he has the Sun conjunct the fourth house cusp and Jupiter on the Descendent. In his birth chart the Sun and Jupiter are in succedent positions in the second and fifth houses and are not activating the major power points of the chart as they are in Lake Tahoe, California. Jupiter is also in favorable trine aspect to Mr. Sinatra's third house cusp of travel, indicating that he would enjoy traveling to this area to perform. His astrocartography has a Jupiter and Sun line running through Northern California, where he was a huge success.

The discrepancies surrounding Princess Diana's astrology chart is an obvious one for there are two known conflicting birth times. I decided to put my analysis in this book for all of those people out there looking for love. Although Princess Diana met and fell in love with Dodi Fayed in St. Tropez, he was from Alexandria, Egypt. In using the approximate 2:10 p.m. birth time for Diana's astrology chart (the time that was given to astrologer Penny Thornton by Diana herself), her astrocartography has a Venus line

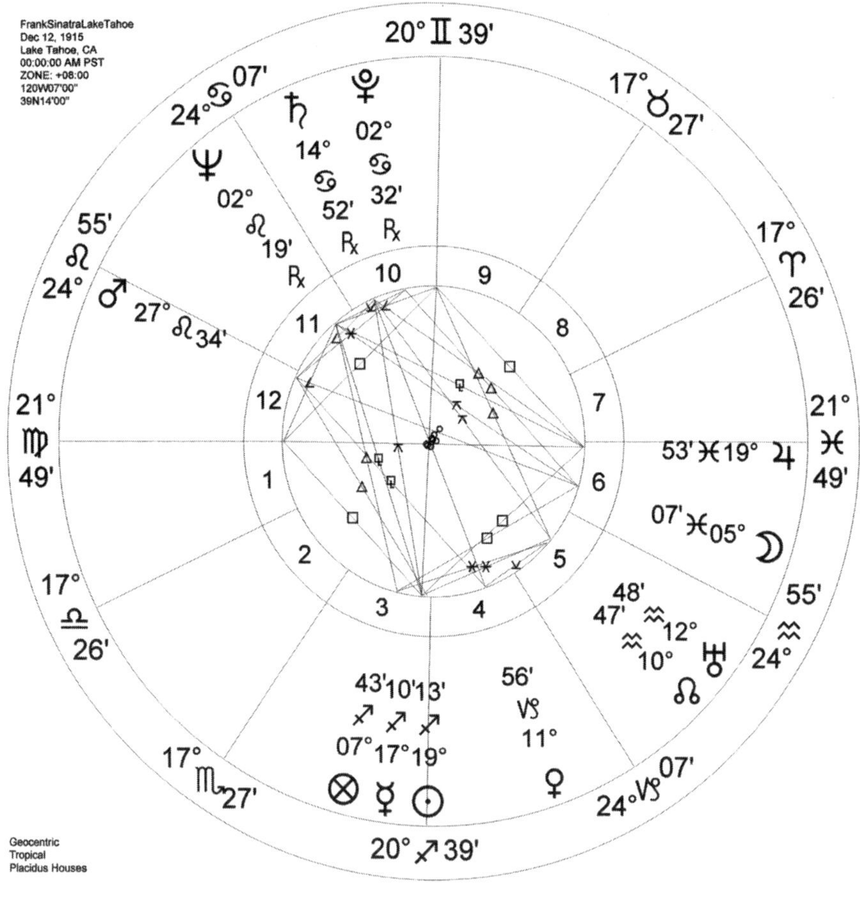

running through Alexandria, and the relocation chart for Alexandira, as well as St. Tropez, shows the planet Venus on all of the angular points. Having Venus and/or Jupiter on the angular power points brings a person the opportunity for romance and/or great personal success. In this case, Diana attracted a wonderful relationship into her life that unfortunately was short lived, most likely due to Uranus adversely aspecting Venus and the angular cusps. In an alternate astrology chart with a birth time of 7:45 p.m., Venus is on the IC, fourth house cusp of the home, and Jupiter in the twelfth house sector is on the Ascendant in Alexandria, which could also cause one to question Diana's 2:10 p.m. time of birth, given that both Jupiter and Venus are emphasized. However, Venus in Taurus in the seventh house sector of relationships and marriage in the 2:10 p.m. chart is a strong argument.

Whether you are using relocation or astrocartography, knowing the planetary effects of the places you are traveling to can dramatically influence the outcome of your trip and is clearly worth your time and energy in figuring it out for the best results.

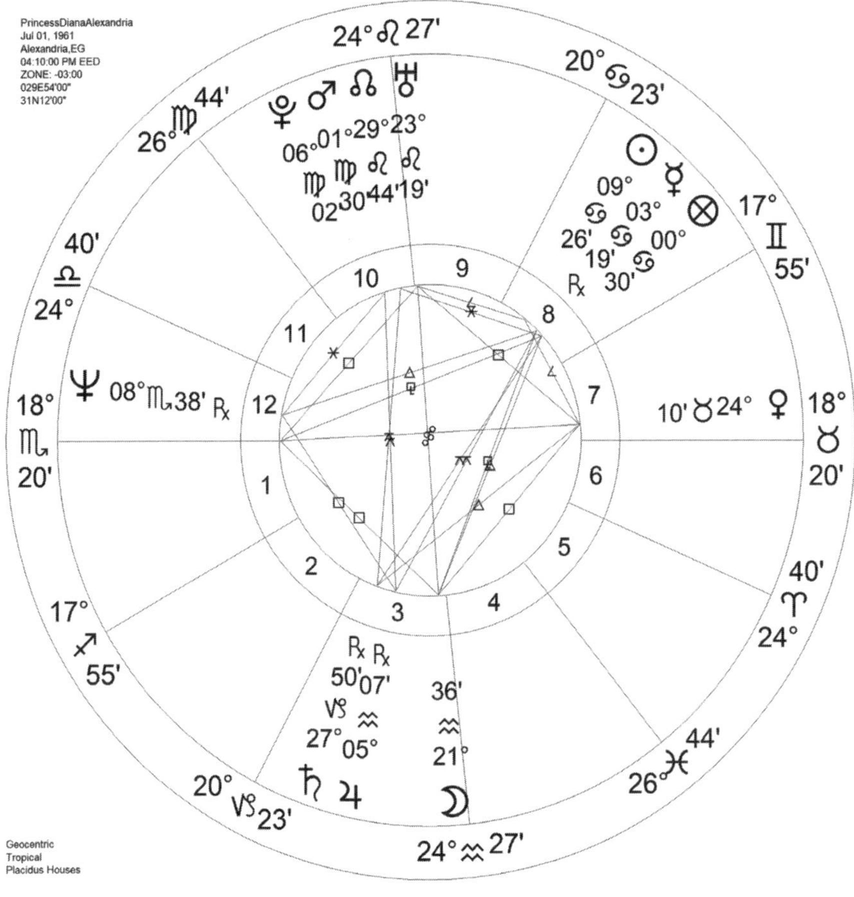

GLOSSARY

Ascendant: Cusp of the first house, pertaining to the self, one's personality, physicality, approach to life goals, and first impression on others, located on the horizon line of an astrology chart. Angular power point is abbreviated as "ASC."

aspect: When a planet by degree interacts with and influences another planet or significant astrological point, thus forming a geometry angle such as 0 degrees, 60 degrees, 90 degrees, 135 degrees, or 180 degrees, with outer space as the backdrop.

astrocartography: Plotting geographic locations on a global astrological map that emphasizes the use of power points—the Ascendant, Descendent, Midheaven, and Imum Coeli, which indicates where you will be able to maximize your potential. A planetary-mapping method used to relocate to ideal astrology zones.

astrology: The study of the stars, including planets, zodiac signs, and house sectors that help us understand the past, deal with the present, and guide us into the future.

benefic: A planetary influence that attracts opportunity, favors, and benefits. Jupiter and Venus are known as the two benefic planets.

Descendent: Cusp of the seventh house, pertaining to close relationships and marriage, which is located on the horizon line of an astrology chart. This angular power point is abbreviated as "DSC."

element: Fire, earth, air, and water are the four elements used in astrology that describe the definition of each planet or significant astrological point.

horoscope signs: Referring to the zodiac, of which there are twelve signs: Aries, Taurus, Gemini, Cancer, Leo, Virgo, Libra, Scorpio, Sagittarius, Capricorn, Aquarius, and Pisces. The signs describe the experience.

houses: Divided sectors of an astrology chart that describe an area of one's life. There are twelve house sectors in a chart. This is where the experience happens.

Inum Colei: Cusp of the fourth house, pertaining to home, property, the mother, and one's roots, which is on the meridian line of the astrology chart. This angular power point is abbreviated as "IC."

malefic: A planetary influence that is adversely nefarious in context, inferring evil intent. Saturn is known as a malefic planet, especially when in adverse aspect to Mars.

Midheaven: Cusp of the tenth house, pertaining to career and social status, which is on the meridian line that divides the astrology chart. This angular power point is abbreviated as "MC."

midpoint: The middle-point degree between a pair of planets or other significant astrological points of interest. Midpoint energies are calculated by changing the zodiacal degrees of two planets to a 360 degrees of a circle of notation, then adding them together and dividing by two.

nodes: Commonly known as the *dragon's head* (North Node) and the *dragon's tail* (South Node). The Moon's North Node indicates the future direction that you should be headed for that is in line with your destiny. The Moon's South Node indicates what you have experienced in a past life and are consciously moving away from to experience something new. One needs to release the symbolism of the South Node and reach for the symbolism of the North Node to attain their highest potential.

orb: The allowed degrees within an aspect. The distance between an astrological angle that emphasizes an influence. A common conjunction orb is 6 degrees.

planets: Cosmic bodies in our solar system, which includes the Sun, the Moon, Mercury, Venus, Mars, Jupiter, Saturn, Uranus, Neptune, and Pluto. In astrology, planets are the experience.

progressions: Transits that are calculated by using an ephemeris and counting a day for a year of your life (after the Greenwich Meridian Time has been refigured and an Adjusted Calculation Date derived) to predict future developments.

relocation: Moving to a particular latitude and longitude that differs from your birthplace, which may astrologically indicate an improved place to live. Relocating your birth chart to another geographical area.

transits: Planets in motion in our solar system that while traveling through the constellations form aspects (mathematical angles) to other planets, be they stationary or in motion.

CHRISTINE RAKELA is an internationally known astrologer. She is officially recognized as a certified astrologer through the National Council for Geocosmic Research and has had a full-time practice for over 30 years. Christine has produced and hosted an independent television program, "Astrology Connection," in New York City for a wide audience for 22 years. She has also been a featured guest on national television and radio, lectures throughout the country, and is a published author. Christine resides in the Greater New York Area.